Afro-Jewish Encounters

ALSO BY WILLIAM F. S. MILES

Jews of Nigeria. An Afro-Judaic Odyssey

My African Horse Problem

Zion in the Desert.
American Jews in Israel's Reform Kibbutzim

Political Islam in West Africa.
State-Society Relations Transformed (ed.)

Bridging Mental Boundaries in a Postcolonial Microcosm.
Identity and Development in Vanuatu

Imperial Burdens.
Countercolonialism in Former French India

Hausaland Divided.
Colonialism and Independence in Nigeria and Niger

Paradoxe au Paradis:
De la politique à la Martinique

Elections in Nigeria.
A Grassroots Perspective

Elections and Ethnicity in French Martinique

Afro-Jewish Encounters

From Timbuktu to the Indian Ocean and Beyond

WILLIAM F. S. MILES

With a Foreword by Ali A. Mazrui

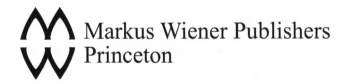

Markus Wiener Publishers
Princeton

Illustrations: All photos, including the cover image ("Faralu, a Nigérien Muslim, tasting matzah for the first time"), are by William F. S. Miles, except that of Rabbi Aby ben Serour in chapter one, which is from *Société de Géographie de Paris*, circa 1874. The illustration of the Torah on the camel in chapter 3 is courtesy of David Clark.

For information, write to:
Markus Wiener Publishers
231 Nassau Street, Princeton, NJ 08542
www.markuswiener.com

Library of Congress Cataloging-in-Publication Data
Miles, William F. S., author.
Afro-Jewish encounters : from Timbuktu to the Indian Ocean and beyond / William
F. S. Miles ; with a foreword by Ali A. Mazrui.
pages cm
Includes bibliographical references.
ISBN 978-1-55876-581-8 (hardcover : alk. paper)
ISBN 978-1-55876-582-5 (pbk. : alk. paper)
1. Jews—Africa. 2. Judaism—Africa. 3. Miles, William F. S.—Travel—Africa. 4. Africa—Description and travel. 5. Africa—Ethnic relations.
I. Title.
DS135.A25M55 2013
960.004924—dc23
2013025407

Markus Wiener Publishers books are printed in the United States of America on acid-free paper and meet the guidelines for permanence and durability of the Committee on Production Guidelines for Book Longevity of the Council on Library Resources.

Contents

To the Brymans

Cousin Helen,
Who Inspired Me to Write as a Youngster

Cousin Douglas,
Whose Discoveries of the Universe Continue to Awe Me

Aunt Hannah,
Whose Afternoon Noshes Got Me Through Hebrew School

and

Uncle George,
Whose Gentleness and Dignity Remain
a Precious Memory to Us All

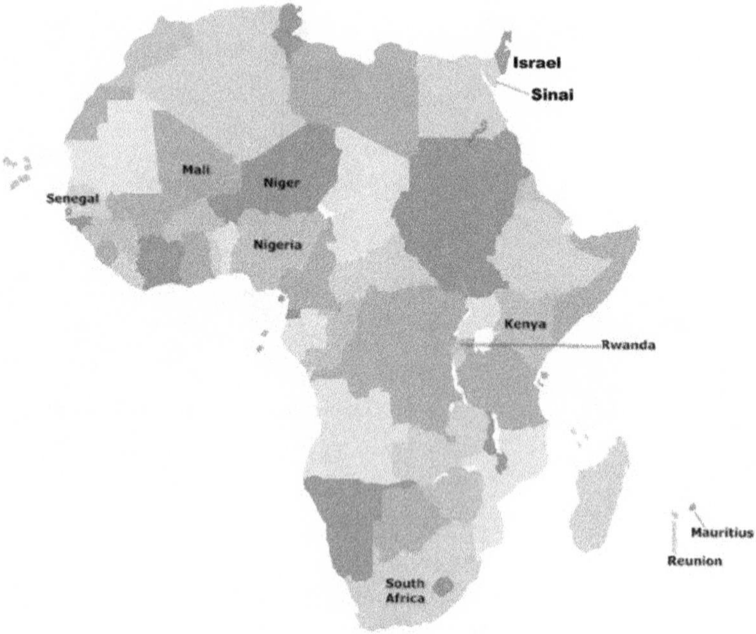

Countries and locales visited for this book

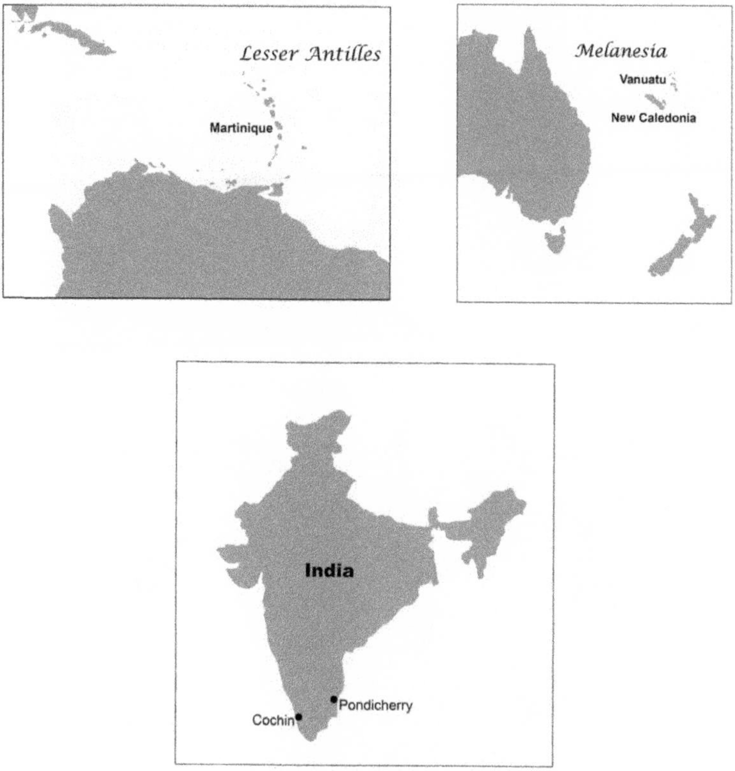

Countries and locales visited for this book

Foreword

BY ALI A. MAZRUI

The Jewish presence in Africa in the first half of the twentieth century consisted of four distinct groups. Perhaps the oldest of these groups consisted of Arab Jews in Morocco, French-ruled Algeria, British-controlled Egypt, and elsewhere in North Africa in that period.

Competing with Arab Jews in duration of settlement in Africa were the so-called "Falasha" (Beta Israel) Jews of imperial Ethiopia right up to the last decades of the twentieth century.

The most prosperous Jews in Africa were the Euro-Jews of southern Africa (Afro-Ashkenazi). Ethnically they were counted among the white citizens of southern Africa, in solidarity with the English-speaking elite.

The least recognized African Jews are those of West Africa, especially the Igbo Jews of Nigeria. In this book they are sometimes referred to as the Jubos (Jewish Igbos).

These four Jewish groups manifested different vulnerabilities as the twentieth century unfolded. Arab Jewry was damaged by the creation of the state of Israel. Large numbers emigrated to Israel under the Law of Return. Most French Jews in Algeria emigrated to France.

The vulnerabilities of the Ethiopian Jews (Beta Israel) included periodic intolerance from their Christian compatriots and from the emperors of Ethiopia. At first, Israel denied them eligibility under the Law of Return. Ironically, it took a natural disaster—draught and widespread famine—for the "Falasha" to be welcomed with open arms by the Israeli Jews. These events triggered large-scale emigration of Ethiopian Jews to Israel.

The vulnerabilities of the Euro-Jews were the threat of a racial war (Black vs. White) in the last days of apartheid and the collapse of the racial system in the 1990s. Many Jews joined the white exodus and emigrated to Europe, Israel, Australia, Canada, or the United States. There were still enough Ashkenazic Jews in southern Africa to make them a strong economic presence.

What were the vulnerabilities of the fourth Jewish group—the Jubos of West Africa? The fate of the embryonic Jewish Igbos was partly, but inevitably, affected by the fate of the Christian Igbos more widely. This wide-ranging volume takes us through many regions of sub-Saharan Africa and its offshore and Indian Ocean diasporas. The tumultuous experiences of the Igbo Jews in wartime and during the uncertainties of relative peace merit particular attention.

Three of the Afro-Jewish groups (North African, Ethiopian, and southern African) have been vulnerable through depletion. Their numbers in Africa have declined. In contrast, the Jubos of Nigeria stand a chance of expanding in number.

Can large numbers of Nigerian Jews abandon Christianity and embrace Judaism? William Miles draws our attention to this demographic potential in the following terms: "When [Jews in America] wake up to the Jubos' demographic potential—Igbos in Nigeria number in the tens of millions—there is bound to be an intra-Jewish scramble for Africa."

The majority of the Igbo Jews of Nigeria do not regard themselves as converts to Judaism. They claim to have rediscovered their Jewish ancestry. "As Igbos, we circumcise our sons on the eighth day. We pray especially at the coming of the new moon. We blow the ram's horn. This we have done as Igbos. But we did not know then we were continuing the acts of our Jewish ancestors."

There are other customs which are widely believed to be "Israelite survivalisms." These include Sukkot, the Feast of Tabernacles, and the Harvest Holy day.

What Professor Miles's chapter on the Jubos leaves open is a remarkable paradox within Nigeria. While a significant number of Igbos regard themselves as descended from ancient Israel, a large number of Yorubas of Nigeria regard themselves as descended from ancient Arabia.

The population of Yorubas in Nigeria is of comparable size to that of the Igbos. That the Yoruba should claim descent from ancient Mecca, while these Igbo claim descent from ancient Jerusalem, is one of the paradoxes of ethnic ancestry in Nigeria.

There is a difference between Igbo identification with Jerusalem and Yoruba identification with Mecca. The Igbo under consideration are relating to a religious legacy—*Judaism*. The Yoruba, on the other hand, are relating to a geographical identity—Mecca as an Arab city rather than as a Muslim metropolis.

Are "tribal myths of origin" a form of genealogical memory? Nigeria's second ethnic group, the Yoruba, does indeed possess more than one myth of ancestry. Ironically, one of these ancestral legends traces Yoruba origins to Arabia and the Persian Gulf. The Yoruba are thus seen as the remnant of the children of Canaan, who were of "the tribe of Nimrod." In a book by the distinguished Yoruba historian and sociologist N. A. Fadipe, published by Ibadan University Press in 1970, a case is made that the Yoruba came to West Africa from Arabia via the Nile Valley: "The cause of their establishment in West Africa was . . . in consequence of their being driven by Yarrooba, son of Kahtan, out of Arabia, to the Western coast between Egypt and Abyssinnia. From that spot they advanced into the interior of Africa till they reached Yarba, where they fixed their residence."[1]

It is tempting to conclude that the word *Yoruba* and the word *Arabiyu* (Arabic adjective for "Arab") are interrelated etymologically. The Yoruba and the Arabs may have more in common than either may have assumed, or would prefer to concede.

According to a related Oyo mythological tradition, the Yoruba migrated from Mecca to their present abode, having been forced out of Mecca following a civil war involving Oduduwa, son of

---

[1] This myth of ancestry is quoted by N. A. Fadipe in *The Sociology of the Yoruba*, edited by Francis Olu Okedji and Oladejo Okedji (Ibadan: Ibadan University Press, 1970), p. 31.

King Lamurudu of Mecca. Oduduwa became the common ancestor of the Yoruba as an *African* people, and Ile-Ife was the place from which the African phase of Yoruba culture flowered on the West Coast of the continent.[2]

Robert W. July traces the West African invasion associated with Oduduwa to about A.D. 1000:

> According to Yoruba myth, the national origin is traceable to Ife where Oduduwa, a prince of Mecca, came seeking refuge from Muslim persecution and remained to live among the local people. . . . What can be inferred from this tradition is that there were invasions of the forest country from the north, one of these being associated with the name of Oduduwa and occurring about 1000 A.D. at a site called Ife.[3]

But whether these ancestral myths are factually true or only symbolically suggestive, Arab-Africa and Africa south of the Sahara are linked among the Yoruba, while Jewish Africa and Africa south of the Sahara are linked among the Igbo.

William Miles draws our attention to theories of the genetic relationship between Yemeni Jewish ancestry and the Lemba of southern Africa. There is passing reference to the Abayudaya of Uganda, who practice Judaism but do not claim a genetic or ancient descent connection to ancient Israel.

Among Jubos of Nigeria, Judaism has not been received by conversion. William Miles asserts: "There is no danger of Jewish missionaries doing in Nigeria what Muslim jihadists did during the pre-Colonial era, Christian missionaries did during the Colonial era, and both are doing now: encouraging any and all Africans to join their respective folds."

---

[2] Ibid., pp. 32-34.

[3] Robert W. July, *A History of the African People* (New York: Charles Scribner's Sons, 1970), p. 108.

Millions of the Yoruba became Muslim by conversion. Did the Jubos become Jews by genetic descent? William Miles argues that it is beside the point: for him, orthopraxis (normative Jewish practice) trumps orthodoxy (canonical identity via birth to a Jewish mother).

This Ashkenazic Jew engaged in participant observation among the Jubos and emerged substantially vindicated. The other Afro-Jewish encounters he vividly describes in this fascinating book are similarly worthy of close reading and serious attention.

Ali A. Mazrui
Albert Schweitzer Professor in the Humanities
Director, Institute of Global Cultural Studies
Binghamton University, New York

Preface and Acknowledgments

The Africanization of an Ashkenazic Jew

When I first encountered Joseph Williams's *Hebrewisms of West Africa: From Nile to Niger with the Jews* (1930) as a graduate student in the 1980s, the book struck me as both intriguing and bizarre. Here was an exhaustive, highly detailed, well-referenced treatise by a Jesuit scholar from Britain who purported to establish an ancient Jewish presence in the most unlikely regions of Africa. Williams's ethnic springboard is the Ashanti, a noble people of what was then known as the Gold Coast and is today Ghana. Drawing on a host of ritualistic, linguistic, and theological similarities, Williams "demonstrates" that the Ashanti are the descendants of ancient Israelites who, over the course of millennia, had made their way from Egypt to the Sahara. But the trail did not end there: Williams's introductory chapter, "Ashanti Influence on Jamaica Customs," maintains that Ashanti "Hebrewisms" survived the Middle Passage and could be detected not only in Jamaica but in Haiti, the Virgin Islands, and the southern United States. And back on the Mother Continent, Hebrew influences could also be discerned, inter alia, among the Yoruba, Songhay, and Tuareg.

Skepticism trumped my fascination for three reasons. For one, I had recently spent three intensive years in West Africa, had met members of several of the ethnic groups identified by Williams, but (with one memorable exception) had not encountered any African claimants to common Hebraic ancestry.[1] Second, the

[1] The one exception was my Peace Corps French teacher in Niger, a Fulani whose name I recall as Ba, who informed me that we were cousins: *les Peuls* (he told me in French) were descendants of a Hebrew tribe that erroneously headed west instead of east during the Exodus from Egypt, and wound up in West Africa instead of Israel. For an interesting polemic in the scholarly literature regarding the "Israelitish origin" of the Fulani, see Jeffreys (1953).

author, a member of the erstwhile militant Catholic Society of Jesus, seemed to be perpetuating the "Lost Tribes of Israel" mythology that had been popular among nineteenth-century Christian missionaries looking for Jewish converts to fulfill the theology of supercessionism;[2] so by the twentieth century, the number of "found" tribes had vastly exceeded the original lost ten. And third, having had a solid Jewish education as a youngster (Hebrew School, Hebrew High School, National Bible Contest winner, International Bible Contest contestant), I "knew" that the existence of Black African Jews was confined to the maladroitly labeled Falasha, from Ethiopia. If we Jews didn't recognize ourselves elsewhere in Africa, then what credence could we give non-Jews who averred such ties? *Hebrewisms of West Africa* made for fascinating reading, but it certainly couldn't be taken seriously as a work of history, religion, or anthropology. Even I, who came to publish essays on re-appreciating the roots of Judaism through living in the Sahel, dismissed Williams as an esoteric, even if philosemitic, Africanist crackpot.

Then came Parfitt.

In 1992, Professor Tudor Parfitt, of the highly esteemed School of Oriental and African Studies at the University of London, published his *Journey to the Vanished City: The Search for a Lost Tribe of Israel.* Though the title evoked more Indiana Jones than Jewish studies, *Journey to the Vanished City* was read by many as a historic and scientific (via DNA) validation of the claims of the Lemba of southern Africa to Jewish ancestry from Yemen.[3] Hold-

---

[2] According to this belief, Jesus will return only when all the Jews have converted to Christianity.

[3] See also Skorecki et al. (1997) and M. G. Thomas et al. (1998) in *Nature*. David Goldstein (2008) has added scientific authority to this perspective in his "genetic view of Jewish history." Nadia Abu El-Haj (2011) masterfully tempers that "ambivalence reigns regarding the significance of genetic evidence to matters of (Jewish) identity: it matters, it doesn't matter; it matters, it shouldn't matter; it matters; it doesn't make the Lemba (or anyone else) Jews." My own view, as it has evolved in the course of writing this book, is that "DNA Jewishness" is irrelevant to actual Judaism: faith and identity are less a matter of genes and chromosomes than of study and practice.

ing the title of Stotsky Professor of Jewish Historical and Cultural Studies from 1998 to 2002 and co-teaching a course on Blacks and Jews in America with historian Professor Robert Hall of the department of African-American studies, I had the opportunity to invite Professor Parfitt to Northeastern University. Professor Parfitt's erudition, bonhomie, and Gentile status only added to the respect the book had already elicited in me. For sure, the Lemba were not West African; but they were just as far from Ethiopia as were the Hausa and Fulani among whom I had lived in Nigeria and Niger. A chink in my dichotomous thinking about Jewish and West African identities had been opened.

But it was a small chink. At about the same time as my encounter with Professor Parfitt and *Journey to the Vanished City*, Dr. Andy Cook—he who had made me aware of *Hebrewisms of West Africa* in the first place—gifted me a copy of Ismaël Diadié Haïdara's *Les Juifs de Tombouctou* (*The Jews of Timbuktu*). Initially, I shelved the book unread, mentally consigning it to the same skeptical location in my mind as I had placed Joseph Williams's *Hebrewisms of West Africa*. Not even the notoriety gained by my Tufts University confidante, the musicologist Rabbi Jeffrey Summit, with his dissertation on and Grammy-winning album of the Abayudaya of Uganda, shook me out of my deep-rooted, binary separation of Africanity from Judaism. After all, even if the Lemba had descended from Yemenite Jews, they had long ceased to practice Judaism. And even if the Abayudaya did practice Judaism, they made no claim to have inherited it from any Hebraic forebears: Ugandan Judaism is of twentieth-century origin. Moreover, I was surely not the only Ashkenazic Jew to have harbored doubts about the ulterior motive of these and other Third World ethnic minorities seeking recognition as Jews. Was it not about seeking financial assistance from world Jewry? Or about invoking the "Law of Return" in order to emigrate to the Middle East economic miracle of Israel?

A word about my own self-perception as an Ashkenazic (and, indeed, Diasporic) Jew is here in order. In the course of pursuing doctoral research in the French West Indies in the early 1980s, I discovered a vibrant Jewish community on the island of Martinique. Virtually all of North African descent, these Sephardi Jews had begun migrating from France in the 1960s but still maintained their Algerian and Tunisian liturgies and accents in Hebrew prayer. Their familiarity as Jews but "exoticism" as Sephardim has intrigued me to this day—so much so that I have most recently pursued research among the Francophone Sephardim of Montreal.[4] That was how I came to meet Daniel Amar, president of the Congrès Juif Québécois and the offspring, as he nonchalantly mentioned over lunch in the gleaming Montreal Jewish Community Center cafeteria in 2010, of Berber Jews. In fact, he had actually visited the Berber village of his father's family and remembers meeting the last of the Berber Jews there.

Berber Jews? To this I shall return.

Sephardim were certainly, to my mind, "authentic" Jews. Expelled from the Iberian Peninsula in the fifteenth century, they reestablished themselves into Jewish communities throughout Mediterranean Europe and, especially, the North African coast. The latter had incorporated the language and lifestyles of their Arab neighbors but maintained distinctively Jewish communities. Whether in Morocco, Martinique, or Montreal, the Sephardim were, to my mind, Arab-inflected Jews. But still Jews. Not "Africans." "North African," often; but not at all related to sub-Saharan Black Africans, like the Lemba or the Abayudaya.[5] Richard Hull's *Jews and Judaism in African History* (2009) similarly accords primacy to the Sephardim of North Africa and the Ashkenazim of South Africa and Zimbabwe; his treatment of Lemba, Abayudaya, and other non-Ethiopian Black African Jewish communities, in his otherwise admirable and comprehensive study, is

---

[4] "Between Ashkenaz and Québécois: Fifty Years of Francophone Sephardim in Montréal," *Diaspora. A Journal of Transnational Studies* 16 (2007/2012).

[5] A similar Sephardic chauvinism is expressed, rather humorously and in cinematic form, in *The Rabbi's Cat*. In that delightful animated film version of the graphic book series by Joann Sfar, the protagonist rabbi initially resists the preposterous notion of traveling to Ethiopia to encounter African Jews by protesting that his Jewish community, that of Algeria, already are Africa's Jews.

rather cursory. Conversely, although Mark and da Silva Horta characterize *Jewish Communities in West Africa* as the (subtitled) subject of their 2011 book, their otherwise fascinating and eminently scholarly study is really limited to two communities of Portuguese Sephardic traders on the coast of Senegal in the seventeenth century. Only with Edith Bruder's *The Black Jews of Africa* did I become aware of serious scholarship on multiple communities of Black Africans throughout the continent who have come to practice Judaism, some of them only within the past few decades.[6] Until then, I had written rather about the ways in which life in West Africa, among Muslims, had made me feel more Jewish.

And why there? Why in West Africa?

For over twenty-five years I had been returning to West Africa following Peace Corps service in the Republic of Niger. My principal purpose was to trace the evolution of two neighboring Hausa villages—one in Nigeria, the other in Niger—that had been divided by an artificial Anglo-French colonial boundary and have remained juridically separated on account of that border ever since. Periodically, I would pursue scholarly endeavors elsewhere in Nigeria (such as lecturing in Port Harcourt on American democracy or in Ibadan on traditional rulership). From time to time I would publish essays (included in the present collection) that reflected on Jewish themes emanating from these West African experiences. The very first one was prompted by Professor Ali Mazrui, whose Triple Heritage thesis, popularized in both print and film, included an "Afro-Semitic" component that spurred me to comment (revised here as "Jewish in Muslim Black Africa") in a publication of the African Studies Association (ASA). A decade later my encounters with a Hausa-speaking chief from Chad presiding over a neighborhood in the Old City of Jerusalem resulted, in that same professional association's journal, in my essay "Black African Muslims in the Jewish State." (The version here includes my later encounters, as

---

[6] My review of Bruder's book appears in Part II as "African Judaism, Race, Romance, and My Mother."

a Hausa speaker, with West Africans in Israel.) A companion piece was "'Take Me to Your Leader': A Jerusalem Story."

Between the two ASA essays, I wrote in *Moment Magazine* about sharing Passover fare in the Sahel ("Luxury Matzah"), Islamic village images of my Hebraic tribesmen ("Out of Egypt"), and commemorating the first *yahrtzeit* (death anniversary) for my father among Hausa friends in Nigeria ("Reburying My Father in Africa"). "Kaddish for My Muslim Chief"—which first aired on National Public Radio in 2011—recounts my recitation of the Jewish memorial prayer for the chief of that same Nigerian village. With my daughter, Arielle, I also wrote about our lighting of Hanukkah candles in a West African village without electricity ("Hanukkah in Hausaland"). A later trip with my son, Samuel, resulted in a book, excerpts of which appear here as "Horse Inheritance, Jewish Soul." "T/Sadaka by the Sahara" recounts the ensuing complexities when my rabbi in Rhode Island offered to provide assistance to the same village. Part I includes my tribute to the late Israeli historian who did so much to illuminate Muslim West Africa ("The Jewishness of Nehemia Levtzion's Legacy").

Somewhere along the Afro-Judaic line I clipped and filed away a Jewish magazine article (Palmer 2006) I had stumbled on about the so-called "Chief Rabbi of Nigeria," Rabbi Howard Gorin of Temple Tikvat Israel in Rockville, Maryland. Despite all the parallels I had been expressing in print and on air between Jewish identity and Sahelian Islam, my initial instinct was to mentally file the piece on Rabbi Gorin and Igbos claiming Judaism alongside Williams's *Hebrewisms of West Africa* and Haïdara's *Jews of Timbuktu*; in other words, among the curious, fanciful, eccentric angles to the Afro-Jewish connection. The Bruder book, whose treatment of judaizing communities in West Africa included Nigeria, impelled me to retrieve the actual clipping and contact Rabbi Gorin. That contact led to my spending all of Hanukkah in 2009 with what I came to call the Jubos—Jewish Igbos—of Abuja. "Among the 'Jubos' on the Festival of Lights" was my first essay to emanate from that life-changing encounter. Because Abuja—and my Jubo experience there—serves as religious fault line between Christian and Muslim Nigeria, it should be read as a bridge chapter between Part I (which focuses on Islamic societies in the western region of the continent) and Part II, "Beyond West Africa."

Bruder's treatment of a judaizing Nigeria in *The Black Jews of Africa* constitutes but one fascinating revelation among many. Another, surfacing in her chapter "African Jews in Western and Central Africa," is on Zakhor (Hebrew: "Remember"), the movement of Muslim descendants of Jews in Mali. This reading, plus an opportunity to travel to Timbuktu in 2011 (despite a U.S. State Department travel advisory and ban on official government travel then in effect on account of Al-Qaeda in the Islamic Maghreb [AQIM] attacks), reminded me of the unread book on my shelf by Ismaël Haïdara. I packed the book, tracked down the author in Timbuktu, and had a felicitous (for he spends half his year in Grenada, Spain) and extraordinary encounter with Monsieur Haïdara at his Fondo Kati research institute and archival collection. The takeover of Timbuktu a year later by Tuareg rebels and then by AQIM-sympathizers retroactively renders that meeting all the more poignant.[7] My interview with Haïdara appears here for the first time and serves as the springboard for Part I.

Reading about and discussing with Ismaël Diadié Haïdara the history of the North African Jews in Timbuktu helped me close the circle from my earliest Jewish reflections in the Sahel. So did visiting the house in Timbuktu where had dwelt the inimitable Saharan rabbi and desert guide of the 1860s, Rabbi Mardochée Aby Serour. North African Jews had long lived in the Sahel and Sahara, I had learned from Professor Hunwick's *Jews of a Saharan Oasis* (my published review of which is reproduced here in chapter twelve as "Passover Reflections on a Saharan Genocide"). But I

---

[7] So does the knowledge that, fearful on account of other depradations by Islamist marauders, the institute then had to hide its thousands of ancient manuscripts.

had no idea that Jews had a presence in Timbuktu as late as the colonial period. Jacob Oliel's *Les Juifs au Sahara* (*Jews in the Sahara*) and his biography of Serour ("Rabbi, Caravaneer, Guide to the Sahara") took on added immediacy for me when Daniel Amar in Montreal recounted to me his childhood visit to N'tifa, the Berber village home of his father's family: there they encountered the last Jew of the village, who served fig liquor in the furnished cave where he was still living in 1972. Berbers, the original inhabitants of North Africa, maintain their distinctive language, ancient script, and many of their pre-Islamic customs. Berber offshoots, particularly the Tuareg of Mali and Niger, have plied the Sahara, linking Africa North and West, for millennia. Their salt caravans are especially famous. Rabbi Serour, in his own inquiries and publication (1880) about Jewish traces in the Sahara (sponsored by the Alliance Israélite Universelle), claimed to have identified a subset of the Aoullimeden Tuareg who, while long Islamized, freely claimed their Jewish origins—perhaps as descendants of the surviving members of the Jewish community of Touat, otherwise decimated and dispersed in 1492.

No longer would Judaism and West Africans occupy two separate spheres in my brain. From Berbers to Tuaregs to Igbos, West Africa had been, and is increasingly, populated by Jews. With his documentary *Black Israel* and journal *Aleph-Beth*, Maurice Dorès offers evidence to make a similar claim. And the establishment of the International Society for the Study of African Jewry (ISSAJ) now provides a scholarly home for like-minded researchers and students of Judaism in Africa. ISSAJ complements the pioneering New York–based lay organization Kulanu, whose mission is to "support isolated and emerging Jewish communities around the world, many of whom have long been disconnected from the worldwide Jewish community" (www.kulanu.org; see also Primack 1998 and El-Haj 2011). Thanks to Kulanu, in 2012 we hosted at Northeastern University Serge Etele, representative of the emerging Jewish community in Cameroon. Even if most of Joseph Williams's assertions of Hebrewisms in West Africa might indeed have been fanciful, I was wrong to have for so long thrown out the

Mosaic Israelite baby with the trans-Saharan bathwater.

I am certainly not the only Africanized Jew to emerge out of academia. Indeed, the very founder of African studies in the United States, Melville Herskovits of the University of Chicago, undertook training for the rabbinate before doing a Ph.D. at Columbia and immersing himself in the cattle culture of East Africa for his dissertation. Although Herskovits problematically differentiated Jewish from African diasporas (Frank 1997, 2001), he—like his mentor, the pioneer of American anthropology, Franz Boas (1923) —openly reflected the influence of Jewish background and sensibility upon his comparative, Africanist, and African diaspora scholarship (Herskovits 1927, 1949). Many scholars of Africa and the African diaspora today are also Jewish and have privately congratulated me on essays I have published to date, sharing with me their own fascinating Afro-Jewish encounters, including Islamo-Jewish ones. Curiously, though, despite the supposedly liberating postmodern and multicultural turns the academy has taken, the crossover kind of reflections that Herskovits and Boas articulated combining their diasporic Jewish and African interests have fallen out of vogue. In that regard, *Afro-Jewish Encounters* is in part a salute to those pioneering scholars and a call for contemporary ones to join in.[8]

Coincidentally, in the same year (2008) that Edith Bruder published her *Black Jews of Africa*, Ali Mazrui released his *Euro-Jews and Afro-Arabs: The Great Semitic Divergence in World History*. That collection of essays contains Professor Mazrui's long-gestating thoughts about the underappreciated influence of Jews in Africa. Part of the Jewish influence in Africa, writes Mazrui, is indirect, via both Islam and Christianity:

[8] Although drawing mostly from the field of literature, the edited collection by Rubin-Dorsky and Fishkin subtitled *Thirty Scholars Reflect on Their Jewish Identity* is an excellent model.

> Virtually all Jewish prophets are honoured by both Christians and Muslims in Africa. And the Jewish myth of origin—Genesis and Adam and Eve—has been replacing Africa's own tribal myths of origins from one corner of the continent to the other. Monotheism has been conquering Africa under the banner of the cross or the crescent—but behind both banners is the shadow of Moses and the Commandments he conveyed.

Whereas Mazrui in his book emphasizes the *divergence* of the Semites from their shared familial origins in Africa, the more recent trends I illuminate in this collection (particularly with respect to the Jubos) point to a *reconvergence* between Judaism and West Africa. I am greatly honored by the willingness of Mwalimu Mazrui (who, among many honors, was recognized in 2012 by the Royal Islamic Strategic Studies Centre of Jordan as one of the five hundred most influential Muslims worldwide) to write the foreword to *Afro-Jewish Encounters*.

Coinciding with my completion of the present volume was the release of two other books that point to the emergence (or, upon closer reading, the reemergence) of Western interest in the existence of Black Jewry and Judaism. In *African Zion: Studies in Black Judaism*, Edith Bruder and Tudor Parfitt team up to present the contributions of twelve scholars, in addition to their own, on various aspects of Black Jewish identity and identification in Africa and across the Atlantic. With respect to West Africa per se, Janice Levi's chapter on the House of Israel movement in Ghana fills a geographical gap in the present book; chapters by Edith Bruder, Johannes Harnischfeger, and Daniel Lis supply key historical and foreign policy context for my more biographical and religio-autobiographical treatments of the Jubos (Jewish Igbos) both here and in my stand-alone book on them (*Jews of Nigeria: An Afro-Judaic Odyssey*). In a series of equally fascinating Harvard University lectures compiled under the title *Black Jews in Africa and the Americas*, Tudor Parfitt raises compelling ontological issues regarding

Black, Jewish, and Black-Jewish identity and identities. To my mind, Professor Parfitt honorably distances himself in these lectures from, or at least more clearly tempers, the significance attributed to his earlier collaboration in genetically testing the Lemba of southern Africa for validation of their claim to Jewish descent. With respect to *West* Africa, the erudite historian documents centuries-old searches and claims by multiple European and American scholars, travel writers, and missionaries, Gentile and Jewish alike, to establish Israelite, Hebrew, or other Judaic lineages. So humbling is Parfitt's historical scholarship to my initial exuberance about African Jewish "discoveries" that I feel compelled to balance the Pliny epigraph in *Jews of Nigeria*—"There is always something new out of Africa"—with the famous observation by Proust: "*Plus ça change, plus c'est la même chose.*"[9]

Not all of my African peregrinations have been in the western and Muslim parts of the continent. Unexpected Jewish encounters on the offshore African islands of Réunion and Mauritius (where I lived with my family for one year thanks to the Fulbright program) and spontaneous interfaith conversations in Kenya (where my daughter served as a Peace Corps Volunteer for two years) have given rise to the findings, observations, and reflections in Part II. So did my efforts, as the Stotsky Professor of Jewish Historical and Cultural Studies, to bring an Africanist dimension to the study of the Holocaust. Hence my essays sparked by visits to South Africa (with special thanks to Dr. Sinclair Wynchank) and to Rwanda (with special thanks to the then prosecutor of acts of genocide, Gerald Gahima). It is in the spirit of diaspora studies (with nods to colleagues Gabi Sheffer, Ilan Troen, and Khachig Tololyan)

---

[9] "The more things change, the more they remain the same." My combined review of *African Zion* and *Black Jews in Africa and the Americas* can be found in Part II ("The 'White House' of Judaism: Under Renovation, New Hues May Apply").

that I include in Part II two chapters relating to Jewish life and history on Martinique, the Caribbean island populated by descendants of West African slaves that I know best.[10]

I thank Markus Wiener for initially suggesting that I contribute my Nigerian Jubo research to his extraordinary imprint and then for recognizing the value of a broader collection of my Judaic Africanist essays. I also thank *Moment Magazine* for first publishing several of the essays that are included here. Given the disparate styles between scholarly journal and "reader-friendly" writing, I hope that you the reader will not be overly jarred as the chapters toggle between the two. Please also forgive the occasional repetitions of background information and sources that are unavoidable in an essay collection such as this.

Rabbis Wayne Franklin, Joel Seltzer, and Elan Babchuck at Temple Emanu-El in Providence, Rhode Island, have been extraordinarily supportive of my commitments in West Africa, to communities Jewish and not; "T/Sadaka by the Sahara" (previously published *in extenso* as "The Rabbi's Well") is ample testament. My agent and publicist *par excellence* is Zev Harel. I again thank Rabbi Howard Gorin of Congregation Tikvat Israel in Maryland for introducing me to his friends and followers in Nigeria, and for sharing with me ever since his experiences, insights, and perspectives. It is for good reason that he is so admired and respected in Nigeria.

It is thanks to the sufferance of my wife (and editor!), Loïza, and children, Arielle and Samuel, that I have undertaken as many trips to Africa as I have; the most rewarding trips have been those during which they have, one-on-one, accompanied me. "Hanukkah in Hausaland," "Horse Inheritance, Jewish Soul," and "Israelite in Kenya" reveal the special ways that they have enhanced my own Afro-Jewish encounters.

---

[10] For some notable journalistic autobiographical accounts of encounters with "far-flung" Jewish communities in the diaspora, see London (2009) and Ross (2000).

PART ONE

Jewish in West Africa and West African in Israel

ONE

Legacy of the Rabbi of Timbuktu in the Age of Al-Qaeda: An Interview with Ismaël Diadié Haïdara

Timbuktu. The very name conjures mystery, remoteness, exoticism. I have several friends—highly educated people who happen not to be Africanists—who have *heard* of Timbuktu, without having any idea of where it is. Some confuse Timbuktu with Tibet, others with Shangri-La. One friend confessed that she thought Timbuktu didn't actually exist, and that it was one of those fabulous but unreal places of myth, like Atlantis.

Timbuktu not only does exist, but has done so for at least a thousand years.[1] Its origins go back to the eleventh century when Tuaregs, nomadic lords of the Sahara, first settled on this buckle of the Niger River as an attractive crossroads for camel caravan routes. By the fifteenth century it had grown to be a major center of the Songhay Empire, carving out a reputation as a center of Islamic learning. In 1591, it was captured by Moors from Spain, and in the seventeenth and eighteenth centuries, it experienced decline. France added Timbuktu to her French West African empire in 1893.

Today, Timbuktu is a designated provincial capital in the Republic of Mali, which has been independent since 1960. Since the 1990s, the country's reputation was burnished by a robust system of democracy—until 2012, when a military coup d'état unexpect-

[1] Although the title may not be politically correct, see Horace Miner's (1965 [1953]) pioneering work of scholarship on the city.

edly reversed Mali's promising political reputation. Timbuktu is the rough traveler's quintessential lure—at least for Anglophones—the kind of place to which rugged English-speaking tourists slog just to be able to boast that they have been there. For the French, Tombouctou, as they spell and pronounce it (as do Malians) is but one of many former colonial backwaters. And for those Westerners who do use the waterway to get there, they will be surprised to realize how far the Niger River actually is from the settlement's original location: the river journey ended, they still have to negotiate the twenty-some-odd kilometers overland from Korioumé to Timbuktu proper. Since there are no international commercial flights to "The Woman of the Big Navel,"[2] if you want "Tombouctou" stamped in your passport, you can get it done at the post office.

Two phenomena not usually associated with this legendary city converged in May 2011 to bring me face-to-face in Timbuktu with Ismael Diadié Haïdara, an extraordinary Malian philosopher and historian. Jews are the first; Al-Qaeda is the second.

As Oliel (2007) documents, Jews have been plying the Sahara for a thousand years. As a center of Islamic learning, however, Timbuktu itself became off-limits to them, at least by the end of the fifteenth century. Yet in the middle of the nineteenth century, an intrepid Jewish adventurer and camel caravan merchant from Morocco, Mordochée (Mordechai) Aby Serour (1826-1886), managed to break the anti-Jewish ban, secure a commercial foothold in the town, and establish for several years there a small Jewish community with kith and kin. If that was not extraordinary enough, think about this: Aby Serour was not "just a Jew," but an actual rabbi to boot. Based on the records of this community, Haïdara Ismael Diadié—himself a native son of Timbuktu—wrote his book, *Les Juifs à Tombouctou*, on the by then long-departed Serours. As I relate in the Introduction, it was by chance and thanks to a good

---

[2] Miner, *Primitive City*, p. 2. Miner admits the etymology of the word is uncertain; a seventeenth century Arabic manuscript merely notes that "a slave called Timbuktoo" looked after the property of the earliest passers-through.

Rabbi Aby ben Serour

Timbuktu home of the late Rabbi Aby ben Serour

friend that this Bamako-published book made its way to me the very year it was published, in 1999.

In the intervening twelve years, not even the remote Sahara was spared the fallout from the attacks of September 11, 2001. Even as Al-Qaeda was being routed from Afghanistan by U.S.-led NATO operations, it began to morph in other remote locales around the globe. One of these was the "Trans-Sahara," a term coined by U.S. intelligence to encompass the vast, supposedly "ungoverned" zone spanning the southern edge of North Africa and the northern ridge of the Sahel; hence, the Trans-Saharan Counter Terrorism Partnership (TSCTP). The TSCTP, set up in 2005 to expand its Pan-Sahel Initiative forerunner, initially linked the U.S. with half-a-dozen other governments in the region, including Mali (Miles 2007a).

Mali became a most sensitive area in the Trans-Saharan front against global terrorism after a violent group fighting the Algerian government aligned itself with Osama Bin Laden and relabeled itself Al-Qaeda in the Islamic Maghreb (AQIM). Even before the rebranding, the group—pushed into the rugged Sahara as a result of Algeria's successful anti-insurgency operations—had been kidnapping tourists in and near Mali and hiding its hostages in that nation's remote northeastern corridor.

As AQIM began ramping up its rhetoric and attacks, the region of Timbuktu, including its fabled city, was put on the no-go lists of both the French and American governments. Tourists were strongly advised not to travel there; official U.S. government personnel were categorically prohibited from so venturing, without explicit approval of the Embassy's top security officer. The toppling of Moammar Qadaffi further destabilized the region, as heavily-armed Tuaregs flooded back into Mali's north after their presence in Libya became untenable. It was the Tuaregs' restoked rebellion, and the civilian government's feckless response, that stoked the 2012 coup. But the Tuaregs' revived quest for an independent Azawad was soon upended: they themselves were soon routed by a fleeting and opportunistic ally, an AQIM-affiliate known as Ansar Din ("Defenders of the Faith"). In Timbuktu, this storied Saharan city and historic repository of Islamic scholarship—a UNESCO-designated world heritage site—a fundamentalist Ansar Din set about desescrating and destroying Sufi shrines, tombs of long-revered Muslim saints, and even mosques that preserved architectural traditions at variance with strict Salafist creed.

Providing hope and opportunity for young people is still one of the TSCTP strategies for countering terrorism in the Sahel. That is the context that brought me to Timbuktu in 2011. Under the auspices of TSCTP, I flew to Mali to help conduct an assessment of U.S.-funded development programs in the country. Since several of those programs occur in and near Timbuktu, the Embassy's security officer in Bamako was petitioned to allow the assessment team to travel there. As long as we observed certain security measures and restrictions, he decided, we could go.

My luck held: not only could I get to Timbuktu, but Ismaël Diadié Haïdara, who otherwise spends half of his year in Spain, would be there at the time. I could meet him at the historical research institute he has established in Timbuktu: Fondo Kati.

As Monsieur Haïdara recounts in the interview below, his is a struggle to preserve memory, particularly that of his city's religious tolerance in a region not otherwise known for it today. He does so by preserving the precious evidence: historical documents that would inconvenience the fanatics of today who will countenance no mention of yesteryear's Jewish presence in Timbuktu. He recounts the negative, even hateful, reactions to his completely nonpolemical published work of economic history. On a continent otherwise known (and sometimes apologetically so) for oral history, Haïdara attaches supreme importance to written documentation. He does so at some personal risk.

For Haïdara, as a citizen of Mali, as a Muslim, and as a descendant of the Kati family line of historians, history is an obligation. As a son of Timbuktu, he effuses immense city pride, but in a modest and quiet scholarly way. Haïdara seeks no limelight; neither does he glamorize Zachor (Hebrew: "Remember"), the organization of self-identifying Muslim descendants of Saharan Jews in the region of Timbuktu. Zachor has been written about by visiting Jews and Jewish scholars, but not always accurately: Haïdara nuances the purpose and status of Zachor.

Ismaël Diadié Haïdara

Timbuktu research institute

Timbuktu manuscripts

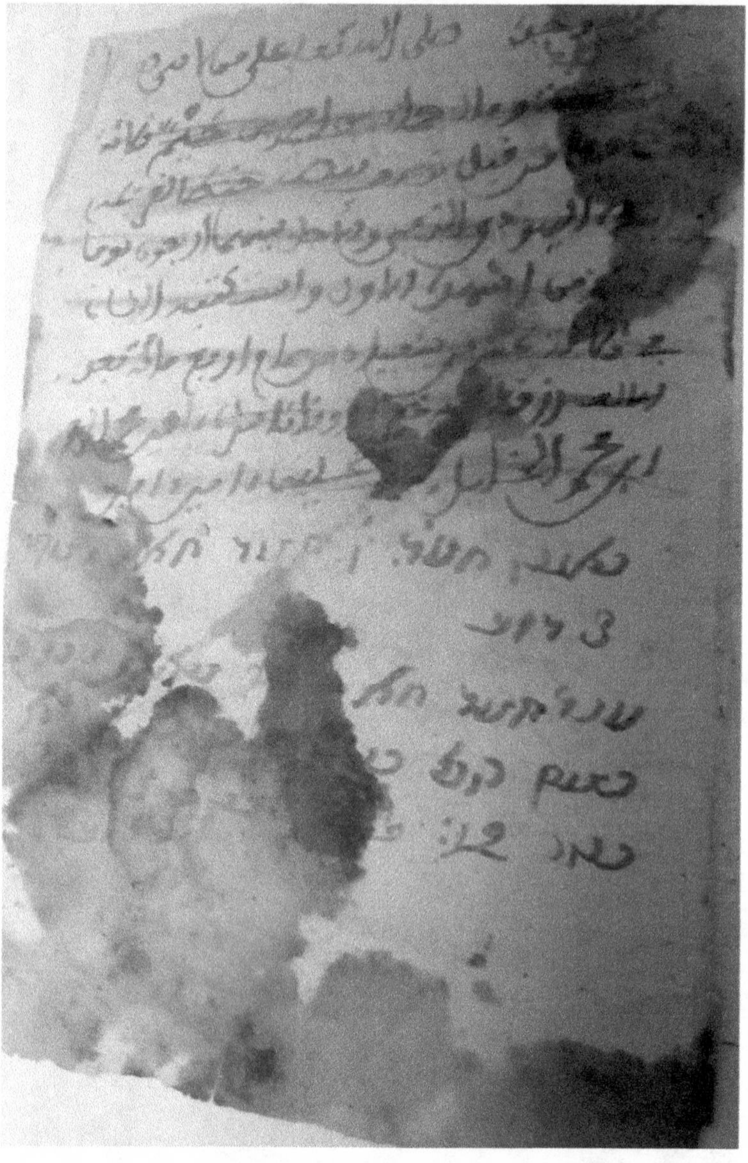

Timbuktu manuscript in Arabic and Hebrew lettering

My training is in philosophy rather than history. But I come from a family of historians, since I belong to a family of Spanish origins—Islamized Visigoths—that has been writing history for centuries. My family left Toledo, in Spain, to wind up settling here [in West Africa] in the fifteenth century, in 1467.

First, by crossing the Straits [of Gibraltar], they went to Fez, where things weren't going well for the Jews. This was before the expulsion of the Spanish Jews on the 31st of March, 1492. Like in Fez, Lisbon, there were anti-Jewish uprisings. But my family had already left, was already here. In fact, they were to defend the Jews here, in Timbuktu.

After coming to the city of Bongou, my family went to Gao, marrying into the royal family.

Our ancestor was Kati the Historian [for whom the Foundation is named]. He was born out of the union of the marriage of this Spaniard, Ali bin Siyad Kati, and the elder sister of Askiya Mohammed.

So this historian, Mahmud Kati, born from this marriage, is one of the first greatest African authors, and the father of African historiography. Since then, my family has always written history. So, by family training and family tradition, I have been involved in the writing of history.

In 1492, there was a persecution of Jews here in Timbuktu, as well as in Gao and elsewhere along the Niger River bend. As in Lisbon, in Fez, along the Straits.

My first interest was purely as an historian, uncovering this period of history of the Niger River, the "buckle." First I wrote about the Moors, about Muslim Spain, about relations between Spain and Mali. After that, I wrote about the Jews of Timbuktu.

In the nineteenth century, there was a movement of Saharan Jews. Some of these, from Morocco, moved down to Timbuktu. It began in 1860 with Mordechai Aby Serour. He was followed by Abraham ben Serour, Issou ben Serour. Then there Isaac came down, too. Eliyahu arrived with another [Jewish] group that came to settle here in Timbuktu. They were observant Jews. They thus had the *Alyahu du-Hu*, the House of Jews, in Timbuktu, where they practiced their religion, and were defended by the great imams of Timbuktu. That is, when a certain portion of the population began to protest against there being Jews, it was the great imams who said that it was their duty to protect the Jewish presence in Timbuktu. It is one example of tolerance, of peaceful cohabitation [*convivance*]. This is very important.

Even before them, there were other communities of descendants of Jews. I don't know if it is wrong to call them Jews. In any case, they had Jewish ancestors. They recognize, for example, the cohens [priests], which they call *kuhin*. They were Cohens from Fez and from Rabat who settled in the region in the eighteenth century. They had already converted to Islam in Morocco, but they retained their Jewish family name. They married here, had children, and their descendants live in riverside villages. It is known that they are different from the others—by their family names, by a very endogenous system of marriage. Among them they have retained this identity. There are documents which show that these families are indeed cohens from Fez and Rabat. It is known that they took root here and, having lived here for centuries, are recognized as such. Incidentally, certain branches of the historian Mahmud Kati intermarried with some of these Cohens from Fez. So this branch also has direct relations with Jews.

Outside of these documented families, there are other ethnic groups of Jewish origin, but we can document their claim only through the oral tradition. They are semi-nomads who live on the other side of the Niger River and who also preserve a certain identity, a certain memory of their origins. It was these families whose ancestors were persecuted by the Emperor Askiya in 1492.

The descendants of all these families constituted the group Zachor.[3] Zachor was founded as an association to preserve and defend Jewish cultural heritage in the Niger River Valley. And not only

[3] Hebrew: "Memory."

Jewish, because it includes [descendants of] the Moors who had been expelled from Spain. So there were also [descendants of] Spaniards of Muslim origin, along with the descendants of Sephardic cohens, who found themselves in the same association. It was set up first to defend the heritage of the Jews (We are Muslims. But be careful—no anti-Judaism!), and then of the Moors. There remains the House of Jews, yes. Nothing more exists from the ten Jewish cemeteries of the region. But the places exist. And so the spirit of Zachor is there to defend this heritage. And also to protect the manuscripts which speak of this population. Because they are part of the cultural heritage of this country [Mali], and also of the Jewish people. . . .

There was a great debate between historians of the colonial period who wrote about Timbuktu, the Niger River Buckle, the Songhay. "Yes, there were Jews; no, there weren't Jews." My position is that you need to base your historical arguments on texts, archaeological evidence, or written testimonies. It was in this sense that, in the 1980s, I discovered the first texts—letters sent by merchants from Rabat, in Morocco, to Timbuktu. I also found copies of answers to these letters. Together, they constituted six exchanges of correspondence.

Later, I continued this research in the Ahmed Baba Institute, part of the National Library where I was working. I was able to discover another twenty or so documents—bills of sale. Commercial documents, in other words, of the type that were discovered in the Genizah in Cairo. With these, and also by being in contact with Niger River Buckle families of Jewish origin, I started working on this book [*The Jews of Timbuktu*]. From the outset I vowed that my writing be based solely on the written sources at my disposal, and that's why the book covers only the nineteenth century.

Unfortunately, the book was very badly received by a public at large that never read it. A book of economic history. People were opposed merely to my writing about Jews in Timbuktu. Some people condemned me. I even received threats. In the 1990s, in the general mentality, being Jewish provoked resistance. I noticed this here, in Timbuktu, and in Spain, and in France. It's not a question of a single culture. It's a resistance that one must overcome. By education. By dialogue.

My philosophy at the time was the same that I maintain today: In Timbuktu, Jews—just like Arabs, Africans, Asians—can live. They must live. A people is not great except through its capacity for exchange with others. By the same token, a city cannot be great without being porous, open to other cultures, to other civilizations.

It is in this spirit that I wrote this book. The Jewish minority of Timbuktu must be known. It has every right to its history. And so the book had to be written. The texts had to be saved; the history had to be saved. . . .

There has been much misunderstanding on account of my book and Zachor. Unfortunately, many people have not understood. But I am not the first in Timbuktu to defend the Jews. It goes back to the greatest sages of Timbuktu, from the fifteenth century. It is a tradition of Timbuktu, unlike many European cities, and other African ones. Timbuktu is a city in which Islamic sages have always defended the Jewish presence. Where they have always *written* about a Jewish presence. I have dozens and dozens of documents drawn up by Muslims on behalf of the Jews here, or about the Jews here. It is deontological—our philosophy has been to defend this dialogue between cultures, this dialogue between civilizations, and the right of peoples to exist. This was the philosophy of Zachor.[4]

[It was IsaacNewton who said that] there are too many walls and that we have to build bridges.[5] And it was [Henri] Dominique Pire, the Belgian Nobel Peace Prize laureate, who picked up on this idea and said [something to the effect that], "There are too many walls. Walls between races, cultures, classes. Walls between the North and the South. We have to begin to create bridges."

That's what I try to do with this Foundation. To build a bridge between peoples of different origins—European, African, Moorish,

---

[4] In the interview, Haidara explained why Zachor suspended its activities.
[5] The precise quote is "Men build too many walls and not enough bridges."

Castilian, Christian, Jewish—peoples who came to Timbuktu, who married here, who established roots here. We have to show that it is from all these peoples that we have a culture, a civilization. It's a struggle for tolerance. That's what this Foundation is—just a library with manuscripts, but with this philosophy.

TWO

Semitic Surprises in Sufi Senegal

You have to crane your neck and look up from the Place de l'Indépendance in downtown Dakar if you wish to see it. But if you do, on the third floor of a sprawling multistoried office building, you will espy, fluttering in the tropical hot and humid wind, the blue-and-white *magen david*: the six-pointed Star of David that serves as centerpiece of the flag of Israel.

The capital of Senegal, a 95 percent Muslim majority country on the furthest point of West Africa, is not where I expected to see such an open display of the Jewish state—not in the summer of 2012, when next-door Mali was in the throes of a takeover of its northern half by an affiliate of Al-Qaeda in the Islamic Maghreb. But this is where the Embassy of Israel is located, and if it *is* going to be there, by God, then its flag will fly, in the open, with pride and guts.

It was only one of several surprises of a Semitic nature that I was to encounter in Senegal.

At a time when U.S. embassies throughout Africa (including Senegal) are undergoing green zonification—relocation in fortress-like structures at some distance from their previous urban accessibility—Israel's resolute downtown perseverance is impressive. Not that the Israeli embassy in Dakar takes security lightly. Within minutes of my taking pictures of the fluttering Israeli flag (discretely, I thought, for I had moved back from the busy Avenue du Président Léopold Senghor towards the emptier War Monument park side), two tall Senegalese men—one in uniform—sidle up to me, asking questions. I am really taken for a loop when one of them addresses me by name. But it is his power of memory, not that of Israeli intelligence writ large, that is prodigious: he happens to have been at the Residence of the Israeli ambassador in another part of town three weeks earlier when I first inquired about seeing the ambassador, and had remembered my name from passport and business card. Still… Certainly by the time I was admitted to the embassy for my appointment, the Israeli head of embassy security knew of my picture-taking, and politely asked to see what I had shot.

The view of Senegal from inside the Israeli embassy is enlightening in its own right, and I shall return to it below. But even more insightful were the various invocations of Israel, Jews and Judaism that emerged, spontaneously and unsolicited, among citizens and migrants alike, during my nearly month-long stay in Senegal, and then during a scheduled series of discussions during a return visit five months later.

Had I paid more attention to my readings of Jewish history in sub-Saharan Africa, I would have realized that some of the earliest synagogues on the continent had been built in what today is known as Senegal. I would not have been surprised reading in French, in the home (now a museum) of first president Leopold Senghor's father in Joal, that that old seaside town had been the site of a synagogue built by precolonial Portuguese traders with ties to Amsterdam. Richard Hull (2009: 109-110, 65) provides more detail:

> By the 1620s, Jews were numerous enough in West Africa to have established a synagogue at Rufisque in Senegal and at Joal. . . . [I]n time all the foreign populations mixed with the local Africans and produced a richly textured creole culture. . . . [B]y 1700, . . . nearly all traces of Judaism had disappeared. . . . Today, communities

> in Senegal . . . are rediscovering their genetic heritage through DNA and by uncovering ancient texts found in the homes of Muslim families.

Mark and Horta (2011) provide the most extensive accounting to date of the rise and fall of the Jewish communities in Senegambia. How theological alliances have changed! At a time when Catholic emissaries were putting pressure on local potentates to exclude or expel Jews from new spheres of European influence, the latter strove to persuade Muslim rulers that Catholics, through their reverence of images of the Trinity and saints practiced idolatry, anathema to Judaism and Islam alike. The revered Rabbi Jacob Peregrino made his mark not only by teaching Torah in Senegal but by reconverting to Judaism descendants of those who had been forced by the Inquisition to embrace Christianity ("New Christians"). Ample evidence also exists of Senegalese men converting to Judaism and of the children of mixed Jewish-Senegalese unions being raised as Jews. Poignant indeed is the account of a Frenchman, Nicolas Villault, three decades after the last Jews had repatriated to the Netherlands in around 1635. Villault was coming to the Upper Guinea shore in rough seas, and his locally hired boatman had feared that the vessel he was piloting would capsize:

> [He was] murmuring, and I distinctly heard these words: "Abraham, Isaac and Jacob." [When] I asked him what he was saying, he replied that he was thanking his "Fetish" for having kept him safe at sea; and that all Maures [that is, Blacks] did likewise. (Mark and Horta 2011: 199, my translation)

Such backdrop helps explains the impromptu invocations of Judaism by Senegalese at a public lecture in mid-2012. A seminar on inter-religious dialogue in America and Senegal was being held at the West Africa Research Center (WARC) in Dakar. After about an hour of academic plowing through familiar terrain, the writer Ahmed Khalifa Niass rose from the audience to transcend the usual Muslim-Christian bases of such discussions. He did so by invoking the Jewish legacy in Joal. "Even before the arrival of Christians," Niass stated to the panelists and fellow audience members alike, "we had the first synagogue of Africa, in Joal. That is the origin of the Serer *signares*."[1] Niass also reminded his compatriots and co-religionists of the many echoes of, and references to, Judaism in the Qur'an.

Not to be outdone by Niass, a Senegalese parliamentarian (and vice-president for the World Council for Peace), Mansour Sy Djamil, then rose to recount his encounter in New York with a "prominent" Jewish leader. It was during Ramadan, and Richard Marker, of the United Nations Coalition for Inter-Faith Partnership, invited Djamil to his home to break the fast. To good-natured laughter among the audience, the parliamentarian recounted that Marker said that he agreed when the Senegalese parliamentarian Djamil presented his position on Palestine, but admitted that "he would not accept it if the same exact thing was said by a Palestinian."

All this to reinforce the famous Sufi-inflected Senegalese reputation for religious accommodation and acceptance. Several panelists and audience bristled when the term "tolerance" was raised. "We long ago surpassed the stage of 'tolerance,'" went the general sentiment. "We are a society of absolute recognition, a single social community . . ."[2]

In his concluding remarks, the WARC director—who, in his no-

[1] Serer is a coastal ethnic group; *signares* were the early, socially privileged mixed offspring (female mulattoes) of European (originally Portuguese) traders and African women.

[2] . . . and more tolerant towards Jews than the French who were colonizing northwest Africa in the late nineteenth and early twentieth centuries, it would appear from Abitbol's 2001 essay: A well-developed plan to organize and fund Jewish migration from Morocco to Senegal was nixed for reasons that smacked of blatant anti-Semitism.

nonsense, managerial mode can first come across as personally aloof, if not gruff—returned to the theme of religious diversity and pluralism in Senegal and in Islam. "They are not so separate, these different religious traditions," summarized Professor Ousmane Sène. "The Torah, the Evangiles, the Qur'an—they are all links in the same chain." That Muslims, Christians, and followers of indigenous traditions would be the focus of a conference on inter-religious dialogue in this Islamic-Christian-animist nation was not at all surprising. But how is it that Jews and Judaism came up at all?

At a colloquium where I spoke under the auspices of the university named after the renowned Senegalese historian, Cheikh Anta Diop, a graduate student invoked the Jewish diaspora. Now, the subject of my talk—colonialism and decolonization in the French West Indies and French West Africa—had nothing to do with the Jews. But my title did have the word "disapora" in it, and this Senegalese student had obviously read a good deal about modern Jewish history.

"The African diaspora is too diffuse," he said. "There is little that binds it together. Color alone is a weak bond.

"It's different from the Jewish diaspora," he continued, taking a surprise tack for reasons that still intrigue me. "The Jewish diaspora has a specific ideology—Zionism—that the African diaspora does not. That's what binds the diaspora Jews together . . . and assures their identity."

Putting aside the also important religious basis of Jewish identity, and the existence of some anti-Zionist ultra-Orthodox sects (which their professor Ibrahima Thioub and I both injected into the discussion), the student had made a valid point. Even more telling was the non-polemical nature of his remark—a point I had to impress on my host at the Israeli embassy, who would later incorrectly anticipate that my account would conclude with the student harping on overweening Jewish influence and power. No, the student was merely making a comparative observation, without normative judgment, in which Jews were added to the conversation to shed light on the various paths of diasporic identity.

Jews and Judaism, despite virtually no physical presence or external prompt, are yet again surfacing in Senegal, in cerebral as well as Sufi circles.

As a stranger in a foreign country, I tend to seek out "my" people so that I may speak "our" language and commune about matters back "home." Notwithstanding years of Hebrew school and several sojourns in Israel, however, I remain more comfortable in Hausa than in Hebrew, and find it easier to break the ice with Nigériens than with Israelis, with northern Nigerian Muslims than with Middle Eastern co-religionists. That is how I find myself spending my last Shabbat morning in Senegal with Murtalla the Tailor in the Medina quarter of Dakar.

Sewing and stitching (especially traditional West African costumes) is Murtalla's day job; his real avocation is study and teaching of the Qur'an. A migrant from the Maradi region of Niger, his sewing room is lined with religious books. Ostensibly, I am in the sewing room to collect the suit for which he had measured me a week before, and wants to offer me as a present. But I sense that a deeper discourse and exchange is expected by this *mallam*, this teacher, as the Hausa word (similar to the Hebrew *melamed*) has it. In our own ways, both of us are diasporics in this city, neither of us a citizen of Senegal, neither of us a member of Wolof society. But we both speak Hausa and share deep connections to Niger. And, though he is a Muslim and I, a Jew, we share great interest in each other's religion.

"Back in my home in Niger," says Murtalla, who is also treasurer of the Hausa association of Dakar (Kulob Zumunci), "I have a copy of the Torah, in Arabic. If we were there, I would show it to you." I don't quite recall how we got on the topic of Torah. I do remember showing him a picture of my synagogue's Torah scroll from Egypt,[3] and him telling me that his older brother is studying at Al Azhar University in Cairo. "If I were back home," I say, "since this is Saturday, we would be reading from the *atora*."

I show other pictures attesting to my "exotic" religious roots—for example, my wedding under a *chuppa*, the Jewish bridal canopy, with explanations of my bride encircling me seven times, and a final breaking of a glass. Murtalla explains to a fellow Hausa diasporic tailor (who, in swift wide threading movements, keeps sewing exquisite cotton button tabs as he listens) that we children of Israel are closer to Muslims than are Christians. He provides the genealogy of our shared forefather Ibrahim/Abraham and our consequent Is(h)mael-Isaac cousinry. Sports and weather? Nah. If you want to break the inter-faith ice, you've got to talk religion.

"I hope you don't mind," Murtalla goes on, in his graceful and diplomatically polite Hausa, after we had discoursed bric-a-brac on Islam and Judaism. "But I have two questions for you, relating to your religion." It is Ramadan, so any distraction from thoughts of hunger and thirst is useful. I assure him that all questions are welcome.

"The writing and language of the Torah," Mallam Murtalla queries. "Are they used today? Do people ever speak the language of the Torah anymore?"

I momentarily forget the Hausa/Arabic word for Hebrew (*Yahudanci*), and so I introduce Murtalla to the word *Ivrit*, which he subsequently pronounces almost like a sabra (native-born Israeli). I explain the common use of "Ivrit" in Israel today; he is also curious about the letters themselves. So, tearing out a piece of paper from my spiral notepad, I write out all twenty-two letters of the Hebraic alphabet, pronouncing each one as I commit it to paper. After each one, Murtalla repeats my pronunciation: "Alef, bet, gimel, daled, hey . . ." When the intial alphabet is sketched out, he transliterates the name of each Hebrew letter into Arabic. He is delighted when

---

[3] Ever since my rabbi sponsored the construction of a well on school grounds in Niger (see chapter ten), in return visits to West Africa I carry pictures of him in the synagogue and holding its Egyptian Torah scroll.

I conclude this initiation into the language of the *atora* by writing out his name in Hebrew.

The Hebrew lesson has taken so long that I forget that there is a second question in the offing. But Murtalla comes back to it. This one, though, requires much more acumen to tackle than writing out and pronouncing even a Semitic alphabet. It also reflects a surprising level of prior knowledge about Judaism.

"Why is it that, unlike Muslims and Christians, Jews do not proselytize?" Underlying this factually-corrected premised question is a related, suggestive one: "Is it possible for someone who is not Jewish to become so, from any tribe whatsoever?"

So I explain both the reason and the tradition, though I feel more confident in discussing the tradition: that the rabbi approached by a convert is supposed to refuse three times before agreeing to accept the non-Jewish supplicant as a candidate; that conversion only follows a long period of study and then a kind of examination before a panel of three rabbis; but that, following this path, any one from any "tribe" may indeed become Jewish. The conversation then takes a simultaneously solemn and mirthful turn when I describe the additional requirement for the adult male convert to Judaism: circumcision.

Murtalla is contemplative, and again invokes our shared ancestor: "Like when God made Ibrahim/Abraham circumcise himself—as an adult, when he was already forty years old."[4] Murtalla then turns to his sewing companion to point out, via our shared surgical tradition, why Islam is more similar to Judaism than it is to Christianity. But now he can no longer contain his solemn self, and breaks out into laughter after he observes: "With this circumcision requirement, it's no wonder that you don't have a lot of men clamoring to become Jewish!"

As for males born into our respective faiths, I express my own people's wonder that the Hausa wait so late, until a boy is about

---

[4] In the Hebrew account, Abraham was ninety-nine years old. In Murtalla's Islamic rendering, Ibrahim circumcised himself; the Torah is vague on this point, using the passive tense to convey that Abraham "was circumcised."

seven years old, before circumcision. "It is not against Islam to circumcise the newborn," Murtalla answers. "But we believe it is better for the boys' health to do it after his testicles have formed and descended."

We have discussed our respective Scriptures so much that Murtalla wants to gift me his silver-covered Franco-Arabic copy of the Qur'an. I do not have a *Chumash* (a bound version of the Five Books of Moses) to offer in exchange, but I do happen to have a pocket-sized, leather-bound Qur'an that I had recently bought from a sidewalk religious artifacts vendor in Dakar's commercial center. We inscribe and sign each of the exchanged Qur'ans. (When I return five months later and do present him with an all-Hebrew Chumash, Murtalla is delighted and shows it off to friends and customers.)

"I thank you," says the embroidering Hausa scholar of Islam, who has plied me with beautiful, expensive gifts to both wear and read, "for you have increased my knowing."

Thus do I take leave of my new friend-in-diaspora, united by a common Chadic language and shared claims to Semitic ancestry, fellow strangers in Sufi Senegal.

Back at the Israeli embassy, the very friendly, Senegalese public relations liaison has put together a packet of materials reflecting the local press's coverage of Israel's activities in Senegal. Much of it recalls the halcyon, pre-1967 days of Israel in Africa, when the Jewish state (itself half-desert) was first and foremost a model of agricultural prowess for the newly independent, hydrologically challenged states of the Sahel.[5] Israeli agronomists train Senegalese farm extension agents in irrigation and market gardening techniques (Kaly 2012). A veritable harvest of clippings detail the

[5] For comprehensive overviews that reflect the evolving stages of Israel's relationship with Africa, from messianic to pragmatic, see Arthur and Gyimah-Boadi 2006, Decalo 1998, Ojo 1988, and Peters 1992.

transformation of the Israeli ambassador's residence into a "Green House," "a model for the emergence of Senegalese agriculture" and renewable energy by virtue of its drip agriculture vegetable garden, fishpond, and solar-powered pump. In the same vein is featured Israel's gift to the Department of Plant Biology at the Université Cheikh Anta Diop in Dakar of composters manufactured in the Jewish state.

Perhaps it is a generational thing, but the local booster of continuing Israeli involvement in agricultural assistance to make the desert (or Sahel) bloom is Sidy Dieng, another parliamentarian who readily invokes Senegal's first president as validator of ties between the Jewish and Senegalese peoples. Ironically, it was in the context of Senegal's severing of diplomatic ties with Israel after the Yom Kippur War of 1973 that Senghor wrote, in a French magazine, of the "trilogy of the suffering peoples": Arab, Jewish, and African. Dieng quoted the phrase in the Israeli ambassador's office; it was the first time I had heard it.

But beyond Senghorian sentimentality, Dieng is most keen about strengthening and expanding the *Club d'Amitié Sénégal-Israël Pour le Développement* (CASID; Senegal-Israel Friendship Club for Development.) Dieng is aware of how active Israel's international development agency, MASHAV, is in certain parts of the continent.[6] Senegal, from his viewpoint, should benefit no less. "Solidarity for development," he intones. "Economic relations." But also trans-cultural and inter-faith dialogue.

And so Israel's generosity is not only of the technical or scientific type. For the end of the Tabaski festival at the end of Ramadan (and to mark Ibrahim's sacrifice of a ram in the place of his son Isaac), the Israeli embassy gives 99 sheep to 99 needy Senegalese (low-income families, orphans, street kids[7]). In his 2009 declara-

---

[6] For an overview of MASHAV, see Divon 2006. For a treatment of development cooperation as an expression of soft power, see Fried 2006. For a linkage of this particular use of soft power with Jewish mysticism, see Beker 2006.

[7] The embassy also acts as local facilitator for the Israeli NGO Save a Child's Heart, bringing to Israel for medical treatment Senegalese children suffering from congenital heart disease.

tion on the offering of the 99 ruminants, then-Ambassador Gideon Behar noted the contribution of "the Jewish community of Senegal" to this religio-philanthropic act (Coly 2009).

"Jewish community of Senegal"? It is miniscule, to be sure—perhaps no more than forty in number, virtually all in Dakar, a combination of French Jewish businessmen, U.S. Embassy and Peace Corps officials and volunteers, and Israeli entrepreneurs and diplomats. ("One of our embassy staff is Arab," clarifies the deputy chief of mission, "but, since she's Israeli, we count her among the Jews.") There is no attempt to downplay the religious dimension of the Jewish state for diplomatic reasons. To the contrary: interfaith dialogue being a veritable *leitmotif* of Senegalese society, the Israeli embassy brought a rabbi from Hebrew University to provide a Jewish dimension to the issue. It also co-sponsors (along with a German organization) a series of conferences and workshops on interreligious dialogue.[8]

In certain respects, Senegal is typical neither of Africa nor of Israel's relationship to Africa. French-speaking, with no history of military coups or religious violence, it has the highest percentage of Muslims, by far, of any of the nine sub-Saharan nations in which Israel has an embassy.[9] At a time when concentrated populations of undocumented Black Africans in Israel (estimated at 60,000, mostly in the Tel Aviv area) have given rise to an unseemly populist backlash (Greenberg 2012; Kershner 2012a, Kershner 2012b), the number of Senegalese in the Jewish state is negligible. There is little evidence in Senegal of Israel's major private sector exports to Africa: arms, munitions and other military materiel, and security expertise (*Africa Confidential* 2009). In a world that has changed

---

[8] Konrad Adenauer Foundation, "Plaidoyer pour le dialogue interreligieux."

[9] The others are Cameroon, Eritrea, Ethiopia, Ghana, Ivory Coast, Kenya, Nigeria, and South Africa. At the apex of Israeli relations in Africa, there were over thirty embassies of the Jewish state throughout the continent. It was in 1973, in the wake of the Yom Kippur War, that all but four of these states cut off diplomatic relations. For an excellent critique of Israel's broader strategy south of the Sahara that bemoans the "absence of a clear Israeli strategy in Africa" and pinpoints the role of "elusive emotional factors," see Naomi Chazan (2006).

dramatically since the independence of Israel in 1948 and of most African colonies in the 1960s, perhaps Senegal (whose Gorée Island serves as epicenter for slave trade memory) best recalls Herzl's original, futuristic vision of Zionism's role for Africa and Black nationalism:

> There is still one problem of racial misfortune unsolved. The depths of that problem, in all their horror, only a Jew can fathom . . . the horrors of the slave trade. . . . Their descendants grow up in alien surroundings despised and hated because their skin is differently pigmented. . . . [N]ow that I have lived to see the restoration of the Jews, I should like to pave the way for the restoration of the [Blacks]. . . . That is why I am working to open up Africa. All human beings ought to have a home . . . (Theodor Herzl, *Alteneuland* [*Old-New Land*], 1902)

Only a visionary like Herzl could have imagined that, one hundred and twelve years after sketching out the above, an Ambassador of the Jewish state to Senegal would be dispensing development assistance to farmers struggling against desertification, sheep to needy families on the Tabaski holiday, and prizes for Qur'anic schools. For sure, there is a strategic dimension to such Jewish engagement with Senegalese society: from the Ambassador's perspective, this entails breaking the simplistic association of Arabism and Islam.

"If there wasn't such confusion [from lumping together] Arabs and Muslims," says Ambassador Eli Ben Tura, "there wouldn't be such misunderstanding between Muslims and Jews." Arabs are a people, he explains; Islam is a religion. "Arab strategy is to tell Senegalese, 'you should support us because we are all Muslims.'" But the more accurate parallel is between Judaism and Islam: "All of our prophets are the same." Nor should one forget the African foundation to the practice of Islam in the Sahel: "culture is not dogma."

There is Arab instrumentalization of religion for the Palestinian cause, Ambassador Ben Tura explains. Sidy Dieng, with whom I met the Ambassador, concurs: "Senegalese understand that the Israel-Palestinian problem is about land and statehood, not a conflict over religion."

"The Arabs make a lot of promises to their African 'brothers,'" the Ambassador observes. "But it is Israel which really does good deeds, provides assistance. The Arabs don't contribute concretely. They give mosques to obtain political support, but that's it."

Diplomacy and agriculture go together, according to Eli Ben Tura, metaphorically as well as literally. "Drop by drop," the Ambassador says, invoking the name of the world famous Israeli technology for irrigating desert climes. It is his same approach to diplomacy. "Little acts here and there, drop by drop. They add up."

The Ambassador does have his work cut out for him. According to two scholars of Islam whom I encounter, Abdoulaziz Kébé who is based in Dakar and Gallaye Ndiaye who teaches in Brussels, there are crosscutting tendencies in local religious thinking that would challenge the Israeli Embassy's outreach plan. Senegalese intellectuals may distinguish between Judaism as a religion and Israel as a state, but the population at large does not. When tensions flare up in the Middle East between Israelis and Palestinians, there is a small but vocal group of Islamists who reframe the contemporary conflict in terms of Qur'anic accounts of betrayal of the Prophet Muhammad by the Jewish Arabian tribe of the Banu Qurayza.[10] Personification of Jewish "hypocrisy" also goes by a name—Abdulahi Ibn Saloul—although since he is not actually mentioned in the Qur'an, some Islamic scholars question his very existence. Africans who have studied in Arab nations are particu-

[10] Taji-Farouki (1998:15) dates this "essentialist" tendency (attributing to Jews of the Qur'an an "unchanging nature" across centuries) to the late 1960s, in the context of Pan-Arabism and Arab confrontation with the young state of Israel.

larly susceptible to this judeophobia, even though verse 75 of the Surat "The Family Imran" directly attests to the trustworthiness of the People of the Book.

It is the Islamists who strive to stoke the image of Israel as an outlaw Jewish state that defies international law and the United Nations, and who conflate "chosen people" with "Jewish arrogance." While the overwhelming majority has no problem with Israel's existence per se, says Ustaz (Teacher) Kébé, others portray Zionism essentially as a project of domination.

Professor Ndiaye has a somewhat different take on perceptions of Jews and Judaism among his countrymen. According to Ndiaye, a political scientist, negative stereotypes about Jews are commonplace, largely as a result of unsophisticated religious teaching and preaching in neighborhood mosques. "Don't take my word for it," he says. "Let me just call over one of my neighbors." So from his balcony Ndiaye calls out to his neighbor to come over.

That is how I meet "Champion," a one-time boxing star from Dakar's northeast coastal neighborhood of Guediawaye. Champion is the nickname of the still brawny Jibril Kanjé, who now runs a school for young and aspiring boxers. Champion's smile neutralizes his physique, which is otherwise quite formidable. But his facial expression morphs into shock when Ndiaye asks him, "How would you feel if I called you a Jew?"

Without missing a beat Champion responds, "I would be offended." His tone is wounded, almost as if his neighbor *had* called him "a Jew". "I was raised by my parents to be a good Muslim. To be honest. Why would you call me that?" Champion has most certainly never met a Jew before, and we didn't want to embarrass him by letting him know that he was now doing just that. But I sense it still wouldn't have mattered—I am sure he still would have walked me around the neighborhood as he did, showing it off to me and me off to it.

"Most people do not distinguish between being Jewish and Israeli," Ndiaye explains to me. "Certainly not the man in the street. Among intellectuals it is different—that's where the work needs to be done, to involve them in the rehabilitation of the image" of the Jew-as-Israeli. "But the political context does not favor it. One risks being labeled 'pro-Jewish,' accused of being paid off." As for the government, when it comes to religion, it still abides by the constitutional provision of "secular neutrality."

Then there is Idrissa Ba (2006a, 2008), a young historian, whose specialty is medieval Jewish communities of the Western Sahara. Ba confirms the role of Jewish traders in sixteenth-century trans-Saharan trade and advances the probability of a significant presence for them in the Black African zone just below, Soudan. While pursuing a variety of trades, they are especially known at that time and in these locales as roving goldsmiths and jewelers. Depending on the particular ruler in a particular place, they are alternately valued and persecuted, invited and expelled. In Walata, a significant junction between North Africa and Timbuktu, they are, according to a contemporary account in 1506-7, "very rich but very oppressed."

Idrissa is a Fulani, otherwise known as Peul (or Pulaar), an originally nomadic herding people who launched a jihad to revitalize West African Islam in the late eighteenth century. Thirty-five years earlier, as a young Peace Corps Volunteer in Niger, I was informed by my French language teacher—also a Fulani—that by virtue of my being Jewish, he and I were cousins. But this was the first time I was hearing of the Jewish-Fulani connection from the mouth of a certified historian. It was certainly the first time I was asked to consider cultural borrowings *from* Africans *to* Jews, and not only the other way around. Part of Ba's one-thousand-plus page doctoral dissertation (2006b) is devoted to exploring the ancient Hebrew-Fulani relationship.[11] But rehearing the connection through his family lore, from Fulani adulation of King Solomon to intricate interpretations of the Fulani Hexagram/Star of David was something

---

[11] To be clear, Ba himself does not claim a Jewish ancestry to the Fulanis/Peuls. Rather, his position is that, through contact with neighboring Jewish communities in Medieval Sahara, in the course of time and acculturation they wound up "integrating into their mental and material culture obvious elements of Jewishness [*judaïté*] that have intrigued researchers and brought a certain number of them to wish to turn them into one of the lost tribes of Israel" (Ba 2004:740).

else. For all of the associations Jews have with the *magen david*—the six-sided figure that is worn around many a Jew's neck and is often taken as a symbol of Israel—I had never before heard its specific mystical and symbolic meanings. Here in Dakar, at the university named after the eminent Senegalese historian, Cheikh Anta Diop, I was at last being initiated into the mysteries of "my" star . . .

There are some ancient—and outright comic—associations between Jews and Senegalese, too. Yet these come neither from Jews nor Senegalese but from European Gentiles. Back in 1506, Valentim Fernandes of Portugal wrote that:

> In this [Wolof] and Manding country there are Jews who are called 'Gaul' and are black like [all the people there]; however they don't have synagogues and do not practice the ceremonies of other Jews. They live separately from the other Blacks in their villages. These Gaul are often jesters.[12]

The ensuing description would be understood by all those familiar with the phenomenon of West African griots. And how does one say "griot" in Peul, the language of the Fulanis? *Gaulo* (the "Gaul" relayed by Fernandes). Centuries before Jewish comedians became an American cultural epiphenomenon, in some erudite but misunderstanding circles, it was in Senegal that Jews were thought to be funny for a living.

It turns out that one of the most recent hires at the Israeli embassy is a former student of Ousmane Sène, the director of the West Africa Research Center. Before leaving the country, I thank Dr.

[12] I have translated from Raymond Mauny's (1949) rendition. The final word in the passage, as rendered by Mauny, is *bouffons*.

Sène for his remarks at the Center-sponsored talk on inter-faith dialogue, at which he had invoked the Torah as one of the three links (Mosaic-New Testament-Qur'anic) in the tripartite scriptural chain of Islam.

"I had no idea you were Jewish," says a surprised Ousmane in French, in his deep and booming voice. "Not that it would have made any difference, of course. But now I will tell you that, as a professor of English literature, I was the first to introduce Jewish authors into the curriculum at the University here. In particular, I had them read Bernard Malamud—*The Tenant*, *The Assistant*. Malamud is my specialty. So I am glad that you have told me."

An uplifting philosemitic coda to a stereotype-busting sojourn in Senegal.

THREE

Jewish in Muslim Black Africa[1]

Ethnographic Reversal

As a Jewish political scientist who has lived, taught, and conducted research in Muslim areas of sub-Saharan Africa (particularly Niger and Northern Nigeria), I was more than intrigued with that aspect of the debate between Ali Mazrui (1984) and Hailu Habtu (1984)—two African Africanists, at least one of whom is of Islamic origin—concerning "Jewish cultural influences on Black Africa." As a reflection on the revolution in Africana studies that has occurred over the past few decades, it is refreshing to note that Westerners (including Jews) may now find themselves to be the objects of intellectual discourse and historical analysis by African scholars—and not, as has traditionally been the case, the other way around. As an illuminating exercise in academic and cultural role reversal, reading the erudite comments by African scholars upon what is familiarly referred to as the greater *mishpocha* engendered a feeling somewhat akin to what African students must have felt (and perhaps often still do) when their cultures, languages, histories, etc. have served as grist for the primarily European and North American academic mill.

Both Professors Mazrui and Habtu, even while in internal discord as to the legitimacy of the double "Triple Heritage" thesis

[1] This essay is slightly adapted from the version, subtitled "Reflections on the Mazrui-Habtu Debate," originally published in *Issue: A Journal of Opinion* 15 (1987), pp. 45-48. The Dave Clark illustration in the fourth section (Hebrew Exodus in Hausa Idiom) accompanied (in color) a rendition of that narrative republished as "Out of Egypt" in *Moment Magazine* 26:4 (June 2001), pp. 36-37.

(indigenous, Semitic, and Greco-Roman influences impacting on Africa, and indigenous, Islamic, and Western influences in Nigeria), nevertheless converge in limiting themselves to the rather ethereal, abstract, and esoteric implications of the (especially) Jewish impact on sub-Saharan Africa. The "true" origins of circumcision (i.e., Hebraic vs. Egyptian), genesis (Biblical vs. African), monotheism (Mosaic vs. Melchizedekist), and even Marxism (Jewish or Western European) may be fascinating intellectual conundrums in their own rights, but obscure what is perhaps a more relevant perspective: the present-day perception, significance, and image of Jews among "indigenous"—and even "Islamicized" (as if the two should be separated)—Black Africans. This is the perspective that emerged for this Ashkenazic Jew living in rural West Africa. In so recasting the frame of reference, the misplaced emphasis on "Jewish cultural *influences*" on Black Africa might be amended to the *commonalities between* the two traditions. Also, the trap of falling prey to ultimately futile (for unresolvable) arguments over historical precedence may be avoided. In this way, Mazrui's perhaps exaggerated notion of "Jewish influence" upon Black Africa may be mitigated, without completely dismissing (as Habtu might do) the otherwise fascinating phenomenon of a Jewish-Black African "Connection."

Hausa-Hebrew Linguistic Commonalities

When I, as a young, naïve, East Coast American liberal arts university graduate was first parachuted into the West African Sahel to begin a two-year stint as a Peace Corps Volunteer, my expectations that I would ever remotely discover anything akin to my own Jewish cultural heritage were nil. Even when my French language instructor soon insisted that we were indeed cousins—for he, as a Fulani from Guinea, was also a descendant of a tribe of Israel (but one that, instead of returning east to Canaan with Moses, headed west into, and across, Africa)—I still assumed that I would live for two years in an environment *sans* Judaica.

In only my first week at my in-county assignment, however, I was struck—and momentarily disoriented—when a cry strangely resembling that of a long ago-learned *mitzvah* greeted me as I walked down a sandy thoroughfare. *"Sadaka"* went that part of the chant which I could recognize. "Charity!" or "Alms!" cried the beggar, using a word I had learned in Hebrew School eons before (as *tsadaka).* When months had passed and my mastery of Hausa had grown, I could recognize the remaining part of the beggar's chant *("Sadaka. Saboda Allah da al-Nabi"),* and related it even further to my previously assimilated knowledge of Hebrew: al-Nabi—meaning "the Prophet" (i.e., Muhammad)—was the same root as the Hebraic *navi*—used in *Eliyahu ha-Navi* ("the Prophet Elijah," particularly known as a Passover Haggadah chant). Just as Mazrui links Arabic and Kiswahili through a common vocabulary of politics, the vocabulary of religion links Hausa (via Arabic) with Hebrew. Linguistically, the connection does not end with a common religious vocabulary, however; even numerically, Hausa and Hebrew, through their similar Semitic linguistic heritage, converge *(ashirin-ashirim* = 20; *arba'in-arba'im* = 40; *hamsin-hamishim* = 50; *saba'in-sheva'im* = 70). I am sure a true linguist could trace many more linguistic similarities than those indicated here. For this initiate to Semitic-rooted languages, however, it sufficed that the transition from Hebrew to Hausa was so remarkably smooth.

Muslim Hausa-Jewish Religious Commonalities[2]

More than linguistic ties, however, bridged the cultural gap. Without a doubt, my integration into Muslim African life was facilitated by my Jewish background. It was not so much as an American, but as a Jew (or, better, Hebrew descendant) that common links with

[2] Lange (2012:139) posits "the possibility that Israelites played a leading role among . . . state builders in Hausaland," a suggestion that would be astonishing to even the most liberal members and chroniclers of the Hausa people today.

my Hausa hosts were discovered, and bonds created. The ritual and timing of daily prayer—*asabar* (morning), *azahar* (mid-morning), *la'asar* (afternoon), *almuru* (evening), and *magariba* (night) in the one case, and *shacharis* (morning), *mincha* (afternoon), *ma'ariv* (evening), and *aravit* (night), in the other—was a common topic of conversation. (On the subject of daily prayer, it strikes me how the Tijani imperative of communal prayer parallels the Talmudic one of forming a ten-member *minyan.*) During Ramadan, we would compare their thirty-day daylight fast to the dusk-to-dusk one of Yom Kippur. (They professed that the latter must be more arduous for it lasts an entire day.) At funerals, I would be asked how "our" custom of "sitting *shiva*" for seven days differs from the Hausa mourning ritual. (The differences are not all that great: in Hausaland, prayers are made, and alms distributed, on the day of the burial, and seven days hence. The *Fatiyya* takes the place of *Kaddish.*) Friends liked to hear the sound of a Hebrew *brocha,* the equivalent of the *bisimillahi* benediction. And when asked if "we" practiced *suna* (the naming ceremony for seven-day old infants), I could not but describe a Jewish *bris.* (Hausa boys, in contrast, are not circumcised until about seven or eight years of age.)

Beyond the links that were strengthened by a parallel religious tradition, life in rural, Islamic Hausaland brought me to a closer understanding of my own historical and spiritual roots. How could I look at a sand-swept, stalk-thatched shelter of the nomadic Fulani, and not see a *sukkah*, the Israelites' hut of branches and leaves, as they wandered throughout the Sinai wilderness? (*Sukkot* are still reconstructed by modern-day Jews, during the holiday of the same name.) How could I observe the slaughter of a sheep on *Sallah,* and not think of the ancient Hebrews' animal sacrifice on the Day of Atonement? (Falashas, incidentally, do retain the sacrificial rites in their Judaic practices.) Or what about the almost mystical veneration held for the religious scholar, be he a *malam* of the Qur'an (as the Hausas would call him), or a *melamed* of the Talmud (as the Hassidim would)—is the chasm so great? On Fridays, I would admire Hausa fathers leading their sons to mosque in their majestic, flowing gowns, fingering gingerly their fringed prayer mats.

Is this not the spirit and trappings of *shabbas,* when the observant Jew dons his own prayer shawl and *davens* with his children by his side? (The Orthodox, like the Muslims, practice sexual segregation during prayer.) I rediscovered the meaning of a Jewish calendar, for here too time was marked by the phases of the moon. But most of all, I lived in a world where every project, every plan, every conversation paid deference to "the will of the Lord"; where human survival is conceptually inseparable from divine design; where the daily cycle of life entails a constant stream of prayer and praise for the Almighty; where no act, no matter how small—be it waking, eating, working, travelling, or sleeping—is performed without expressed recognition of its accordance with God.

Little of this bears a resemblance to modem Jewish life, especially in the United States today. Yet is this not the same existential and environmental fount out of which Judaism originally sprang? It has little to do with UJA fund drives and big bash bar mitzvahs: it does reconnect, however, with the *roots* of the people and their religion. Out in rural Hausaland, I feel, what has been lost by Jewish Americana persists in Muslim Africana.

Hebrew Exodus in Hausa Idiom

Four years after my Peace Corps experience, I returned to Hausaland to conduct research under the auspices of the Fulbright program. This time, I found myself even deeper in the Hausa countryside than my previous experience had allowed me. My exposure to village life was all the more profound, and the conversations I held all the more unforgettable. As regards the theme of the present article—commentary upon Judaism by Black Africans—I will excerpt from the journal I kept during this period (1983). The exchange occurred one night, after I had just finished sharing information about some local history with Dan Mallam and friend. Dan Mallam was one of the most wiry and physically expressive persons I have ever known anywhere. His facial expressions were as animated as his bodily ones. His every sentence pulsed with excitement. He was also one of those otherwise anonymous millions known in academic textbooks and development reports as "the poorest of the poor."

> After I finished, Dan Mallam, a Muslim priest, wanted information on another subject. When he first asked me, I understood the words but thought I must have misunderstood his meaning, for it seemed so unlikely a question, and so implausible in the context. But, after verifying, I was astounded to realize I had understood from the beginning.
>
> "Is Isa [Jesus] going to come back?" he asked. We were seated on a straw mat, with a friend of Dan Mallam crouching next to us. Once again, I was at a loss. It was one of those questions that required another bit of background information, and personal explanations that I didn't feel like going into—such as my not subscribing to the "Jesus-as-Messiah" theory.
>
> So, to skirt the question, I just answered, "How am I supposed to know?" But I had not counted on the effect my storytelling would have. I had just proven that I knew so much, that my *ilmi,* my learning, was boundless. And now Dan Mallam was asking me in all sincerity, not as a query into my personal beliefs, but factually. He wanted to know if it was indeed true, as he knew some claimed, that Jesus would return.
>
> When I professed ignorance, he insisted that I *did* know, but just wasn't telling. After all, I had just told him the history of his own people, the Hausa of Daura emirate. I realized that the only way to get out of it was to tell him that I was not an *Anasara* (a Christian), as he had been assuming, and therefore I was not a follower of the Prophet Jesus.

"Oho," he said. "You don't follow the prophet Isa. You follow the prophet Musa (Moses)." Dan Mallam then explained to his friend that in the Western world there were Anasara, followers of Isa, and the Yahudawa, or B'nai Israilia, as they are known to the readers of the Qur'an. "It is they who follow the *atora* [Torah]." Then, turning back towards me, he asked: "You were under the *faruna*, weren't you?"

Faruna? What was he talking about?

"You don't know the faruna? Harsh masters, they made your people work hard, so finally you left them."

A flash of recognition struck me. Pharaoh!

Turning to his friend, but pointing to me as an example, Dan Mallam started to give the account of my "brothers'" exodus from Masar (Egypt), the Faruna's pursuit, and the splitting of the Red Sea. All of a sudden, his friend bolted upright. Recognizing the story, he finally put everything together, and now understood who the B'nai Israilia were.

"That was you?!" he exclaimed in utter amazement and admiration. "You were the ones who did all that?"

I shyly admitted that it was indeed "us."

Then, with clenched fist, he raised his arm and shook it, in the Hausaland salute given to kings and rulers. *"Ranke ya dadi!"* he declared, May you live long! In the same exuberant tone, he recited the story of the flight from Egypt complete with miracles and the parting of the sea, with an immediacy, enthusiasm, and believability greater than I have witnessed in the more than twenty Passover Seders that I have attended in my life. The rod of Moses seemed to have made a particular hit.

He saw it all in his mind's eye; I now saw it, with his vivid retelling, as if for the first time. He had been impressed with the exploits of the B'nai Israilia since he first learned their *tarihi* [Hausa: story]. And now, he was meeting one of them.

"Your brothers did all that! Ranke ya dadi!"

"Well," I explained, now in false modesty, "we had to. After all, we were living under a harsh regime" (I used the term *mulkin malaka,* which usually refers to Nigeria's colonial era) and we "were put under slavery." (Hausaland too experienced internal slavery).

Artist's rendition of Dan Mallam's Torah tale

"Do you have the atora here?" Dan Mallam asked, expectantly.

His friend interrupted. "No, he has it at home. How could he bring it here? One needs a camel to carry the Torah."

I didn't bother to correct him. But the image of a Torah-laden dromedary parading around the synagogue on Simchas Torah is one that I just can't shake.[3]

Middle-Elite Perceptions of Late-70s Israel

While a Peace Corps Volunteer, I lost all compunction about sharing my own religious identity with non-Westernized Africans. These included marabouts (Islamic holymen) as well as ordinary Muslims. They related to Judaism on the Biblical—or better, Qur'anic—level. For them, the Jews were also (in addition to Muslims and Christians) a "people of the Book." They knew "our" prophets, "our" miracles, (a part of) "our" history. They share them, in fact. But what about the Westernized Africans—specifically, my colleagues, teachers at the secondary school? How far would their tolerance go? Would they not voice the (by-then) common Afro-Islamic condemnation of Israel, Zionism, etc.? Would they not jump to the defense of their Palestinian brethren?

I was relieved—and surprised—to discover that however informed these African Muslims were about the Middle East and Palestinian situation, their opinions of modern Israel still reflected her early African post-independence image: a young, developing state, whose principal exploit, for these educated Sahelians, was that of desert-buster. Even when the conversation drifted to politics and Palestinians, they exhibited a balance and perspective rarely

[3] Simchas (or Simchat) Torah is the festival marking the end and recommencement of the annual cycle of reading the Five Books of Moses. During services the synagogue's scrolls are removed from the ark and paraded/danced with.

encountered in discussion, wherever, over the Middle East. I realized that despite Black African rhetoric and voting at the U.N., among the unknown, unasked, unquestioned middle-level African intelligentsia, there persisted admiration, and a degree of empathy, for the Jewish state. "Afro-Arab Solidarity," I learned in this and other contexts in Africa, is more diplomatic myth than attitudinal reality: at this level, that of the high school teacher or young university student, Arabs were not universally embraced as fellow Muslims; more common was a certain caution, if not suspicion, due to suspected anti-Black racism.

These are generalizations, however, and my aim has been just the opposite—to communicate the unexpected ways in which ordinary, individual Black African Muslims have related to me, as a Jew, to the Jewish people, and to Judaism. This has not been a rigorous study about the image of Jews and Judaism in Black Africa, and some may argue that the impressions and experiences recounted here are rather anomalous. No matter—any such criticism would be a positive contribution to the debate.

In the meantime, I will continue to applaud Ali Mazrui and Hailu Habtu—both Black Africans—for having raised the theoretical issue of Jewish-Black African culture influences. I will then beg the reader's indulgence for having considered this personalized flip-side approach to the question: one Jew's empirical and grassroots perspective on this very same issue.

FOUR

"Take Me to Your Leader": A Jerusalem Story[1]

During one of the regular Shabbat tours of the Old City conducted by the city municipality, our guide took us through a narrow archway tucked away in the Muslim Quarter. It opened onto a cramped courtyard populated by dark-skinned Jerusalemites. "This is the 'black neighborhood,'" she explained matter-of-factly. "These people are from Africa."

Falashas—Ethiopian Jews—we all know about. Ethiopian Coptic monks—living on the rooftop above the Church of the Holy Sepulcher—we had just seen. But Black African Muslims in the heart of Jerusalem? For a normal tourist, this was an authentic curiosity. But for someone who had spent years just south of the Sahara, it was absolutely beguiling. I vowed to return soon to the African neighborhood in the Old City.

Given the religious and racial sensitivities and tensions that undergird life in the misnamed City of Peace, though, I needed cover. So I invited a colleague who was also spending a sabbatical at the Hebrew University—a scholar from Nigeria who, even after two months in Yerushalayim, had not set foot inside the Old City.

Emeka, an Igbo, readily agreed to come. Although a Christian, he, too, wanted to see what kind of Black African populated the Muslim Quarter of the capital of the Jewish state.

From the Western Wall I knew which covered passageway to take towards the Muslim Quarter. But from there I was soon lost

---

[1] Originally published, in shorter form, in *Moment Magazine* 27:5 (October 2002), pp. 44-46.

in the labyrinth of tiny alleys and byways that in and of themselves make the Old City a mystery.

After some minutes of disorientation and indecision—immobile in the incessantly moving crowd of purposeful Arabs—I espied and hailed a disheveled young Palestinian teenager. He was black.

What else could I say but some pale version of "Take us to the others who look like you"?

He looked at me askance, without betraying any inclination to assist. But glancing at my companion—a tall, dignified-looking Black African—he decided not to just blow us off, after all.

The boy brought us to an older Black man, who was also dressed in shabby but more traditional Arab attire. He viewed us only slightly less suspiciously than did the boy. From this point on I let Emeka do the talking, and tried to fade away as his (slightly) less conspicuous sidekick. It was Emeka, then, who was left to pose again the pale variation upon "Take us to your leader."

And so we were led even deeper into the maze of the Muslim Quarter, to a side street tomb near Bab-El-Nadir (Prison Gate) in a neighborhood that used to house the old Ottoman jails. Inside the tomb we were greeted formally by the *mukhtar*—the chief—of the Black African Muslim community in Old Jerusalem. Jet-black El-haj Jadeh was dressed in dignified white robe and checkered Arabic kaffiyeh.

Understandably, the chief addressed himself to Emeka, who at least looked like he might have belonged on this alleyway spelled Al-al-Din but more easily remembered as Aladdin Street. There was only one problem, however: Although the chief could speak Arabic and a smattering of Hebrew, and Emeka was fluent in both English and Igbo, the two Black Africans had no lingua franca.

After a few awkward minutes of Emeka and Jadeh casting futilely about for a common language, as a last resort I piped up from the sidelines: *Ka iya Hausa?*

I feared that El-Haj's eyeballs would pop out of his face.

Indeed, not only could the Black mukhtar speak Hausa—which I had first learned as a Peace Corps Volunteer in Niger and fine tuned as a Fulbright Scholar in Nigeria—but it was the language that he had spoken as a youth, growing up in West Africa more than half a century prior. He had rarely spoken it since.

Thus began an unusual friendship in the heart of Muslim Jerusalem, between the wise old chief from Chad and this Jewish *bocher* from Boston.

At first, El-Haj Jadeh relied on me for "news" from Nigeria, the country where he had first learned Qur'an. Since our respective Nigerian experiences were several decades apart, however, it was more interesting to discuss his current life. (He recounted it in a Hausa laced [perhaps for my benefit] with a little Hebrew.) What was he doing here? How did he get from N'Djamena to Jerusalem?

Basically, he walked—across Africa.

Author with El-Haj Jadeh in Jerusalem

"I was born in N'Djamena, but at that time they called it Fort Lamy," El-Haj recounted. "At the age of ten I went to a Beri-Beri speaking settlement in Nigeria: Maidugari. There I began to study the Qur'an. I also travelled to Jikwa and Dayarwa. Afterwards, we went to a village called Murakarawa—a Manga village, part of which was 'French' and part of which was 'English.'[2] After five years we returned to N'Djamena and stayed there for one year.

"Then my uncle Aminu and I travelled overland to Sudan. Just the two of us. We started off by foot, walking some during the daylight hours. Yes, there were horses in those days but not on that route. Sometimes we did ride on donkeys, until we reached Sudan. It took us two months like this. I was about fifteen years old.

"We eventually arrived at Haile Selassie's town.[3] Then we were placed in a boat to take us to Yemen. The king in Yemen at that time was Imam Yahiya. Then from Yemen we walked to Mecca.

"We arrived in Mecca. After performing the *hajj* we went to Medina. After that, we set off for Jerusalem.[4] We spent two days travelling on water before setting off again on foot. First we walked to Jordan, and afterwards, we arrived here, in Palestine.[5] We settled here in Jerusalem.

"There were already people here from Sudan and from Nigeria and this is with whom we stayed, in this very ward. There were lots of Hausa, too, who came here as a kind of pilgrimage. Our 'brothers' here gave us a place to live. At the time, the mukhtar of the community was Muhammad Sidika. After he was gone, they appointed Sani. When he got old, another had to be chosen in his stead. The people were gathered and were asked to choose between his son and myself. There were many, many on my side. They said

---

[2] In other words, a border settlement that was divided into separate colonies ruled by France and Britain.

[3] Presumably, Addis Ababa, capital of Ethiopia.

[4] El-Haj here used the traditional Arabic-derived Hausa term for Jerusalem, *Kudus*. At other times, he employed the anglicized form.

[5] During the British Mandate, it was common to add Jerusalem to the Muslim pilgrim circuit. Jadeh and his uncle were welcomed by a community of established migrants from Sudan and Nigeria.

that I knew many languages but the other one knew only Hausa, not Arabic. That is why I was chosen *mukhtar.*

"I was married when I was about twenty. My wife had been born here. Her mother, too, was born here and spoke only Arabic. But her father was a Fulani born in Nigeria, from Sokoto, and came here during the time of the Turks. He did as I did, marrying an Arabic-speaking woman. He fathered thirteen children, five daughters and eight sons. Now they have all gone to Saudi Arabia and live in Mecca and Jeddah. My own wife gave me three daughters and six sons, but one of the sons died. We've been together for forty-five years now.

"When I arrived there was a big war going on, between Germany and England. But it didn't affect us much. There was plenty of food; there was money; the markets were full. The big powers brought us large markets.

"As a mukhtar, I'm responsible for all kinds of things. I approve marriages. If someone does something affecting the authorities, I am informed. If someone wants to travel from Jordan, the mukhtar helps him.

"People used to come on pilgrimage a lot, but now they don't come so much. If they come, they may stay for some time and return. There was one man who came not so long ago from Nigeria. He stayed for five or six years, then went back to Nigeria to get married. He's in Kano now. Now, all told, there are about ten Hausa-speakers left."

In the weeks and months that followed, despite the strange stares from his neighbors, I brought my wife, children, and even mother to meet my African friend in the humble house on Al al-Din Street. He always received us in the best Arab/African tradition of hospitality. Ours was the kind of bond that could only have been forged between two marginal diasporics sharing an exotic language in an otherwise forbidding and fractious city.

There is a dark side to this otherwise happy multicultural

encounter, however. The mukhtar himself was a political moderate, a wise sage who prided himself on maintaining good relations with both Jewish and Palestinian camps. In the course of befriending Jadeh and his family, however, I also spent time with one of his eight surviving children—the son who spent seventeen years in Israeli prisons. In the late 1960s, Jadeh junior had planted a bomb in the Jewish sector of the city. Even if he had long since renounced violence and paid for his offense by doing hard time, it was for me a chilling and unsettling encounter—certainly not the kind that I would ever have had were it not for my relationship with his kind, elderly, Hausa-speaking father.

My African oasis in tense Old Jerusalem, then, was not as impervious as I had imagined. It had led me to meet, face-to-face, with a former terrorist.

When you're taken to the leader, you never know where it may lead.

FIVE

Black African Muslims in the Jewish State: Lessons of Colonial Nigeria for Contemporary Jerusalem[1]

This chapter extends the discussion on Afro-Jewish cultural reciprocity conducted in an organ of the African Studies Assocation. In 1985, the pages of *Issue* carried a debate between Ali Mazrui and Hailu Habtu concerning Western and Semitic (Arab and Jewish) cultural influences in sub-Saharan Africa. In response to Professor Ali Mazrui's argument on the Jewish religious, metaphorical, economic, and political impact on Black Africa (foreshadowing Greco-Roman and Islamic influences), Professor Haile Habtu vigorously rejected the "hidden premise . . . of an African cultural vacuum, or near-vacuum, destined to be filled by 'universalistic' civilizations" (Habtu 1985:26).

In that 1985 exchange, neither Professor Mazrui nor Habtu cited Joseph Williams's 1930 curious but relevant book, *Hebrewisms of West Africa*. In this eclectic and exhaustively referenced work, the author marshals hosts of linguistic and cultural coincidences to buttress the thesis that "[s]omewhere in the dim past, a wave, or more probably a series of waves, of Hebraic influence swept over Negro Africa, leaving unmistakable traces among the various tribes, where they have endured even to the present day." Williams focuses on the Ashanti of the then Gold Coast as the repository

---

[1] Originally published in *Issue: A Journal of Opinion* 25 (1997), pp. 39-42, with a slightly modified title. As with some of the succeeding chapters, I have made stylistic modifications and updated content and references.

of this Hebraic influence. The primary intermediary of this trans-Saharan Judaic migration, which began in Upper Egypt and took strength in Abyssinia, is held to be the Songhay ("Songhois"). Williams also conjures a common migratory link between the Songhay and the Hausa.

Also published in 1930, the autobiography of Bata Kindai Amgoza lbn LoBagola ("a Black Jew, descended from the Lost Tribes of Israel, a Savage who came out of the African Bush into Modern Civilization and thenceforth found himself an alien among his own people and a stranger in the Twentieth Century World") identifies northern Dahomey as the repository of West African Judaism. Two-thousand Africans concentrated in twenty villages are said to descend from the tribe of Ephraim and follow seven hereditary rabbis. For all its detail, there are serious doubts about the veracity of many aspects of LoBagola's narration.[2]

Two years after the Mazrui-Habtu exchange-but unacquainted with either Hebrewisms of West Africa or the LoBagola autobiography-I joined the discussion by publishing, also in *Issue,* "Jewish in Muslim Black Africa."[3] In that essay I offered the perspective of an American Jew residing in Hausa communities in Northern Nigeria and Niger. Though the focus in my article was the "perception, significance, and image of Jews" among indigenous and Islamized Black Africans, it also contained some autobiographical musings of a Jew temporarily diasporized in Hausaland.

Seven years later, I encountered the flip side to "Jewish in Muslim Black Africa." In the course of sabbatical leave research at the Harry S. Truman Research Institute in 1994, I came across a Hausa elder living in Jerusalem. El-Haj[4] Jadeh is not only a rare Hausa residing in territory incorporated into Israel in 1967 (though of course contested ever since), but the official mukhtar, or chief, of

---

[2] I am indebted to Professor David Killingray for bringing the LoBagola autobiography to my attention.

[3] Republished as chapter three in this collection.

[4] I use this spelling for the honorific denoting "pilgrim to Mecca" rather than the more usual *alhaji* because this is how it appeared on Jadeh's business card.

the African community of the Old City of Jerusalem.[5] In the previous chapter I have introduced the reader to the extraordinary life path of El-Haj (Alhaji) Jadeh, the Hausa-speaking chief who lives in voluntary diaspora in Jerusalem. Plans to meet with the other Hausa-speakers of Jerusalem did not materialize: El-Haj Jadeh's health was not the best, and his official duties onerous. According to El-Haj Jadeh, there are three hundred Black Africans living in the Muslim quarter of Jerusalem's Old City. During the Mandate, he claims, there were up to three thousand.

Lest my title—"Black African Muslims in the Jewish State"—be construed as tacit endorsement of Israeli sovereignty over all of East as well as West Jerusalem, let me clarify that I employ "Jewish" and "Israeli" rather than "Palestinian" when referring to governance in Old Jerusalem because this is the way does. El-Haj Jadeh's politics are more grounded in reality than swayed by ideology and thereby reflect, even in hot button Jerusalem, fundamental Hausa norms of *hakuri, sulhu,* and *zaman lafiya:* patience, compromise, and peace. Whether such African-derived pragmatism can survive the torrents of Middle East politics is another question. It is in any event useful to review briefly the historical geography of Black African Muslims in Jerusalem.

---

[5] The significant influx of refugees and economic migrants to Israel from South Sudan and elsewhere throughout sub-Saharan Africa since 2000 begs here for mention and this anecdote: Literally within minutes of being dropped off in the teeming Third World outdoor market in the Neve Shanan neighborhood near the Tel Aviv bus station during my sabbatical in 2009, I overheard (and then joined) a conversation going on in Hausa between "illegals" from West Africa. Our trading of cell phone numbers gave rise to the subsequent strange sensation of fielding phone calls in Hausa in Israel.

Diasporic Hausa

It is not known when Black Africans first came in significant numbers to the Muslim Quarter of Old Jerusalem.[6] We do know, however, that towards the beginning of the Ottoman empire, two wards *(ribat)*, Ala al-Din (Alladin) and Mansuri, whose thirteenth century buildings originally housed notables exiled by the Mameluks and their *medrassas* (religious academies), were given over to "Tukarina" (Burgogne 1987: 119-121). While the term Tukarina was used to describe Africans coming from Darfur in Sudan in general, today it more accurately describes (as Takari) the descendants of Hausa and other West Africans who settled in large numbers in the Sudan at the beginning of the twentieth century.

The Ottoman-era Africans were taken by the Turks to guard the gates to the Haram esh-Sharif, particularly to prevent non-Muslims and foreigners (including visiting royalty) from entering. It was during the Ottoman period too that Ala al-Din Street was converted into two prison facilities: one for convicts awaiting the death penalty, the other for less serious offenders.

During the First World War, for the first time a significant number of West Africans, Christian as well as Muslim, came to Palestine. (They included, if we can believe him, LaBagola himself.) These Africans came as railway and water pipe layers of the British engineering corps, facilitating General Allenby's campaign across the Sinai. Soon after taking control of Jerusalem, the British decided to move the prisons from Ala al-Din Street to a different

---

[6] "Old Jerusalem" refers to the walled section of the city. It is divided into four quarters: Armenian, Christian, Jewish and, the largest, Muslim. The Muslim quarter is dominated by the Haram esh-Sharif, or Temple Mount. Until the final half century of Turkish Ottoman rule (1537-1917), the walled city *was* Jerusalem and the population mostly Arab. After 1864 Jews constituted a majority of Jerusalemites and began settling outside the city walls. Growth of Jerusalem outside the Old City continued throughout the British Mandate (1917-1948). Between 1948 (as a result of the Israeli War of Independence) and until 1967 (the Six Day War), Jerusalem was partitioned into Jordanian (Arab East) and Israeli (Jewish West) sectors, with the walled city falling entirely within the East. Today, Old Jerusalem constitutes a very small proportion of the total landmass of the city.

location. Established Tukarina reclaimed the old ribat for residential purposes but were reduced, according to contemporary accounts, to begging (Burgoge 1987:121).

Though Allenby's African Muslims did not settle in Jerusalem, their descriptions of the Holy City encouraged others, now that Palestine was part of the same British Empire, to follow suit as pilgrims. It was during the British Mandate, particularly in the 1930s, that groups of Chadians, Senegalese, Sudanese and Nigerians made their way to Jerusalem as part of an extended pilgrimage to Islam's holy sites, joining Mecca and Medina as part of the hajj (pilgrimage) circuit. Relatively few of those who decided to settle in the holy land did so in Jerusalem. While the number of Takari families now inhabiting the African Quarter has been reported to be as low as one hundred, 20,000 Black Palestinians are reputed to live in Gaza, the West Bank, and Jordan (Sissung 1992:11).

Those African pilgrims who did decide to stay in Jerusalem settled principally on Ala al-Din Street, converting former prison cells into living quarters or building hut-like dwellings in the prison courtyards. These have been described as "tiny villages with small alleys running the length and width of the courtyard settlements" (Millgram 1990:256) and do not exude an air of economic prosperity. The gate at the end of Ala al-Din Street is still called Bab el-Nadir: Prison Gate. Also intact, near the Prison Gate, is the cenotaph of Sheikh Ala al-Din, founder of the ward who died in 1294. The tomb has been regarded as a sacred site from at least 1537 and remains under the care of the mukhtar of the ribat. In 1971 the building in which the cenotaph is housed was dedicated as the official mosque of the African community in Jerusalem.

Black Skin, Palestinian Masks

None of El-Haj Jadeh's children speaks Hausa. Their maternal language is Arabic and their secondary languages are English and French (the latter from schooling in the local Catholic Collège des Frères.) None of the other youngsters of African descent whom I encountered speaks any African language, from East or West. Linguistic and cultural assimilation into Muslim and Arabic culture is the norm—just as Ethiopian Jews are being assimilated into Jewish, Israeli, and Hebrew norms. Assimilation of the Takari in Jerusalem has gone even beyond that occurring in East Africa, where there is no "cultural or 'ethnic' continuity between the communities of Hausa and their descendants in Sudan and the Hausa of northern Nigeria" (Duffield 1983:45-46).

Unlike in America, where Minister Louis Farakhan's Million Man March on Washington aimed to unite African-Americans regardless of denomination, in Jerusalem, religious identity transcends racial solidarity. Negritude has played no role whatsoever in Jerusalem social life. Except for maintaining a tradition of marital endogamy and urban spatial proximity, there has been no attempt to preserve indigenous African culture, education, or language. From as early as the second generation onward, Arabic language and Palestinian identity seem to have completely replaced African self-referents. Black Palestinians have likewise been drawn into the political drama of Arab-Israeli relations, including the *intifada.* One female of African origin, Fatima Barnawi, is a member of the Palestinian National Council and as such spent many years in exile in Tunis. Indeed, as mentioned in the previous chapter, one of El-Haj Jadeh's own sons spent seventeen years in Israeli prisons for planting a bomb in the Jewish sector of Jerusalem in the late 1960s.[7]

Through the Gate of the Prison beyond El-Haj Jadeh's home, there is an Israeli security station. It is not uncommon for the station to be manned by Israeli soldiers originally from Ethiopia. These Afro-Israelis are guarding the Temple Mount as Jews; their commonality with the Muslim Afro-Arabs who pass their way is

[7] Ali is said to have been released from his sentence early as part of the Jibril Prisoner agreement of 1985, during which 1,150 security prisoners held by Israel were exchanged with the Popular Front for the Liberation of Palestine-General Command for three Israeli soldiers taken during the war in Lebanon. I thank Professor Victor Azarya of Hebrew University for his personal communication on certain details of this subject.

skin-deep, and by some accounts tinged with hostility (Dent 1992: 10). Neither group has much truck with the even older Christian community in Jerusalem represented by the Ethiopian Church. Religious rivalries in Jerusalem cast cold water on ideologies of pan-Africanism and the solidarity of hyphenated-Africans.

El-Haj Jadeh himself has resisted radicalization. He prides himself on maintaining good relations with all sides, Israeli as well as Palestinian. He has not abandoned hope of finding a middle way through the thicket of contested sovereignty over Jerusalem and speaks only of living in peace with the Jews. As a local-level leader, of course, El-Haj Jadeh does not have to grapple with the intricate architecture of the larger peace process. Yet on another level, that of the Hausa *mutumin kirki,* the virtuous man, El-Haj Jadeh is himself an embodiment of the peace process.

Non-Sovereign Islam: From Sokoto to Jerusalem

It is possible that Jerusalem will one day become the shared capital of an independent Palestine, as the Palestinian Authority insists. Yet is also possible that, long after the Palestinians in the territories of the West Bank of the Jordan River attain actual sovereignty, the Muslims of East Jerusalem will remain residents of the capital of the state of Israel. As such, whether or not they choose Israeli citizenship (an option they have held since 1967 but of which only recently have they begun to avail themselves), the Muslims of Jerusalem will remain for many years to come a religious minority within the greater city and the Jewish state. Although Jewish-Muslim relations in Israel proper are, in an ecumenical sense, actually quite good, the importance of the Haram esh-Sharif for Islam makes Old Jerusalem an unusually explosive religious locale. The extent to which both sides, Jewish and Muslim, manage to channel and contain religious passion will determine how much blood is spilled in and over the so-called "City of Peace."

Can the entente worked out in Northern Nigeria at the turn of the century between (Christian) British rulers and Muslim subjects be of any comparative interest in managing the Middle East conflict? Is there no analogy to be found between Old Jerusalem and post-jihadic Sokoto, two cities central to Arab-Palestinian and Hausa-Fulani history? Both recall Muslim majorities administered, however indirectly, by non-Muslim rulers. In Sokoto, British rule, fiercely resisted at first, was smoothly accommodated by a Hausa-Fulani aristocracy which invoked classical Islamic rules of *taqiyya*: externally submitting under conditions of physical weakness to infidel rulers while internally retaining the Faith. Lord Lugard's proclamation after the conquest of Northern Nigeria by the (Christian) British attempted to legitimize such accommodation:

> All [that] the Fulani by conquest took the right to do to rule . . . to levy taxes, to depose kings and to create kings now pass to the British. . . .You need have no fear regarding British rule, it is our wish to learn your customs and fashion. British rule is just and fair . . .

Though the Caliphate of Sokoto as a politico-religious polity was permanently undone by British occupation, Islam as such thrived—indeed, it significantly expanded—under the tutelage of colonial indirect rule. When independence came, Muslim rulers retained extensive powers, even if Nigeria as a whole was declared a secular state. By adopting a combination of accommodationist *taqiyya* and conciliatory *sulhu,* Islam in the Hausa-Fulani emirates not only survived but prospered, even under (and partly due to) European colonization.

There is no question here of comparing the Jews of Jerusalem to the British in Sokoto: whereas the former have ancestral ties and have maintained a three millenia presence, the British conquered only in 1900 and stayed for a mere six decades. More important, Jerusalem and Zion have held a central place in Jewish liturgy and consciousness throughout the ages; for the British, Nigeria was a mere colony and never held an affective place in the national psyche. Nor can one equate the colonization of Nigeria with the unification of Jerusalem (though both were unilateral measures which initially required force). From the Islamic perspective, however, there is this one parallel: Muslims, who once enjoyed uncontested sovereignty, have become political minors.

I am not, of course, legitimating the colonization of Nigeria, on account of its benefit to Islam, any more than I am championing the annexation of the Muslim quarters of Jerusalem into greater Israel. My point is that the experience of Sokoto and Northern Nigeria shows that, even on Islamic grounds, accommodation with rulers perceived to be theologically "infidel" can be nevertheless bloodless and relatively peaceable. Though political sovereignty was withheld for well over half a century, Muslims in colonial Nigeria did during that time enjoy widespread religious freedom.

One cannot, especially from the outside, counsel for the Palestinians of Jerusalem the same strategy employed by the Nigerians of Sokoto. But this, essentially, is El-Haj Jadeh's disposition. Though his knowledge of Hausa may be idiosyncratic in Jerusalem, as a local leader concerned foremost with the daily needs of his constituents, this alhaji's inclination to favor *hakuri,* patience, over intifada is probably not. Sixty years may be too long for those Palestinians anxious for the disincorporation of Arab Jerusalem from the Jewish state to wait; but if Israeli sovereignty over the Muslim and African Quarters of Old Jerusalem lasts only as long as did British rule over Northern Nigeria, they are already half way there.

Afterword

During my search for El-Haj Jadeh back on Ala al-Din Street in the Arab Quarter of Jerusalem's Old City in 2009, I was told that he had passed away a couple of years before. In 2013 I returned, meeting again with his formerly incarcerated son and, for the first time, El-Haj's cousin Muhammad Adam Jeddah. This older cousin had been born in Jerusalem of a Chadian father with roots in Saudi Arabia; I was told that in 2000 the cousin's own son was "martyred" on the Mount of Olives at the beginning of the second intifada.

There are no longer any African-born or African language-speaking residents of the Black African neighborhood of the Muslim Quarter in Old Jerusalem. Nor is there any more a mukhtar, because, I was told, El-Haj Jadeh had "cooperated" with the Israeli government. Instead of a mukhtar representing the Palestinians of Black African descent, there is now a committee.

SIX

Luxury Matzah[1]

Sharing the portable food gift

As a political anthropologist specializing in Third World countries, I travel widely in remote locales—West Africa, South Asia, the South Pacific, the Indian Ocean. Sometimes I'm away for more than a year. And deciding what to pack for food is never very easy. Yes, I take cans of tuna and the add-hot-water-and-eat meals in a

[1] Originally published in *Moment Magazine* 6:2 (April 2001), p. 48.

packet. But after years of traveling, I have made a counterintuitive culinary discovery. The perfect travel food was actually created by Jews in the desert some 5,000 years ago. Think matzah. Consider: Matzah is lightweight but filling; it never goes stale; and if it breaks in the suitcase—so what?

In the hinterlands of Niger (often ranked as the world's least developed country, according to the United Nations), matzah is a luxury. That's because Nigériens don't have much variety in their diet. Breakfast, lunch, or dinner, the main course is always the same: pounded millet or sorghum in hot sauce. Wheat is exotic, bread a rarity. When I share my matzah with African friends, it isn't exactly viewed as a "bread of affliction." Food "affliction" occurs when it is absent, and villagers resort to eating leaves or boiled grass.

All food (and matzah is no exception) is consumed in a certain context. In the hinterlands, that context is one of scarcity. I shared matzah with Africans in Muslim Niger not to be symbolic, but as a simple way to stave off hunger. It's the most portable fast food you can pack: no fuss, no muss—just open and crunch. Deep in the African bush, matzah is appreciated perhaps even more than at the Seder. Every piece is chewed slowly and mulled over, down to the very last crumb.

My decision to share the matzah has had an unintended consequence. At least in this corner of Africa, tucked away from Western civilization, a certain number of people think of matzah as just another thing that Westerners eat. They see it as a typically American snack, rather than a ritual Jewish food. Thus far, I have not managed to convey this distinction to my hosts. Which means that for now, at least, unleavened bread is as American to some Nigériens as apple pie.

Faralu, a Nigérien Muslim, tasting matzah for the first time

SEVEN

Reburying My Father in Africa[1]

A year after my father's death, I received a letter from my mother. She suggested I find a synagogue and spend the *yahrtzeit*, the anniversary of his death, with other Jews. There was just one problem: I was living in a remote Muslim African village on the outskirts of Nigeria, where I was a Fulbright researcher. The nearest *shul* was then thousands of miles away, and there was no way for me to get there.

I thought about my father as his yahrtzeit approached. Then, two days before the anniversary of his death, I found myself bantering in Hausa (a major language of Niger and Nigeria) with security officers at the university in Kano, the nearest big city from my research site. They taught me an existential African riddle:

Question: What is sweeter than sweet?

Answer: The fact that you don't know in advance the day that you'll die.

At nine in the morning on the day of the yahrtzeit, I heard crying and wailing from next door. The wife of Ilu the Tea Man, my neighbor, had just died.

That day, I followed the gravediggers to the cemetery, an unmarked sandy field on the outskirts of my village. All the village men were already there. The grave diggers dug a grave two feet deep. Then they dug another hole within the first. They carried the corpse, wrapped in a shroud and covered by a straw mat, on a bier to the burial ground. They removed the straw mat and placed the

---

[1] Originally published as "Sweeter than Sweet" in *Moment Magazine* 26:6 (December 2001), p. 48.

body deep in the ground. From one side they filled in the grave using a shovel; from the other side they pushed in the sand with their hands. Everyone sat on the ground and followed the imam, the Muslim priest, in Arabic prayer. It was not the ideal minyan for my father, but it would have to do. After a thought for Ilu's wife, I said Kaddish and thought about my father.

I had first come to Africa years before as a Peace Corps Volunteer. My father had initially opposed my joining the Corps, saying that those two years of teaching high school in Africa would be better spent in law school. But Dad came around to supporting me, and a year and a half later, he actually journeyed to Niger to check up on me.

Initially I feared it would be awkward. Since he was unfamiliar with the land and culture, I, the son, would be leading him, the father, for the first time. But he took his vulnerability in stride. "I'm in your hands, boy," he said. "I can't even speak the language."

Dad related to other Peace Corps Volunteers and American diplomats with surprising ease. He was the hit of the Peace Corps director's Hanukkah party. I listened in amazement as he regaled seasoned expatriates with his own travel tales and life stories. Top on the list was the bar mitzvah gift he gave my younger brother: fulfilling Alex's dream by bringing him, at real maritime peril, onto Devil's Island. This is the tiny spit of land off the northeast coast of South America, surrounded by rough and shark-infested waters, to which Alfred Dreyfus, the late nineteenth century Jewish French army captain, had been deported and spent over four solitary years on trumped-up charges of treason.

But it was Dad's bearing with my African friends that impressed me most. Even when he, a quasi-vegetarian, discovered that the goat the imam presented to him was to be slaughtered and skewered in his honor, my father preserved his unflappable calm. He greatly impressed members of my adopted culture, who place a premium on age, and who automatically accord the elderly the status, as we would say back home, of *chacham*—a sage, a wise man. That trip bonded us, and we remained closer than ever for the last three years of his life.

After the funeral of the Tea Man's wife, all the men gathered outside Ilu's home. According to custom, the imam distributed sadaka (the Hausa word for "charity" is identical to the Hebrew: tsadaka) to all the mourners: three *kobos* (cents) to men, one *kobo* to boys. More prayers (this time the Islamic Fatiyya) were recited. It was the start of a week-long vigil.

During the sadaka ceremony, they asked me how people in my land mourn. The question posed a challenge I had faced many times: providing a single satisfactory answer to sweeping questions about the customs and religions in *Ameriyka.* How do Americans marry? How do they pray? How do they grieve? To answer "they mourn in different ways" is not to answer at all.

"We, too, gather the community at the home of the bereaved," I explained, "though we do not at that time give tsadaka. Tsadaka is given in the name of the deceased some time later. It is given not to the mourners directly, but to support our 'mosques,' to purchase 'Qur'ans,' to support 'imams,' to help the poor."

Hundreds of villagers sat silently around me, thinking about Ilu the Tea Man and his wife. I whispered to a friend that today was the first anniversary of my own father's death. He nodded, understanding. I repeated the Kaddish, reburying my father in Africa.

EIGHT

Kaddish for My Muslim Chief[1]

This morning, I learned that my chief—an African chief of a Muslim people—died. And while some of my Orthodox co-religionists may frown upon the idea, tonight I shall say Kaddish in his honor. For he was not only my chief—he was the very embodiment of peace, tolerance, and forgiveness to which every leader should strive, and for which every religious person should pray. It's on the forgiveness front that he sorely tested—and taught—me.

Precisely half my life ago—twenty-seven years before, to be exact—I first appeared before Alhaji Harou Sarkin Fulani Mai-Gari da Mai-Guduma na Yardaje Zangon-Daura. At the time I had no idea what all those titles meant, only that he was the one who presided over the village in which I was hoping to live. Together, I eventually learned, those honorifics conveyed that he had already undertaken the prescribed pilgrimage to Mecca; that he was the chief not only of my desired village but over all the surrounding territory; and that he was a royal of the nomadic tribe credited with Islamizing the entire region by jihad two centuries ago. Today, that land is part of the strategic, often violent, oil-spouting giant about which we usually read only trouble—Nigeria. And the ethnic group among whom I would live as one of his subjects is the same as that of the would-be airline underwear bomber of December 2009—Hausa.

By agreeing to host me in his community—and never asking for a thing in return—Alhaji Harou became my chief. I have lost

[1] A version of this essay first aired over National Public Radio ("This I Believe—Rhode Island") in August 2011.

track of the number of times I returned to Yardaje, in Nigeria's far Muslim north, since that first year I spent there in 1983. Right before I last called upon him, also in December 2009, I was warned that his vision had sorely dimmed and his hearing greatly diminished. But he unfailingly asked after each individual member of my family, even remembering to ask about my mother (and not my father, who had already died before I first visited the chief's domain in 1983). And, as was his custom, soon after my arrival, he gifted me some birds (usually doves, this time a chicken).

"Power of God!" and "That's how it is"—along with his irrepressible chuckle—were my chief's trademark expressions. "Practice patience!" was another common phrase he used, especially when administering justice, or reconciling quarreling couples. And, as in all Hausa speech, he would rarely go three sentences without invoking *lafiya*—peace, well-being, health.

An Orthodox Muslim, one would be hard-pressed to describe my chief as a progressive. He had four wives—simultaneously—and more children than even he, in his final years, could probably keep track of. But not only did he approve Mom's and Aunt Hannah's funding of a shelter for blind women in his village, it was he who provided the precious plot of land right in the middle of it, just across from his own royal compound.

It was upon returning from safari with Elly from the Bronx that our personal relations were sorely tested. In our absence, someone broke into my hut and stole my only source of information from the outside world—a shortwave radio. My chief paid for the town crier to announce that, if the radio were not returned within three days, he would have a Qur'anic curse cast upon the culprit. It *was* returned, but I also wanted the thief to be punished.

I was the last in the village to learn what everyone in the village, including the chief, knew for some time—that it was a younger, favorite son of his who had committed the burglary. My courtesy visits to the chief were difficult for me in those days—especially when I knew that he knew that I finally knew what everyone had known all along. But not a word of the one thing that preoccupied me was uttered.

That's when I really learned to "practice patience."

Over more time—a quarter of a century's worth—I also learned from my Muslim chief the greatness of leadership through hospitality, generosity, and religious tolerance. And when I happened to be back in Yardaje three months after 9/11, in extending condolences over what had happened to "my brothers in America," my Muslim chief reaffirmed the greatness of faith and compassion over tribalism and fanaticism.

I grew up less than twenty miles from the World Trade Center. Why do those from afar who so fervently oppose a Muslim community center near its site so adamantly strive to associate Islam with the likes of Al-Qaeda? Why this urge to fear and reject a religion represented the world over, rather, by people like my chief, Alhaji Harou?

I believe that if more people, when they heard the word "Muslim," could evoke my chief's gentle face, infectious laugh, and soothing words—rather than the sinister mug and murderous deeds of a Bin Laden—then fewer people would automatically recoil at the idea of an Islamic center on sacred ground in a city that we all share.

Yes, I will say Kaddish for my departed Muslim chief. And, in his honor, I shall add (as do many Jews) to the prayer's affirmation in Hebrew that the Holy One will bring "peace over all of the people of Israel," the words *v'al kol yoshvei tevel*—and that He will bring peace "over all the dwellers of this world."

And I shall also say, as they would in Hausaland, "Amin."

NINE

Hanukkah in Hausaland[1]

(with Arielle P. Miles)

Prologue: African Genesis, Jewish Mother

Never, in my twenty-five years of periodic sojourns to Muslim Black Africa, have I concealed my Jewish heritage. Even despite the advice of my mother, late in the summer of 1977 . . .

I had just completed college. Mother finally accepted that, despite her concerted campaign against it, I was about to enter not law school, but the Peace Corps. In fact, I was about to leave the United States for a two-year stint in an Islamic country just south of the Sahara. It was not what a nice Jewish boy from New York was supposed to do—particularly given the global climate of anti-Israeli diplomacy at the United Nations and Palestinian airplane hijackings, kidnappings, and assassinations directed at US and Zionist targets alike.

So Mother finally relented—under one condition: "Promise me," she implored, "that you will not tell the people over there three things."

"Yes, Mother."

"First, don't tell anyone that you are an American." (So what if representing America is the very essence of being a Peace Corps Volunteer?)

"Yes, Mother."

"Second, don't tell anyone that you are Jewish." (This too was

[1] An abbreviated version of this essay, co-written with Arielle P. Miles, first appeared as "Hanukkah in Niger" in *Hadassah Magazine* (December 2004).

a strange request, given that my parents had always raised me to be proud about my heritage.)

"Yes, Mother."

"And finally," she said, still in a tone of utmost gravity, "don't tell anyone that you're white!"

Needless to say, I didn't follow my mother's instructions. (For the filial record, though, let me claim that it was the only instance ever . . .)

No, I never concealed my Jewishness in Muslim Black Africa. But neither did I make a show of it. When, chatting in the local language of Hausa, the subject of religion came up, I invariably pointed out that I was not, as they had assumed, a devotee of "the one from Nazareth," but rather a follower of the *Nabi Musa* (Prophet Moses) who brought us the *atora* (Torah). Still, for most villagers, it was rather abstract theology.

Until Hanukkah of 2003, when I visited Hausaland with my then-sixteen-year-old daughter, Arielle.

Excerpts Adapted from the Journals

Father

More than at any time during the two decades I have been visiting a distant Muslim village in the poorest country on earth, the issue of religion—my religion—has become prominent in conversation. Is it because of the war in Iraq and the alleged conspiracy of Israel and America? Because of the global terrorism perpetrated by al-Qaeda and cohorts? No, it is simply because this time I am accompanied by my young lady of a daughter for whom observing our holidays, as we do at home, is essential.

Daughter Continues

It was the fourth night of Hanukkah when we arrived in the village. I brought the menorah, one of those flimsy Chabad ones.

Hanukkah is kind of a messy holiday, because it leaves all that colored wax on whatever surface you place the menorah. In America, you just scoop it up and throw it out, but what are you supposed to do with it Africa? Nothing here gets thrown away. I picked up some pieces of the wax and made a pile of it for the children. I hope they found some entertainment in it.

Some nights we had visitors while we lit the candles. Sometimes they talked while I was saying the prayers, which I found quite disrespectful—I don't make noise when *they* are praying. Once, we lit candles at the home of one of Dad's friends. As gifts to the women and children we gave some of the dozens of wooden dreidles we had brought along.

Father

Only in a Third World setting would the sacrificial nature of ritual candle lighting hit me so. In a community without electricity, where few people own flashlights and even fewer can afford batteries, burning candles merely as a memory device (remember, we are not supposed to *use* the Hanukkah light, only to look at it) verges on the extravagant.

In such a poverty-stricken society, the notion of kids playing with dreidels for *gelt*—even just pennies—is too much. Instead, I say children spin these tops to win roasted peanuts.

Daughter

We also did Shabbat, of course. While we were packing for the trip, I asked Dad how many candles we'd need, and he said enough for one Shabbat. I made a really bad joke and said—knowing there'd be no electricity even-"Ok, I'll bring two candles, and one extra in case there's a power outage."

It turns out we actually spent two Shabbatot and so we only had three candles. I improvised with a makeshift Shabbat candle made of two yellow Hanukkah candles melted together.

Father

The Islamic world as a whole is especially upset with Israel and America nowadays, and this time I wondered before how these unprecedented displays of Jewish ritual would strike my Muslim friends and neighbors here. For sure, most people in Hausaland are too preoccupied with day-to-day survival to care much about Middle Eastern politics. Their knowledge of and interest in Judaism remains Qur'an-based. But you never know . . .

Word of our candle-lighting indeed spread through the village like fire; the deputy imam I interviewed the very next day ("People follow Bin Laden on account of what Israel does," he told me) had already heard about it.

Shariah (Islamic law) also had been adopted as the law of the land. Alcohol (including wine) is now not only irreligious; it is illegal. Celebrating Hanukkah and Shabbat are not the simple matters they were back home. But with daughter by my side, the pressure to observe is irresistible.

Daughter

Shabbat was a treat because that's when we had our little boxes of grape juice. It was our wine. Instead of challah, we used the matzah we had brought. (Dad always packs matzah as "emergency food" because he says it never goes bad and so what if it breaks?) We had salt. Everything was there.

We recited Kiddush from memory. The last night of Hanukkah fell on our first Shabbat, and I was really upset because the wind kept blowing out the candles. Kiddush and Hanukkah were the only similar things my mother and brother would be doing at home, and it made me homesick.

Father

"You are greater than we are," an Islamic preacher friend says to me.

I ask for confirmation, though I believe I know what he meant. "What do you mean by 'you'?" I ask.

"You Yahuds. For your origins go back further than others'," he replies. "Also, you are a people of trust."

Daughter

One by one, I put the headphones of my Discman on the ears of the young boys who had come to visit and let them listen to my favorite CDs. They had never heard this kind of music before. Some of it was klezmer. Their faces lit up in wonder, and they immediately began to dance.

In America, I always lie down and wait until I get sleepy before chanting the *Shema*. In Africa, though, sometimes I fall asleep before remembering to sing it.

Father

We brought dreidels to my Peace Corps town, and I gave one to a school official. He painstakingly copied the Hebrew letters from dreidel to paper, making note of what we explained, in French, each letter stood for.

This principal was an erudite young man impressively familiar with the contours and key dates of Jewish history. Yet he had also heard some rather fabulous things about us.

Daughter

We were talking to the principal of the middle school and it came up that we were Jewish. He said that Jews are a very smart people, "eternal scholars." He also shared with us some of the rumors that people had about Jews. These were new to me. Not mean, just very far-fetched.

Supposedly, we have a special mirror (*miroir mystique*). Anyone who looks in it immediately possesses all knowledge and doesn't need to study anymore because they know everything . . .

Father

. . . Jews have "secret powers" that enable them to "succeed in everything they do," the principal said he has been told. In particular, we are thought to possess "a magical mirror." Anything we decide to see will appear in the mirror and become real . . .

Father

"There is something I want to ask of you," the prince of the region tells me, "but I am afraid to."

"Don't be afraid," I reply. "You can ask me anything."

"I want you to make sallah."

I am momentarily confused. Sallah means prayer. What is so difficult about asking me to pray?

Then I realize the subtext—the prince means that I should pray like he does. As a Muslim.

I have already been asked by a village friend what my rabbi would think were I to convert to Islam. But this is different.

"My father raised me to pray in a certain way," I explain by way of polite decline. The prince knew that my father—who had visited me in that very kingdom when I first lived there—had died long before. "When I use the same words that Father used, in prayer," I go on, "I feel close to him."

The prince nods.

"And were I to change the religion he gave me, I feel that I would be betraying him."

His Highness clucks in sympathy. Invoking the ancestors is usually effective.

Daughter

Our rabbi sent money to build latrines so that the village schoolchildren wouldn't have to go in the bush. But the kids are embarrassed to share stalls and prefer to do it out in nature.

So the money from Rabbi Franklin is instead being used to dig a well. For their drinking water, the kids go home during recreation and often don't return to school. This way, with a well, the kids can drink at school and remain for afternoon class.

Father

"Without bread, there is no Torah," it says in the Talmud. Here in Hausaland, I adapt the maxim: "Without water, there is no learning." How can children concentrate in class if they are thirsty and have nothing to drink?

"Why don't they bring a water container from home?" you might ask. The answer is disarmingly simple: Plastic bottles are simply non-existent. And even if they were, who could afford to buy them?

Daughter

The principal had wanted the well completed for our arrival so that we could have an inauguration ceremony. But the well-diggers haven't finished. They are participating in the annual boxing and wrestling matches going on in the village.

Father

Post-9/11 sensitivities had inhibited my committing in writing the source of the *tsadaka* [charity]. This is the second most Muslim country in all West Africa, after all, and was it not possible that an overly zealous government official might catch wind of the Jewish connection and misinterpret or distort the motives of the donation? Face-to-face I would tell the principal, the chief, the imam, and anyone else who cared to know that the money for the well was actually provided by my rabbi in America. Indeed, I would show them pictures of Rabbi Franklin, of our synagogue, of its Torah, and especially the scroll from Egypt (Masar, in Hausa).

Rabbi Franklin was quite satisfied with my plan. In fact, he said, it didn't matter if his hand in the donation were known at all.

Daughter

At the well itself, Dad gave pictures of him and the rabbi standing in front of the *aron ha-kodesh* [the holy ark]. Dad pointed out the Ten Commandments, written in Hebrew, above the ark. The school librarian asked about the "scarves" Dad and the rabbi were wearing in the picture. "Scarves of holiness," is how the librarian put it in French, after he heard Dad explain what a *tallit* is.

Father

"I tell you all this just so that you know," I say to the principal. "My rabbi does not seek any credit. In our religion, there are levels of tsadaka. The highest one is the charity given anonymously."

"It is the same in Islam," the principal replies. "The imam will announce to the congregation that the mosque needs a new prayer mat. By the next morning, a mat will be inside. But no one will know who put it there. 'Anonymous gift.'"

Postscript: Back Home, Two Weeks Later

Daughter

"It's not fair, the magnitude of the difference between America and Africa."

Father

Amen. She got it. The trip was a success.

TEN

T/Sadaka by the Sahara: Birth Gifts, Bar Mitzvah Projects, and the Rabbi's Well[1]

> There are no totally generous acts. All "acts" have an element of calculation. One black ox slaughtered at Christmas does not wipe out a year of careful manipulation of gifts given to serve your own ends.
>
> *Richard Lee,*
> *"Eating Christmas in the Kalahari" (1969)*

Objectivity versus Philanthropy in Rural Africa

Richard Lee's cautionary tale of blending ethnography and generosity among the !Kung raises fundamental questions about the role of the Africanist in promoting change. Whether the goal is raising living standards throughout an entire society or feeding a Kalahari clan at Christmastime, the academic's interaction with Africa inevitably changes something about the continent.

A cornerstone principle of conventional social science is that the researcher should minimize his or her impact on the population under study. Few fundaments of positivism have retained as much

[1] A much longer version of this essay was originally published as "The Rabbi's Well: A Case Study in the Micropolitics of Foreign Aid in Muslim West Africa" in the *African Studies Review* 51:1 (2008), pp. 41-57. For stylistic reasons, I have excised most of the footnotes and references.

consensus among social scientists. Yet for social scientists conducting fieldwork in rural communities of Africa, this principle represents a major challenge. By virtue of the enormous economic disparity between scholar and subject, the goal of apprehending a community without changing it is as difficult as it is problematic.

Yekuwa (Yékoua) is an agglomeration of two Hausa villages in southcentral Niger, approximately seven miles from the boundary with Nigeria. As such, it lies on the southern zone of the Sahel, so-named for itself being on the southern "edge" of the Sahara. Now exceeding eight thousand in population (double its size from 1986), over the last two decades Yekuwa has experienced a modicum of development. Still, Yekuwa is incontrovertibly ensconced within the nation that the United Nations consistently ranks as dead last in terms of human development. Local economy is based on rain-fed dependent cereal production (millet, sorghum, maize) and livestock production. Outside of the few government-employed functionaries (teachers, medical personnel) there are no salaried workers. There is no electricity or running water: hand-drawn and manual foot-pump wells are the only source of water.

There are no welfare provisions for the numerous widows, blind, and destitute: begging for charity (Hausa: sadaka) is a common practice. In short, conditions in Yekuwa may be marginally better than the average for Niger as a whole, where life expectancy is 44 years, adult literacy barely tops 14 percent, and 85 percent of the population survives on two dollars a day or less (61 percent survive on $1.00). Hardship defines life in Yekuwa as it does throughout rural Niger: There is nevertheless one sustaining force that does impart hope and meaningful existence within grinding conditions otherwise determined by material privation: Islam.

Preliminary T/Sadaka

Upon the birth of my first-born (a daughter) in 1987, I sent word with a request that the town crier of Yekuwa spread the news. As is customary, I arranged to give a small sum of cash to "thank" the town crier for his efforts. The same procedure was followed two years later following the birth of my son.

During intervening visits, ad hoc, I extended modest amounts of sadaka to individuals, as culturally appropriate: to widows of recently deceased friends; to the blind and otherwise disabled; to *almajirai* (young Qur'anic disciples). It was with the impending bat mitzvah (the coming-of-age ceremony for Jewish females) for my daughter that the first attempt at wider scale sadaka distribution was instituted, thirteen years after her birth.

Distribution of sadaka is an integral part of life-cycle rituals within Hausa society. At naming ceremonies for newborns, at public wedding rites between betrothed families, and at mourning sessions following funerals, it is customary for sponsors and attendees to make donations that are in turn recycled to other attendees in the form of kola nuts and to the presiding mallams (Qur'anic masters) as honoraria. *Not* to contribute even a token amount of sadaka in such contexts is culturally uncouth.

Similarly, giving tsadaka (Hebrew: charity) has become an integral part of the coming-of-age ritual for Jewish adolescents in North America. Neighborhood soup kitchens, shelters for the homeless, clinics for abandoned animals—such are typical recipients of bar/bat mitzvah tsadaka projects. Given my longstanding relationship with Yekuwa, and the villagers' oft expressed interest in the growth of my family, we conducted a traditional Hausa distribution of *t/sadaka* in each of the villages in honor of Arielle's coming of age. Instructions went out that the t/sadaka should go to the needy, as defined by categories utilized in the carrying out of village censuses conducted in the course of research.

In each of the villages, an interlocutor-correspondent prepared a list with the names of the t/sadaka recipients. In Yekuwa, one hundred and four people each received fifty naira; in the neighboring village over the border in Nigeria, Yardaje, one hundred and nineteen individuals received the same: this represented approximately one percent of the population of each community. One of the lists detailed the following categories of recipients: blind (or partially sighted); mentally disturbed; extremely poor; crippled (polio, crawling); deaf; widowed; leprous; other.

No doubt encouraged by this expression of religiously inspired beneficence, the Sarkin Makaho (King of the Blind) of Yardaje in Nigeria approached me during a subsequent visit. "Should you be able and Allah so move you," he suggested, "please think about building a village Guest House for the Blind."

Thus germinated the idea for the t/sadaka project tied to my son's bar mitzvah in 2002—thirteen years after Samuel was born and two years after he had accompanied me on a visit to the village. A subsequent visit to the villages generated (1) a realization that the Guest House for the Blind was restricted to blind *men*; and (2) a request from the principal of the middle school of Yekuwa to finance construction of latrines for both male and female pupils. Gender bias with respect to the shelter for the blind was addressed subsequently by construction of a separate Guest House for Blind Women, financed by my mother, aunt, and daughter. Provision of sanitary facilities in Yekuwa became the entry point for rabbinic involvement in this Nigérien community.

Jewish Charity, African Development

Temple Emanu-El was founded in 1924 to serve that portion of the Jewish community of Providence, Rhode Island, adhering to the Conservative movement of Judaism. While "conservative" may have been an accurate characterization of the denomination vis-à-vis the less ritualistic and halachic (Talmud-adhering) Reform movement, it is a misnomer with respect to contemporary notions of politics and social justice. Although Conservative congregations differ considerably (based on membership and theopolitics of rabbi) in their attitudes toward and involvement in policy issues that transcend the Jewish community, by and large, they have come to embrace an expansive application of the principle *tikkun olam* (Hebrew: "repairing" or "mending the world"; the Hausa equivalent is *gyaran duniya*).

It was this spirit of tikkun olam, undergirded by tsadaka, that persuaded the rabbi of Temple Emanu-El, in the course of an informal and informational discussion, to finance the construction of latrines in Yekuwa. Given the potential for political mischief or suspicion that could arise at higher levels of Nigérien officialdom from formal Jewish charitable intervention in this Muslim society—and with such activity occurring at the height of the second intifada in Israel/Palestine—I asked that the rabbi's identity not be divulged in official correspondence. Invoking the Talmudic maxim that anonymous charity is higher than attributed tsadaka, the rabbi readily agreed.

Conceptually, it is unclear whether rabbinic sponsoring of latrines for Muslim children in a West African school should be characterized in terms of "development" (a secular notion) or "charity" (a notion with religious inspiration). Secular developmentalists could easily justify school latrines in terms of general hygiene and especially female empowerment. The rabbi himself employed the language of Jewish theologian Martin Buber (1970 [1923]) to describe his motives: human dignity, respect, privacy. In the context of Muslim-Jewish tensions revolving around the Palestinian-Israeli conflict, some might see the gesture through the lens of instrumental theopolitics. Social scientists, of course, could easily take issue with the hermeneutic, methodological, and indeed ethical propriety of integrating my religious background into the fieldwork locale. That line had already been crossed a year before, however, with the original distribution of t/sadaka funds to mark the bat mitzvah.

A letter dated March 26, 2003, from the principal reaffirmed the need for latrines for the middle school pupils and requested "expedited sending of the promised sum so that the work be entirely completed before the rainy season." A subsequent letter confirmed the receipt on May 15, 2003 (at 16:59), of the money transferred via Western Union and collected at the nearest bank (ninety miles away in Zinder). That same letter went on to explain a change in program plans: "At the meeting of the School Board, the governing body of secondary schools in Niger, it was affirmed that priority here still goes to drinking water. The decision was therefore taken to dig a well"—even though the amount of money made available (for latrines) would not suffice.

Despite the fait accompli, my rabbi not only agreed to the modification of the original project goal, but also decided to underwrite the additional funds necessary to complete the well. When I returned to Yekuwa in December 2003, work on the well had been held up on account of traditional wrestling and boxing matches that had drawn away most of the able-bodied well-workers. With a few apprentices, the master well-digger proceeded on his own, but water had not yet been reached by the time I departed the village. There was also now a planned second phrase of the well project. With the redoubled rabbinic contribution, the principal now envisioned improvements beyond the well project and the provision of regular drinking water for the students. These included a range of school gardening activities and a protective wall around the well to prevent contamination from animals attracted to the water source.

In face-to-face conversations with the principal and other village school administrators, I revealed the identity of the hitherto anonymous donor. Pictures of the rabbi, in liturgical dress and taken in the synagogue, were widely shown and left as mementos. Subsequent correspondence referred to the "salvific actions" of my "spiritual leader, the honorable Rabbi." To all who saw the photos, great interest was taken in the displayed Torah scrolls, skullcaps, and prayer shawls.

Emphasizing the role of the rabbi in the well project had strategic value: I retained my role as scholar-friend of the community, and at best intermediary of t/sadaka development, but deliberately eschewed adopting the persona of donor per se. Maintaining the long-term scholarly relationship without "giving back" to the community had become, over time, ethically problematic; but it also would have been problematic for me to assume the image or title (as a Nigerian immigration agent would later put it) of "philanthropist." It had taken many years, and some strategic personal investments, to earn the status of "son of Yekuwa"; becoming "benefactor of Yekuwa" would ineluctably distort and problematize this position.

Politics of the Rabbi's Well

In anticipation of my return to West Africa in March 2006, I took an empty bottle of drinking water from the repast following Sabbath services in Providence. I vowed that I would fill it in Yekuwa so that the rabbi could drink from "his" well in Niger.

Shortly after arriving, I searched with difficulty for the rabbi's well: village housing had expanded almost to the perimeter of the middle school, and spatial perspective was very different from what I had been familiar with just two years before. The well, when I finally discovered it, was a profound disappointment; in local parlance, it had "died." No longer giving any water, it had been stuffed with bramble to prevent the unwary from accidentally falling into the abandoned pit. I thereupon requested an audience with the district chief, to be attended by the two village chiefs and the principal of the middle schools. Two sets of reasons were proffered at that meeting (and at a subsequent one, with the mayor) for the well's dilapidation: one indigenous and one technical.

The indigenous explanation was that "the eyes of the well" had become "blind" for lack of care. A well must be constantly primed; otherwise it will dry up. Students at the school where the well had been dug were not drinking from it enough—they were studying instead. And the master well-digger—the person who had been paid to dig it in the first place—considered his job over once water had been reached. No one was in charge of maintenance. The technical explanation was that from the outset the well was not geologically, topographically, or hydrologically sound. It had been constructed in artisanal fashion, not scientifically: neither the location chosen nor the technology employed was suitable. Modern wells are made differently, with much more sophisticated equipment. That is why it stopped giving water after only a little time.

As I dug deeper, however, I sensed that the overarching reasons for the well's abandonment were political. According to the new principal, the well was a private, "person-to-person" enterprise between his predecessor and me. The former principal had not informed the staff, he claimed, which included himself. Without saying so explicitly, the new principal made it clear that when he took over the middle school, he had no sense of ownership of, or responsibility for, the well.

Based on the correspondence that I had received from the former principal, this was patently false: it had been in an official parent-teacher meeting that committee members had decided to use the rabbi's money to dig a well rather than latrines. This correspondence also identified the ringleader who supposedly had plotted, be it out of ethnic rivalry or partisan politics, to have the former principal ousted from his position. It was only after I returned to the U.S. that, rereading the correspondence and focusing on the names, I realized who this "plotter" was: the mayor!

Nevertheless, as yet oblivious to these machinations, I leveraged the rabbi's well in separate discussions with the current principal and the mayor. To the principal, with the district chief and two lesser ones witnessing, I asked rhetorically, "What am I going to tell my imam?" I then handed over the empty water bottle "from the rabbi's mosque," expressing the wish that, with the principal's leadership, one day it would be filled with water from the well and the rabbi would drink from it.

One morning, members of a wedding party from both the bride's and groom's side of the family appeared unannounced at my lodgings in Yekuwa. The main purpose was to officialize the marriage of the two families. After Mallam Souleymane, the visiting friend, asked that the parents counsel their children to be patient with their spouse (to the husband: "Be kind"; to the bride, "Do not run away"), Alhaji M. H. seamlessly integrated into the wedding formalities the problems of the rabbi's well: "May all proceed properly, without any problem that might bring us shame or embarrassment. Unlike the well at the middle school. The foreign 'imam' wanted to help, and built the well. Already, after less than a year, she is ruined. The foreign imam was supposed to drink from the well; [our friend] brought a bottle so that his imam could do so. But it could not be. So he put the bottle in the hands of the principal, as a sign of what he needs to do. May nothing like that occur."

Lessons Learned

Job descriptions for "doing good" in impoverished Third World settings ought to bear the requirement "thick skin." One must not be unduly upset by painful human reality, by the misery of the destitute blind, and by the indigence of the deaf-mute. One must be steeled against difficulties attending the transition from helping needy individuals to helping a needy community.

The biblical "Song of the Well" (Numbers 21:17–18) lyrically expresses the joy, accompanied by song, that the digging of new wells occasioned within the water-scarce environment of ancient Canaan: "Spring up, O well, sing-in-chorus to it; the well that was dug out by princes! that was excavated by people's nobles! with scepter! with their rods!" Yet wells also have been "causes of strife" (Miller & Miller 1952:814). Today, both the joyous and conflictual properties surrounding wells are evident more commonly in the Sahel than in Israel.

As outlined, an unusual rabbinic intervention in a Muslim community came to highlight both the positive and negative potentialities of well-digging. On one level, the religious profile of the donor was incidental: the micropolitical machinations surrounding the well's maintenance (or lack thereof) had little to do with its original financing. Yet the religious imperative "to do good abroad" did become enmeshed with local politics in unforeseeable ways.

Local politics render much more complex the goal of accomplishing grassroots, international development than some academics and Western donors imagine. In addition to the contrast between charity and development, the story of the rabbi's well also illuminates the messy contours between morally driven giving and locally directed projects. Faced with the inevitable frustrations and disappointments that such well-intentioned initiatives occasion, what course should one take? One possibility is to view development projects as "experiments" and a "learning process," accepting that experimentation carries with it the risk of failure. Another is to embrace the Hausa proverb, "Better the smallest present than the most magnificent meanness," and join to it the Talmudic maxim: "It is not for you to complete the work. Neither are you free to desist from it" (Pirkei Avoth 2:21).

Afterword

Fifteen American university students in tow, I returned to Yekuwa in December 2006. Leverage seemed to be working: the mayor claimed to have paid for repairs out of his own pocket, and water was again being drawn from the rabbi's well.

ELEVEN

Horse Inheritance, Jewish Soul[1]

A letter from an imam in Niger prompted the unusual dilemma. It came from Alhaji Mallam Harouna, whom I'd befriended sixteen years prior, deep in the West African bush, but hadn't seen since. In his missive, handwritten in Hausa, Alhaji Mallam Harouna informed me of the death of the village chief and the resulting inheritance dispute surrounding the horse the chief was wont to ride. But *whose* horse was it really? The chief's, as his brother—now claiming chieftaincy over the village—claimed? Or was it mine, as Harouna and others in the village distinctly recalled?

The horse belonged to me. And should the owner pass away, the legitimate heir would not be the chief's sibling, but my children.

Trying to resolve the dispute from long distance failed. By the time each successive exchange of letters made its rounds, the situation had deteriorated—the horse was seized; the horse was sold; the horse money was spent. I realized that in order to press my claim, I would have to return in person to Yekuwa, my village in Niger, after more than a decade's lapse. And to impress upon my village friends and adversaries the significance of inheritance, I decided to bring along my son, to show them what a true heir of the horse looked like. At the time, Samuel was all of ten years old.

On account of the legalistically religious aspects of the dilemma, before returning to West Africa with my son, I approached two local authorities for canonical advice: a Muslim scholar and my rabbi. Neither could provide the clear cut guidance I sought.

---

[1] Excerpts adapted from *My African Horse Problem* (Amherst: University of Massachusetts Press, 2008), written with Samuel Benjamin Miles.

"How would *shariah*"—that is, Islamic law—"deal with such a property and inheritance dispute?" I asked Dr. Shawkat Toorawa, a Muslim from Mauritius. Although I knew that in the village itself, African custom might trump Qur'anic law, it would still be helpful to know beforehand how Islamic jurists would adjudge the rightful heir question.

"Well," answered my young but full bearded friend, "it would depend on which school of shariah they follow there. Is it Maliki? Hanafi? . . ." I was stumped. All previous attempts to determine denominational affiliation level had met with the same village response: *Musilimi kawai* ("We're just plain old Muslims"). I never figured out if the answer signaled a front of religious unity or an indifference to high falutin' theological distinctions.

Rabbi Wayne Franklin of Providence did not ask if my Muslim African acquaintances inclined towards the Babylonian or Palestinian Talmud, the equivalent of the Maliki-Hanafi divide. Neither of us actually presumed that *halacha*—Jewish law—carried any weight in Hausaland. But disputed ownership of a dead chief's twice removed horse (for the chief had traded in my original horse for a younger steed, and then done it again) would be precisely up the ecumenical alley of any expert whose legalistic training begins with a case of ox goring. Or so I thought.

As I explained the detailed reasons for my son's and my imminent African journey, seeking some Semitic precedent of possible relevance, Rabbi Franklin took an unexpected tack. Rather than providing a detached Talmudic perspective based on rabbinic reason, this modern, clean-shaven, ever-poised cleric of a Conservative Temple turned kabbalistic on me.

"You've left part of your *neshuma* there," he pronounced.

Even before my likening of the Hausa village to a pre-Holocaust *shtetl*, a community in which everyone is connected and a place to which you viscerally belonged, my rabbi understood. He saw that there still was a part of my neshuma, my soul, still wandering horseback south of the Sahara. Did this neshuma, now sobered by fatherhood, still require an actual horse to claim as its own in Africa?

It is not that I wore my Jewish identity on my sleeve. But no more than would I hide it among those who mattered to me in America would I do so in West Africa. Religion is, in any event, too important a topic *not* to discuss with Nigériens, and my interlocutors were invariably intrigued to learn how Allah is worshiped by others.

My most public Jewish "outing" in Niger had actually occurred long before, with a Catholic friend. Zouménou was a fellow middle school teacher where I taught English as a Peace Corps Volunteer in the late 1970s. He taught history and geography. Zouménou was from Porto Novo in Benin, coastal West Africa, making him almost as much as a foreigner in the Islamic interior of the Sahel as I. He and I would spend entire Sundays accompanying each other to our respective homes African-style, by foot, back and forth, taking long pauses in each other's abode for refreshments. It was Zouménou who, for his lesson on the ancient Near East, invited me to address his class as a modern-day descendant of the nomadic Hebrews described in the students' French-language textbook. On the one hand, it made me feel like a Lubavitcher version of Mel Brooks' Million Year Old Man. On the other hand, I felt a keen sense of responsibility in being most likely the only Jew that any of these West African teenagers would ever be conscious of encountering in their entire lives.

The two decades following my Peace Corps service saw the spread of fundamentalist Islam in northern Nigeria and in Niger. But I refused to allow whatever fanaticism had taken hold outside of "my" villages to color my relationships within them. To do so would have meant ceding the essential humanity of person-to-person bonding to primal fear and regressive tribalism.

This is no idealistic, let's-all-hold-hands-and-sing-Kumbaya sense of humanity. If I was back in Yekuwa now, it was to protect my own property claims against local interlopers, even if I had to fight to do so. This is also a universal feature of the human condition. And I wouldn't renounce my horse rights in this Muslim land just *because* I was Jewish, and even if amputation for thievery and stoning for adultery were being reinstated as the law of the land in northern Nigeria. I am who I am, and this horse was mine—and my son's.

My pangs of medical guilt rather converged most intensely at the pharmaceutical desk at Rhode Island Memorial Hospital where the receptionist asked me pointblank, "How many do you want?"

It was thanks to the Internet and our pious pediatrician that I'd tracked down the only commercially available bulk source of oral rehydration. These relatively inexpensive packets have been long prescribed by the World Health Organization as the cheapest, most effective way of saving Third World babies from death by diarrhea. Previous sojourns had taught me how painfully common diarrheal death among infants is in Yekuwa and the nearby Nigerian village of Yardaje; indeed, I had once been ecstatically transported by being handed an hours-old newborn by her father, my census assistant in Yekuwa, only to be later plunged into depression to hear him murmur, after I asked about his daughter's health, "Ta raisuwa"—she'd passed away.

So although the major purpose of our journey is to untangle a horse knot, shouldn't my son and I also save baby lives along the way? Indeed, how can we travel to a place of such high infant mortality and *not* pack along some of those lightweight ORT kits?

It's a simple case of Morality 101—until you realize that the hospital receptionist's simple question "How many do you want?" actually translates into "How many babies' lives are you prepared to save?" You then find yourself on that slippery and guilt-wracked slope of insufficient liberalism, knowing that any amount of baby-saving ORT you bring along will still be insufficient, and that there will always be one more village baby dying of simple diarrhea even if you stuff your suitcases with nothing *but* ORT packets. You also can't help confronting your true limits of personal generosity or religious obligation: "How much of my travel and entertainment budget—not to mention life savings—am I willing to spend on baby saving, anyway?" What is the right amount of monetary sacrifice to make in a land where infant death is inevitable, recurrent, and seemingly eternal? Is it moral to travel to these parts for any other reason than to save innocent lives? Why travel there at all, when philanthropy can be just as easily—and much more cheaply—provided from afar?

I have to remind myself: I am not merely another white, middle-class liberal with vague sympathies for Third World babies. I am Mallam Beel/Mista Bello, a quasi-African on a specific horse-recovery mission with his rightful heir. Everybody can understand the ethics of this journey in Hausaland, even if in America nobody can.

In Jewish mysticism, eighteen is a propitious number, for its characters literally spell out *chai*, the Hebrew word for life. Multiples of eighteen are proportionately auspicious. Faced in the Rhode Island clinic with choosing how many hypothetical Hausa babies to save from future death by diarrhea, I transcend indecision by calculating a double chai, multiplying by two (one for each village), and plunking down the odd number of greenbacks to procure a kabbalistically based rate of reduced infant mortality.

Sam is not to remain Sama'ila for long. Apprised of the name change he underwent in Nigeria, here in Niger our Muslim priest of a host decides to further Islamize my son's Hausa name. Henceforth, my son is to be known, at least on this side of the border, as Isma'il.

In Qur'an and Torah alike, Isma'il is no other than Ishmael, son of Ibrahim (aka Abraham, patriarch of the Hebrews). In English, the name is usually rendered as "God hears." The literal Hebrew root for "God" embedded in the name is El, a close-sounding cousin to Allah.

Ishmael, it should not be forgotten, was expelled into the desert with his mother Hagar by a jealous Sarah and henpecked Abraham. But El-Allah took pity and sent an angel to rescue mother and child from the harsh wilderness.

And God was with the lad as he grew up,
he settled in the bush, and became an archer, a bowman . . .

fulfilling an even earlier divine prophesy: "he shall be a wild ass of a man."

Sorry, Samuel.

It's not the horse I most want Sam to remember. It's faithful Faralu, who chose to care for my horse rather than enrich himself with naira; our host and Qur'anic teacher, Alhaji Mallam Harouna, whose unexpected letters triggered our journey in the first place; Mallam Souleymane, our crippled, hand-walking, Muslim priest friend in Magaria. . . . It's the blind men with staffs who cheerfully greeted us, the deaf-mute women who patted us in welcome, the ragged beggars whose smiles calmed and reassured us. . . .

"In both villages," Sam writes in his journal, "there are blind men who get around by walking around with sticks held on one end by their sons. The son turns the stick to direct the father . . ."

May my son never forget that we wandered and rode alone, Hebrew songs and prayers on our lips, on horseback, through the wilderness of Hausaland.

TWELVE

Passover Reflections on a Saharan Genocide[1]

An oft-invoked myth, current in academic circles as elsewhere, is that of the pre-Zionist "Golden Era" between Muslims and Jews. According to this revisionist paradigm, until the emergence of the colonial and settler proto-Israeli state in Palestine, Jews and Muslims lived in harmony, if not fraternal solidarity, throughout the Islamic world. Jews were a protected and respected minority, a "people of the Book," as the Qur'an describes them, under beneficent Muslim tutelage. And they prospered. It was only the imposition of a Jewish state in the heart of the *ummah*, goes this baleful narrative, that politicized and antagonized relations between Muslim and Jewish communities in the Middle East and throughout the world. (By implication, the resolution of conflict between Muslims and Jews lies in the dissolution of the Jewish State of Israel.)

John Hunwick's (2006) concise but poignant study of a single Jewish community in the northwestern Sahara provides an African-based refutation to this myth. Thoroughly exploiting the extant (if scant) Arabic writings on the subject, Professor John Hunwick examines the rise and purge of a Jewish communal outpost of Tlemcen (now Algeria), which lay in the Touat oasis more than a third of the way to Timbuktu (where Jews also participated in the trans-Saharan trade). This outpost (or "fortified settlement") was called Tamantit and, at its peak in the fifteenth century, 4 percent of its

[1] A review of Professor John Hunwick's *Jews of a Saharan Oasis: Elimination of the Tamantit Community*, as published in *International Journal of African Historical Studies* 39:3 (2006).

overall population (no aggregate figure is given) was Jewish. That the Jews of Tamantit were not just a minority but a community with means is attested to by the existence of a synagogue. Then arose a man whose name should be as notorious as Pharaoh of the Passover Exodus, or Haman from Purim: al-Maghili.

Muhammad al-Maghili was a Tlemcen-born cleric who, sometime in the mid-1400s, took violent exception not only to the prosperity of the Jews but to their very presence in the midst of Touat. Hunwick implies that al-Maghili's enmity stemmed from economic envy or rage. His public rationale for preaching the expulsion and "degradation" (Hunwick's word) of the Jews was, however, purely theological. It is the kind of invective theology that today we would expect from the likes of a bin Laden or Zarqawi:

> Rise up, kill and enslave the infidels—
> Pigs, who care not for the name of Muhammad.
> Rise up and kill the Jews; they are indeed
> The bitterest enemies who reject Muhammad . . .
> Rise up and kill the Jews and all of those
> Who fight for them; thus will you please Muhammad.

Examples of the objectionable behavior ("foul abomination") of Saharan Jews mentioned in contemporary *fatwas* included: riding horses; using expensive saddles; and wearing spurred boots and turbans. For these and other transgressions, the Jews of Tamantit were routed, their synagogue demolished, and some of them killed at about the same time (coincidence?) as the Spanish Inquisition. Al-Maghili then went on to counsel, successfully, banishment of the Jews from the Songhay Empire. After all, according to al-Maghili's venomous interpretations of Qur'anic rulings governing the status of the *dhimmi* (protected non-Muslim), the Jews of the Sahara had especially transgressed by building a house of worship in an Islamic land; and for that, writes Professor Hunwick, this forebear of anti-Semitic fanaticism preached that "their men should be killed, their women and children enslaved, and their property seized" (p. 14).

John Hunwick, no less prolific for becoming emeritus professor (from Northwestern University) is of course one of the most pre-eminent scholars of Islam in Africa. (With the passing of Nehemia Levtzion—to whose memory Professor Hunwick co-dedicates the book—this circle has grown even smaller.) That he has at last turned a decades-long interest in this tragic but obscure event in Jewish and African history into a book should be of satisfaction to not only him but to two otherwise unconnected academic constituencies: the budding field of Saharan studies; and historians of the Jewish people. The former share in the overall ignorance among Africanists (Ali Mazrui being the most notable exception) about the role of Jews in West Africa history writ large. The latter generally have paid attention almost exclusively to the Jews of Ethiopia, the Lemba of Zimbabwe (cf. Tudor Parfitt) and the Abayudaya of Uganda being rare add-ons to Africanist Judaica.

For sure, the book is slim in length—much of the 67 pre-Appendix text pages are themselves textual translations—but the shadow it spreads on this epoch and corner of the Sahara is long, indeed. Nearly five hundred years after the Jews were routed from their Saharan homes, their descendants in the northern oases, notes Hunwick on page 1 of his book, still concluded their Passover Seder by replacing "Jerusalem" with "Tamantit" in the traditional prayer "Next Year in ______ ." Reading this fine gem during Passover reinforced this reader's faith in the God of Memory, as incarnated in Hunwickian history.

THIRTEEN

The Jewishness of Nehemia Levtzion's Legacy[1]

In the Hebrew language, *kavod*—respect—conveys a sense of obligation reminiscent of that so strongly entrenched in African culture as well. By highlighting Nehemia's Levtzion's contributions in the areas highlighted by the themes of the 2004 African Studies Association meeting (Identity, Language, and Memory, in Africa and the Diaspora) I wish to impart my own measure of *kavod* to one of the foremost Israeli, and Jewish, Africanists.

Who was Nehemia Levtzion? His very name gives us a sense of his origins: Lev Tsion, The Heart of Zion.

The original Nehemiah, of the Old Testament, was the wine taster to King Artaxerxes of Persia in the fifth century B.C. (His job, of course, was not to choose the best Bordeaux or Merlot, but rather to sip and physically react to any poison that enemies of the king may have slipped in to the royal cup.) One day the King noticed that Nehemiah was not looking well. He could have been concerned for his own self, but nevertheless inquired of Nehemiah what was ailing him. The prophet responded that Jerusalem ("the city of my ancestors") lay in ruins. Artaxerxes dispatched Nehemiah on a mission to restore the welfare of the Jerusalemites, who were then under Persian dominion.

"Our" Nehemia was also a true Jerusalemite, similarly making a mark in Yerushalayim (Jerusalem). In his capacity as Dean of Humanities and Bamberger and Fuld Professor of History of the

[1]Originally published in a collection of homages edited by Professor Ann McDougall in the *Canadian Journal of African Studies* 42:2/3 (2008), "Engaging with a Legacy: Nehemia Levtzion (1935-2003)."

Muslim Peoples at The Hebrew University in Jerusalem, as academic chairman of the International Center for University Teaching of Jewish Civilization, and Director of the Van Leer Jerusalem Institute, like his prophetic namesake, Professor Levtzion contributed immensely to the making of Jerusalem as a center of learning. His contribution in this domain was three-fold.

First was his teaching: scholarly, non-politicized study of African history, and especially Muslim African history, to his students at the Hebrew University in Jerusalem. The conference out of which his co-edited *The History of Islam in Africa* grew was convened at the Van Leer Institute in Jerusalem. Though published only a few years ago (2000), it has already become a standard textbook in the field.

Second was the kind of learning with which historians and Africanists are most familiar: the dissemination, within the global scholarly community, of his scholarship on West African history. In our politicized times, some might have expected the prospect of an Israeli Jew uncovering and interpreting Muslim history to be problematic. Yet Nehemia encountered no such protest or barrier: his scholarly integrity transcended even Middle East tensions.

Third, and probably least known, were Nehemia's efforts to promote Jewish studies, in an interdisciplinary, and international, plane. This included, as he put it in his 1990 contribution to the New York University Press volume *Teaching Jewish Civilization: A Global Approach to Higher Education*, "the development of regional approaches to the teaching of Jewish civilization." *Teaching Jewish Civilization* contains a listing of countries and universities included in the World Register of University Studies in Jewish Civilization, and included seven African nations (Cameroon, Côte d'Ivoire, Congo, Kenya, Nigeria, South Africa, and Swaziland).

Nehemia Levtzion thus integrated two complementary scholarly agendas: on the one hand, respectful learning of Muslim civilization by Jewish scholars and institutions of higher learning; on the other hand, promoting respectful learning of Jewish civilization in non-Jewish universities and by non-Jewish as well as Jewish scholars.

In his life and beyond, Nehemia serves as model for integrative efforts of scholarly exchange between the Jewish and non-Jewish scholarly worlds in general, and between the Muslim and Jewish worlds in particular. It is in this context that I take the liberty of summarizing my own project which surely bears this Levtzionian imprint: but before doing so, permit me to invoke the first time that I ever met Nehemia:

I was a graduate student at the Fletcher School of Law and Diplomacy of Tufts University when Nehemia was on sabbatical at the Center for International Affairs at Harvard. Just back from Muslim West Africa after two years in the Peace Corps, I was writing a paper on the role of the chiefs under French and British colonial jurisdiction and eagerly attended a talk that Nehemia was giving in the African Studies seminar series convened by Dov Ronen. Somehow, I had the temerity (or chutzpa) to approach this eminent historian and maladroitly asked, "Why would an Israeli be so interested in African history?"

Nehemia misinterpreted my admiration as a challenge and brusquely replied with a variation on "Why not?"

"Why shouldn't an Israeli choose this as a field?" he replied in his characteristically powerful manner. "Are not Israelis scholars like anybody else?" I then proceeded to compound my chutzpa by asking Nehemia to read my student paper. (This was a decade after he had already published *Muslims and Chiefs in West Africa,* but I was a bumbling grad student and did not yet know it.) I was incredibly naïve about sabbaticals, professors, and pesky grad students. Remember, he was not my professor, he was not at my school, and he was on leave. Yet Nehemia not only agreed to read my paper, but gave it the benefit of his full critique and commentary. In the ensuing years, I was honored by his friendship.

During my first sabbatical, at The Hebrew University in Jerusalem in 1994, I presented my book (*Hausaland Divided*) that expanded from that graduate school paper. Though I was a tenured professor, when Nehemia Levtzion showed up at my talk I started quaking again. Even among friends, could not Nehemia intimidate by his sheer breadth of knowledge?

My project that most bears the influence of Nehemia's integrative scholarship is *Third World Views of the Holocaust.* It began with an international symposium aiming "to assess the contemporary relevance of the Holocaust for the non-Western world":

> Scholars, writers and activists hailing from Africa, Asia, Latin American and the Caribbean focused on the impact of the Shoah on their own thinking writing, and worldviews. The Symposium belied the preconceived notion that among Third World intellectuals hostility towards Israel and the Jewish world is ingrained and endemic, that sensitivity to the Holocaust is conditional and politically framed, and that there is little sympathetic consciousness of the Shoah among peoples and societies not directly affected by it. (*Third World Views of the Holocaust. Summary of the International Symposium*, p. i, 2002)

My inclusion of scholars from Palestine and Muslim Mauritius in the symposium makes me wonder what role my emulation of the Africanist "heart of Zion" played in conceiving such a project in the first place. In any event, I am confident that Nehemia would have sympathized with at least some of my main conclusions:

1. *intellectual globalization* includes the Shoah within the emerging universal consciousness of world history;
2. *reparations claims* for other people's historical injustices derive their moral authority and tactical moorings from precedents established for Holocaust victims;
3. *H/holocaust parallelism* is a strategy employed by otherwise ignored groups under fire to gain support and sympathy from the West;
4. *post-Shoah moral responsibility* redounds upon an Israel whose overall legitimacy, despite criticism of certain policies, is respected; and

5. *denial of Holocaust* (along with fictionalization and self-suppression) is replicated in instances of Third World genocides. In short, the Third World *indigenizes* the Holocaust and its legacies in diverse manners.

August 1999 in Jerusalem was the last time I spent with Nehemia, one-on-one. He was very generous with his time, taking me on a tour of his favorite spots in his favorite city. These included the Haas Promenade panorama of the Old City near the old United Nations headquarters and the American Colony Hotel in the eastern part of the city. I distinctly remember being surprised by the unsolicited theological admission he made to me.

"On *Yizkor* [memorial service for the dead] for those who are close to me, I say Kaddish; for High Holidays, I go to synagogue. But I don't go in the whole superstition of it.

"I have my own *shulchan aruch* [observance rules]: I don't write on Shabbat. It's something I do for my children, as an example."

The memory of Nehemia unites scholars across disciplines and geographical boundaries. He embodied strong commitment to education in one's homeland, and about one's homeland in the diaspora. He was the consummate sabra—an Israeli-born Jew, named after the desert fruit that is prickly on the outside, sweet on the inside. For sure, no colleague I know called Nehemia "sweet"—but inside, he was certainly a *mensch*, a good man who did good things. We are lucky he was also a scholar.

FOURTEEN

Among the "Jubos" on the Festival of Lights[1]

24th of Kislev, 5770—Erev Hanukkah, Nnamdi Azikiwe International Airport, Nigeria

"Shalom, Prof!" the stocky, dark man calls out as I begin to queue up at the arrivals Immigration counter. "Come with me." I follow as we circumvent the normal line of people queuing up to be stamped into the Giant of Africa.

In exactly two weeks, while I am still here, the would-be underwear suicide bomber will set off from this same country to try exploding a device as his plane—of the same airline that just left me off here—begins its descent into Detroit. He will do so as the first-known global jihad terrorist from Nigeria. I am here, as far as I can gather, as the first Jew to travel to Nigeria expressly for the purpose of spending Hanukkah with a handful of Igbos who, in Black Africa's most heavily Muslim-populated nation, proudly but incongruously identify as Jews. I do not yet know, of course, that in a fortnight, the world's attention will be focused on the nexus of

[1] This is an expanded version of the essay that appears in the "Blacks, Jews, and Black Jews" issue of *Transition. An International Review* 105 (2011), pp. 30-45. It is informed by a return visit to Abuja and interviews in Tel Aviv with Nigerian Jews residing there. It is also enhanced by scholarship published in 2012, especially on Igbo identification with Jews and Judaism by Edith Bruder and by Johannes Harnischfeger, and on the relationship between Nigeria and Israel by Daniel Lis. For an account of spending the holiday of Purim with the same community, see Afsai (2013).

Nigeria, Islam, and terrorism. Nor do I realize, due to a misunderstanding arising from a hurried flurry of pre-flight e-mails, that the man I am following out of this airport named for the Igbos' greatest hero is not, as I had assumed, a Member of the Tribe (Igbo or Jewish), but rather a Muslim, from the Ibara, a small tribe related to the Yoruba.

Then again, every visit to Nigeria is illuminating in its own way. And that's even without the benefit of the Festival of Lights.

Ever since the nineteenth century, when Christian missionaries began venturing into the colonies to ferret out remote peoples for whole scale conversion, discovering any one of the ancient Ten Lost Tribes of Jews has become an evangelical growth industry. A Hebraic past fit perfectly well into the New Testament perspective of an evolutionary approach to the Judeo-Christian faith. It also was tactically useful. "Primitive tribes" shown to have derived from lost Israelite clans could be induced to continue travelling along the theological continuum from superseded Old Testament ritual to post-rabbinic Christianity. Such seemingly academic tomes as Joseph Williams's 1930 *Hebrewisms of West Africa* distilled the work of a host of Biblical-minded colonial officials and anthropologists to identify a multitude of West African peoples as Israelitish descendants. Doctor (of theology) George Basden had already titillated readers regarding customary commonalities with the Hebrews in his earlier *Among the Ibos*, and would do so again with his later *Niger Ibos*. Even the most widely known Igbo in the Western world, the former slave (and devout Christian) Olaudah Equiano, seems to have imbibed earlier missionary belief in Hebraic West African origins, as reflected in his late eighteenth century autobiography. Thus identified, millions more West Africans could more easily be corralled into Christianity in the colonies.

Mainstream Jewry, both Ashkenazic (European) and Sephardic (Mediterranean and North African), has traditionally been reticent about discovering their putative long lost cousins in "exotic" lands. It is true that two British rabbis provided Hebrew-English letters of introduction for members of an 1841-2 European expedition in case they encountered any Igbo-speaking Jewish communities along the Niger River. But with the partial exception of Ethiopian Jews, whom Jewish lore long identified (despite lack of historical evidence) as descendants of King Solomon and the Queen of Sheba, both Ashkenazim and Sephardim alike looked askance at supposed Lost Tribe descendants who looked so different from them. Prior to the establishment of the modern State of Israel, surviving as minorities both in European Christendom and Islamic Caliphates was a sufficiently difficult enough task, trumping any desire (or facility) to track down or claim Lost Tribe descendants. After Israel's founding, consolidation of a Jewish majority within the Jewish State has been challenging enough, what with Orthodox rejection of Reform and Conservative Judaism and their converts from overseas, tensions between North African and East European Jews over political supremacy, the battle of Ethiopian male "Falashas" to be considered Jewish without further circumcision, and the massive influx of new Israeli Russian spouses and in-laws who never claimed to be Jewish in the first place. Looking for ancient remnants of Hebrew ancestors in Africa was the last thing the modern State of Israel was set to do.

So it is little wonder that *The Search for a Lost Tribe of Israel*—subtitle of a groundbreaking crossover in Jewish and African studies—was undertaken by a non-Jewish scholar, Tudor Parfitt of the School of Oriental and African Studies at the University of London (*Journey to the Vanished City* 1999/1992). Using a combination of classical anthropology, oral history, and genetic testing, Professor Parfitt helped confirm the claims for the Lemba of southern Africa (even if his own conclusions are more guarded) of Jewish Yemenite-Southern Arabian ancestry. The recurrent trope of Hebrew or Israelite origins of supposedly superior tribes—in shorthand, the "Hamitic Hypothesis"—is elegantly exposed in Parfitt's later work, *Black Jews in Africa and the Americas*.

Mainstream Jewish reticence to African Judaica has been

replaced in some circles by certain outreach, if not outright embrace. A single-century old community from Uganda, the Abayudaya have become the object of intensive engagement by American Jews: Jewish education, community development, ethnomusicology. A New York-based Jewish organization, Kulanu ("All of Us"), pro-actively seeks out "lost" communities with claims to Judaism throughout the developing world. So does Be'Chol Lashon ("In All Languages"), based in San Francisco, whose mission is to "grow and strengthen the Jewish people through ethnic, cultural, and racial inclusiveness." From Jerusalem, The Elijah Project of Amishav actively searches for Jewish-identifying descendants of the ancient tribes of Israel (both the Lost Ten and those of the tribe of Judah whose ancestors were forced to convert to Christianity during the Spanish Inquisition) to reintegrate them within Judaism and modern Israel. Also in Israel, Shavei Israel-For Our Lost Brethren similarly "supports, guides and provides assistance [to] all members of [the] extended Jewish family" in countries where they are otherwise unknown. Dr. Edith Bruder, a former student of Professor Parfitt, has synthesized the corpus of recent work on African Jewry in *The Black Jews of Africa* and, together with Parfitt, in their edited anthology *African Zion: Studies in Black Judaism*. The transcultural transformations that these activities and inquiries so keenly pursue (and thereby promote) are a byproduct of globalization. They raise a broader question: to whom does Judaism belong? This is an unspoken question that my Jewish experience in the Nigerian capital thrust to the fore.

My first glimmer of knowledge about Nigeria came in 1967, the year before my bar mitzvah. Walter Cronkite horrified us on the CBS Nightly News with images and commentary about children with bloated bellies dying of hunger. It was happening in a far-off place called Biafra. A civil war was raging; the "Igbo tribe" was trying to break away; Biafra is what they called their would-be country. Israel was on the side of the Biafrans: was it in Hebrew School that I learned that? In any event, regardless of Israeli opinion, in my adolescent understanding Biafran kids were helpless victims, and therefore among the good guys. Little did I know then that the Ibos (as they were spelled then) had, on account of their respected reputation as entrepreneurial merchants, long been called "the Jews of Africa." Even less did I appreciate that, behind the scenes, Israel supported the Biafrans because they were fighting a Nigerian government led mostly by Muslims. It would be many years before I would learn, as a scholar of the Shoah, that lobbyists and diplomats of Biafra strategically cultivated their image to the Jewish world as a people suffering a "holocaust." In the meantime, years of living among the Muslims of northern Nigeria had nuanced my view of the Biafran conflict. In any event, the Igbo rebellion was long quashed (with tacit U.S. support), and I have had little personal contact with Igbos.

Until now. Thanks to e-introductions by Rabbi Howard Gorin of Maryland, pioneering envoy to Nigerian Jewry, I would spend this entire Hanukkah in the company of a people who, not satisfied with having survived the near-genocide of the Biafran war, have assumed an even riskier identity as a tiny minority of Jews in a mega-country that periodically melts down, in pogrom-like riots, along its Muslim-Christian fault line.

Tonight, though, fighting off jet lag, the confusion of tribal identities, and a nagging skepticism born of advance fee and other scams emanating from Nigeria, I am more worried about making cultural or liturgical gaffes as I bring my Long Island Ashkenazic understanding of Hanukkah to the people whom I call "Jubos"—that is, the Jewish Igbos—of Abuja.

Second Night of Hanukkah: Gihon Hebrew Research Center, Jikwoyi, Abuja

Only forty-eight hours before, still in packing mode, I was wondering: Should I bring *latke* (potato pancake) mix to West Africa? What kind of *gelt* (coin-shaped chocolate) is appropriate in the sub-Saharan tropics? Will they know of dreidels, these people from the Niger Delta? How many candles, how many menorahs, should I put in my suitcase? And most stressing of all, will I be the one leading the Hanukkah service?

I need not have been distracted by such details. For the corollary to the question, "To whom does Judaism belong?" is much more compelling. That question is: "To whom do the Jubos belong?"

Hanukkah, in stencil and spirit

Without renouncing their Igbo and African heritage, the Jubos yearn to belong also to the wider Jewish world. This is not a "mere" matter of being recognized as brethren by their counterparts in America or Israel. "Torah, worship, land, and people are inseparable," one Jubo said to me. It is this holistic concept of Jewishness to which Jubos bind themselves. Through belief, study, and practice, they ought to earn entry into the worldwide community of Jews. At the same time, their claim to Nigeria is unflappable. Perhaps most difficult to understand is the Jubos' willingness to accept the mantle of minorityhood within a nation experiencing an already rocky pluralism. Given the background of Biafra—and latent Christian-Muslim tensions—in the wider scheme of Nigerian history, it is difficult enough to feel secure as an Igbo. For an Igbo to quit Christianity is all the more risky. To whom do the Jubos belong? They belong to all those willing to accept the sincerity of their convictions.

No, I needn't have worried about my hosts' lack for objects of Judaica. For the Jubos possess much more precious commodities than I could stuff in my duffle bag: a joy-infused approach to Judaism, an unquenchable thirst for Jewish knowledge, and masterful prayer leaders. And, though it costs fifty dollars at the local market, they even manage to bring to their festivities a bottle of Manischewitz wine for the Kiddush blessing. But that's the least of their sacrifice.

Pinchas ben Eliezer (born Azuka Ogbuka'a) is but one of the several Jubo men I encountered who had lost their wives over the husbands' irresistible attraction to Judaism. Raised as Christians in a profoundly religious country, Igbos who reject the divinity of Jesus for the faith of their reputed ancestors—Lost Tribes of Israel—must often tragically choose between spouse and faith. Now *that* is a humbling commitment to Judaism. In America, the tradeoff is more commonly losing the religion as one marries out of the Jewish faith; among the Jubos, the tradeoff is alienating one's spouse as one enters into the Jewish faith. So whose relationship to Judaism is more meaningful: that of American ethnic Jews or that of Nigerian Igbo Jews?

Personal sacrifice for the Jewish faith: Pinchas

Among the more observant Jewish communities in America, a holdover, self-deprecatory joke from Eastern Europe still pertains: "two Jews, three synagogues." I wonder about its extension to the minoritarian Jubos in Nigeria: in Abuja, I need to shuffle between the Gihon and Tikvat Israel congregations. Each is over 45 maddening African driving minutes away, in opposite directions, from my accommodations in the center of town. If the *mechitza*, the separation between men and women in the prayer hall, is a standard litmus test, we can say that if Gihon is Orthodox, then Tikvat is Conservative. But more striking is the difference in infrastructure. At Gihon, the ceiling is finished, there is an ark for the Torah, and the Hanukkah menorah is large and lovely. At Tikvat Israel, where I lit the first night's candle, the rafters are open, there is no Torah scroll, and the menorah consists of painted coke bottles mounted on a wooden frame. Neither congregation lacks, however, in *kavana*—authentic intent of worship. And neither community appears insecure in its observance of Judaism: it is I, the odd Ashkenazi in a minyan (prayer quorum) of Black Africans, who would look to an outsider like he doesn't belong in this assembly of Jews. But, as one of the hand painted sigs on the outside synagogue wall serves as reminder, *kol Yisrael aravim ze le'ze*—all Jews are brothers. I am an honored guest, but nothing special as a Jew.

For now, the Jubos are largely unknown to, if not mostly ignored by, the wider Jewish world. But when the different denominations in America wake up to the Jubos' demographic potential—Igbos in Nigeria number in the tens of millions—there is bound to be an intra-Jewish Scramble for Africa. The movement with the most at stake is Conservative. Once the largest stream of organized American Jewry, this centrist pole of Judaism has come under stress from the more theologically liberal Reform movement to its left and more traditional Orthodoxy to its right. Holding the middle is never easy, but moderates don't usually realize how hard they need to work to maintain their centrality. Thanks to Rabbi Howard Gorin, Conservative Judaism already has a toe-hold in Nigeria. But if, as a movement, it does not embrace the Jubos, then eventually some

No reflection of vibrancy within: Synagogue signage

strain of Orthodox Judaism will do so, and wind up slighting Conservatives in the process.

Actually, this has already begun to happen. Oriel ben Shlomo, originally from Cameroon, presents himself as a rabbi who has lived in Israel. Soon after arriving in Nigeria, Rabbi Oriel took his hosts aback by reputedly asking, "What kind of Judaism is this?" (As many first-timers to Nigeria, he also supposedly demanded "What kind of country is this?") Dissension among the Jubos reputedly contributed to the rabbi's detention on suspicion of espionage and his expulsion from Nigeria. But it is likely that other Orthodox missionaries will return. And when Lubavitch—the ultra-Orthodox outreach Brotherhood—discovers the Jubos, well, both Nigeria and world Jewry better watch out. They will undoubtedly repeat Rabbi ben Oriel's message that "Only the light of Torah can break the cloud of darkness over Nigeria." This is not a message that Nigeria, dealing with its own shocks from Niger Delta terrorists in the South to the shariah-hardliners in the North, will be happy to hear.

Jubos are only dimly aware of the sometimes keen competition that frames relations between and among Orthodox and non-Orthodox streams of Judaism. In this sense, the embrace of Judaism in Nigeria is in its idyllic phase. But woe to the Jewish world at large if it superimposes its own *mishegas* (craziness) upon Nigeria's homegrown *wahalla* (troubles).

"Where did you put the *aliya*?" I am asked at the conclusion of the Shabbat morning service. I thought my questioner meant the card with the number indicating the order in which I was called to recite the blessing over the Torah, which happened to be the fourth aliya. But no, he meant the bid I had placed for the privilege of being called up to the Torah. Since my arrival yesterday, I haven't had time to change money; fortunately, I have local currency left over from my previous trip to Nigeria.

Actually, I had goofed in the bidding. Two hundred—my original bid—was what the first aliya had gone for. The third aliya had already been auctioned off for four hundred. So, for the honor to have my name, and that of my father, invoked in the benediction over the Torah reading, I had pledged to the synagogue five hundred naira. That's what the Igbo beadle was making sure I placed in the appropriate box, lest the bid be forgotten. Just one of the customs that make Judaism in Nigeria quirky. But no less genuine.

Like the ablutions. In "normative" Judaism, I had never experienced washing one's hands before entering the synagogue to begin prayers. Even *between* prayers (say, between those of Shabbat morning and Shabbat afternoon), the ritual hand washing is practiced. It is an enchanting *minhag* (custom), an appropriate adaptation of Igbo tradition to Jewish religion.

Here is another endearing minhag: men holding hands and dancing, in the middle of the synagogue, around the altar-in-the-middle. Or another: at the conclusion of the Sabbath, the congregation, in song, exits the synagogue backwards, to symbolize their reluctance to leave Shabbat and their continuing facing towards Judaism during the week.

Third Night of Hanukkah

Humbling, too, in their tranquil way are the children. I contrast the squirming, running, yelling kids in most shuls I have known in America to the quiet, immobile, obedient Igbo children taking in the hours-long services in Abuja. They are truly a marvel. If there is one contribution I have made to the celebration of Hanukkah among the Jubos, it is to communicate—through story-reading, Hanukkah song tapes, dreidels, and shekels—that this is a holiday for children. The mothers beam even as the fathers are a bit befuddled.

Then I wonder—am I doing the right thing? Is the child-focus of Hanukkah more an American accretion than a Jewish tradition? How much of what I bring as "normative Judaism" is really a kind of American Ashkenazic chauvinism? Shouldn't I focus on absorbing rather what the Igbo struggle to revive and preserve in Judaism?

In an ironic throwback to the state of Jewry in America, the Jubos express their concern over assimilation. The main problem is the public school system where, here in Abuja, Christianizing influences are prevalent. "My son was beaten up because he does not accept Jesus," is a typical refrain. "We need our own school. Only that way can they remain open and proud Jews."

Throughout Nigeria, pupils in public schools must take either Muslim or Christian studies. You must "be" of some recognized religion in Nigeria, or else you are despised or worse. If you practice something unknown—such as Judaism-you may be accused of being a cultist. This is the reason that Jubos dare not display their Hanukkah menorahs in their windows.

Jewish education: this is the main message that Sar Habakkuk, leader of the Tikvat Israel congregation, wishes to convey. "A teacher. That's all we want. Someone who can come and teach our children. A school. We have a building; we have a room for the teacher. But we need to give our children a Jewish education!" Habakkuk's protégé, Natan, Tikvat Israel's cantor, is the only Jubo in Abuja to have undergone formal conversion.

If there were a rabbi, of course, things would be easier. But the congregations are led by "elders"—venerated Igbo men who, over the last two decades, have invoked Hebraic roots. For most, that path was a circuitous one, taking them first through the detour of so-called Messianic Judaism. For some, the theological contradictions eventually began to gnaw mercilessly. "When I first began thinking about it," says Pinchas, "I could not sleep an entire night. The contradiction was too much. If we are to be worshipping the one and unique Creator as God, then how can we also be supposed to worship Yeshua [Jesus]?"

In the absence of trained and bona fide local rabbis, Igbos are the first historical and thorough-going theological beneficiaries of cyberspace: they are, to a large extent, Internet Jews. While holy books and Jewish texts do make their way to Nigeria, it is by going on-line—however fitfully, given limited computer access and fre-

Sar Habakkuk

quent power outages—that Jubos connect to the greater Jewish world of learning.

Twenty-nine-year-old Moshe, who does seamless Torah readings in a beautiful voice and near flawless delivery, learns his Hebrew online. (The only "defect," a function of the Igbo language, is his inability to chant the *ts* sound of *tsadi*; it comes out closer to a *zayin*.) Moshe's eyes do not project pixels, however, but rather *tefilla* (prayer) and *Torah*: the look of a Hasid. And how does this cantor of Gihon in Abuja make a living? "I am self-employed," he responds vaguely. When pressed for detail, he admits, "I do laundering."

Cantor Moshe of Gihon synagogue, Abuja

Fourth Night of Hanukkah

How many do they say they are? Numeration is vague among the Jubos. At least in Abuja. At Tikvat Israel, I was originally told, there are nine nominal, but seven active, families. But Elder Agbia put the number at sixteen. And now, I am told that there are definitely "more." How many more? It's not worth asking. For the Gihon congregation, at any rate, there seem to be at least double the number of congregants.

Both congregations require that you wend your way down perilously rutted paths and alleyways on the outskirts of town. Gihon is on a small hill, a mound, really. When you look up from the Rabbi Schehr Artscroll prayer book and look out the window, you see goats chomping at the vegetation sticking up among the detritus of the impoverished neighborhood made up of tiny huts. Outside the Tikvat synagogue, nestled within Sar Habakkuk's tidy compound, I see another goat climbing up to take a Shabbat nap on the hood of a car.

On the fourth night at Tikvat Israel, Abuja (candelabra fashioned from Coke bottles)

Shabbat ruminant rests outside the synagogue

In both synagogues, they pray in Hebrew. There is only a smattering of Igbo language in the services—much less than the amount of English at my Conservative shul in Providence. But the Hebrew chants are certainly inflected by this Niger-Congo dialect, as is the body movement. During some prayers, the faithful sway at the hips, swinging their arms at their sides, in a movement more evocative of freedom than the urgent *shukling* of the ultra-Orthodox—a stance they adopt in other prayers.

Kashrut—keeping kosher—is a problem, of course. Just as Muslims in America often go to kosher butchers to get the meat closest to *hallal*, some Jubos will get their beef, goat, and mutton from Muslim butchers. But others observe by avoiding meat altogether. The main course at Kiddush meals, invariably, is fish.

I think back to the animated Torah portion discussion (*Vayeshev—Shabbat Hanukkah [1]*) following last Shabbat's Kiddush meal. Thanks to Rabbi Gorin's online study guide, "Shalom, Africa," we all had a solid basis to consider the implications of Joseph's prophesying, his being thrown into a pit by his brothers, his sale as slave to Pharaoh, his near-seduction by Potiphar's wife, his imprisonment, and, as at the beginning of the portion, his interpretation of more dreams. There is also a curious aside about the serial widowed and long motherless Tamar who eventually seduces her father-in-law on account of her brothers'-in-law refusal to impregnate her. And how does *Vayeshev* play among the Jubos?

Quite well. I ask my hosts about dream preemption and in-law marriage. Both are more common in Igboland than in Israel or Jewish America. "Dreams do have significance," I am told. If you have a disturbing one, you go to a "mature" person—someone you know well—to deal with it, to prevent the negative dream from being re-

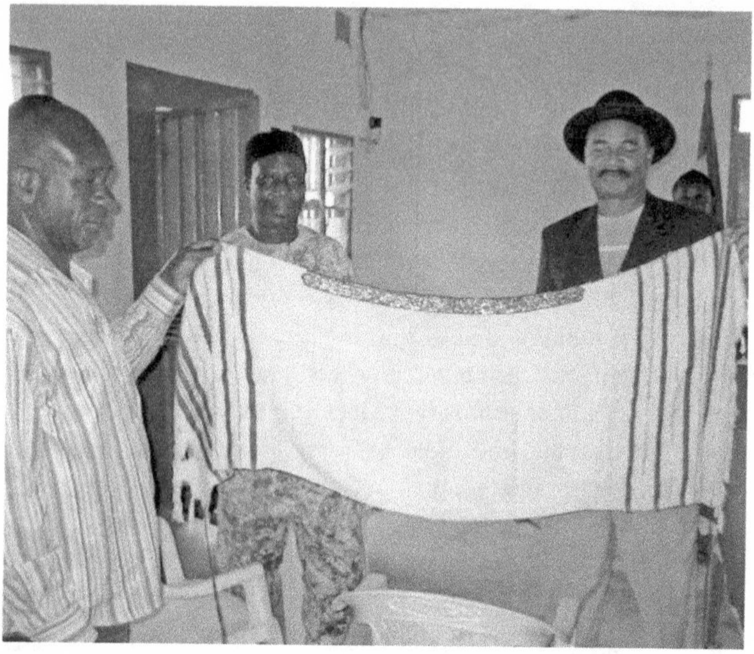

Made in Nigeria: Jewish prayer shawl

alized. As for the levirate obligation of marrying one's childless sister-in-law: the custom, long abandoned in Judaism itself, lives on among the Igbos. Just as do many other Jewish observances—"proof" that the Igbos are descendants of a Lost Tribe of Israel.

Fifth Night of Hanukkah

"As Igbos, we circumcise our sons on the eighth day. We pray especially at the coming of the new moon. We blow the ram's horn. This we have done, as Igbos. But we did not know then that we were continuing the acts of our Jewish ancestors." These are not the only Igbo customs now believed by Jubos to be Israelite survivalisms. "As Igbos, we have always observed Shavuot"—the Harvest Holiday—"as *Ufegiku*. And Sukkot"—the Feast of Tabernacles—"as *Afigolu*."

And the women? When they speak of the matriarchs, of Rachel and Leah, they invoke them wholeheartedly, as living models with whom they identify. Personally.

The *mechitza* that separates the sexes in the "Orthodox" Igbo synagogue is low enough so that the women can easily see what is going on up front. As the Torah scroll wends its way around the synagogue during the procession, Jubo women approach and do a little curtsey before touching their prayer book to the Sefer Torah and then kissing it. Some do an additional bob and twist, so that their babies, wrapped around their backs, get to see the Torah. How often do you see *that* in shul?

For a few Igbos, living as Jews is a conscious anti-colonial position. Paradoxically, it is both a modern and traditional way of reclaiming their authenticity as Igbos, severely undermined under the British. Going back to the practices of their immediate precolonial forebears would be retrograde—how can you advocate worshipping a multiplicity of forgotten gods and goddesses in the twenty-first century? But Judaism—a universal, recognized faith—is an acceptable alternative to both Christianity and Islam. Others emphasize the distinction of their claimed Judaic roots to justify a re-emergent Biafra, independent of Nigeria, or an Igboland allied with Israel.

Western scholars of the Jewish Igbo—Edith Bruder, Daniel Lis, Johannes Harnischfeger, and Tudor Parfitt—similarly focus on the anti-colonial and political dimensions of Igbo identification with the Jewish people and state, with Jewry and Israel. Their arguments are cogent and engrossing. Few Jubo congregants and worshipers themselves, however, make such connections. For them, faith trumps politics and observance counts more than historicism. And why not? When it comes to religion, at some point, scholarship ought to defer to theology. When it comes to Jewishness, at some point *kavanah* and tefilla transcend deconstructionism.

Sixth Night of Hanukkah

I have gotten used to the regular greeting to me: "Shalom, Sah [Sir]." On the telephone, Jubos call each other as "My Teacher." And they are constantly invoking, as the Orthodox refer to God, *Ha-Shem* (The Name).

Recognition by world Judaism is critical to their sense of identity. That is why there was such a reaction to some religious deviancy by members of one of the congregations. "We don't want to bring Voodoo into the synagogue," says Pinchas with emphasis. "With the Sefer Torah, and the blessing of Ha-Shem, we keep Voodoo out."

Because this is Africa, it is here that I am reminded, as a Jew, of my tribal roots. Yes, my hosts are keenly conscious, and proud, of being Igbo. Yes, it would be a *faux pas* to mistake them for Yoruba "tribesmen" (also from the south, about evenly split between Muslims and Christians). It would be even more incongruous to take them for members of the Hausa-Fulani (from northern Nigeria, overwhelmingly followers of Islam). But it is listening to Cantor Moshe's schoolchildren singing out the names of our common tribes that is most humbling. Seated in the white plastics chairs of the synagogue of Gihon, beginning with Reuben and ending with

Benjamin, they melodically recite, in Hebrew, the names of the twelve children of Jacob, foundation of the twelve tribes of Israel. In America, Jews may humorously wonder in code if somebody else is also an MOT (Member of the Tribe). Other Diasporic Jews take seriously their status as descendants of the tribe of Levi, as either cohens (priests) or levites (assistants to the priests). That is because these designations still count in Jewish ritual. But only among the Jubos (because this is Africa? because these kids chant the twelve eponymous tribal names?) do I begin to think that I have neglected my tribal heritage.

If I am called a "Jew," it is because I descend from the tribe of Judah. Along with Levi, Judah is the only tribe known to have survived the conquest of 722 B.C.E. by the Assyrians. But if it had been some other tribe that had survived instead, I would not be a "Jew" but, perhaps, a "Reuben" (mistaken for the sandwich?) or a "Simon." My co-religionists from Ethiopia, after all, claim to descend not from Judah but from his brother Dan. Are they any less J(uda)ish for it?

To be honest, my claim to be a "Jew" really rests on the greater Tribe's acceptance that I descend from Judah, or that some forbear of mine did. I don't have papers to prove it. Even if my grandparents' extended families hadn't been killed in the Holocaust, I doubt that they could have proved their descent from the tribe of Judah, either. (And please don't ask me to "prove" I am Jewish—especially after I have just invoked the eugenics-driven Shoah—by undergoing some kind of DNA test.) But how far back can any Jew-by-heritage trace back his or her ancestry? How many hundreds of years back can even those with the greatest *yichus* (Yiddish: familial status) in their lineage go? Remember, we are talking about almost three thousand years since the tribe of Judah (with its clerics from Levi) became the last historically traceable Israelite tribe. Paper proof? Proof positive?

"Israel," it bears remembering, is the name of the kingdom that composed the Ten Tribes who were vanquished, dispersed and henceforth considered "Lost." When modern Zionists decided to call the restored nation the State of Israel, in a sense they were semantically conjuring up not the descendants of Judah, (the "Jews" of the diaspora,) but rather, those of the Ten Lost Tribes. For most early Zionists, that's what the enterprise was all about: recreating a non-europeanized, non-ghettoized, non-Yiddish-speaking people—"Israelis," not "Jews"—with Hebrew roots and language. Working the land of their tribal ancestors is what they envisioned, not recreating the shtetl economy of Euro-Jewish merchants and money lenders. The model tribes of the Zionists were the primordial Lost Ones, not the adulterated one of Judah.

A Jew is not necessarily an Israeli, even if both happen to be Zionists. An Igbo is not a Hausa or a Yoruba, even if both happen to be Nigerians. When African ethnicities struggle to retain their particular identities, we dismiss it as tribalism. But when anti-Semites "accuse" all Jews of being overt or covert Zionists, we resent the oversimplification.

Yes, we Jews need to be more conscious of our own tribal status and internal tribalism. Another lesson from this Hanukkah with the Jubos.[2]

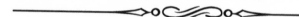

"This is the first time that many of our families have menorahs (candelabras) in their homes," Pinchas says, referring to the gift from my Rabbi in Providence, Wayne Franklin. "It's the first time they've ever seen such candles—even I, it's the first time I've seen these colored, twisted Hanukkah ones." The miracle of lights lives on.

The men kiss the coin shekels that I have brought as *gelt* for the children to play with their dreidels. "It is only money," I protest. "Yes," comes the response, "but it is from the Holy Land."

---

[2] In the context of southern Nigeria, Johannes Harnischfeger (2012:75) also writes of the importance of the "model of the scattered tribes that lost contact but have to recover their Jewish origins" and the "paradigm of a 'multi-tribal origin' of the Jewish immigrants."

Not only Igbos claim Israelite ancestry:
Abdulmalik Badamassi, an Ibira

Seventh Night of Hanukkah

If you are ever in need of marble fixtures or other "High Quality Italian & International Building Materials" in Nigeria, you can't do better than going to Pated Marble, owned and run, not by a Jubo, but by a Holocaust survivor from Transylvania. He is Teddy Luttwak, whose younger brother Edward chose the capital of the U.S. rather than that of Nigeria to carve out his career (in academia). Teddy the septuagenarian has limited contact with the Jubos but is raising his young son—fruit of a late marriage with a rather younger Nigerian woman—to be a Jew. If you can tutor the boy in Hebrew, you've got a job in Abuja. But Teddy's Nigerian Jewish expansiveness is not shared by all expatriate Jews in the capital.

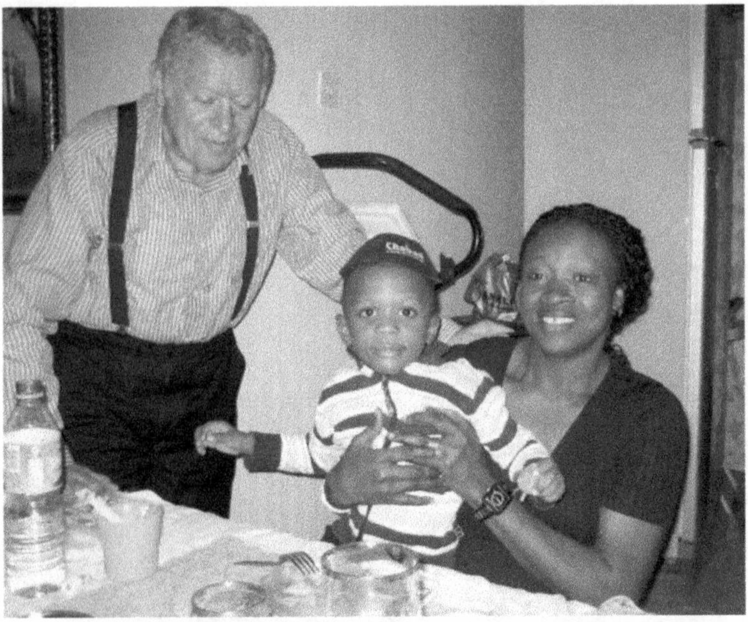

Africanized Jew: Teddy Luttwak and his family

"The last thing we need," says a source close to the Israeli embassy, speaking of the Jubos, "is for some crazy rabbi to fly over from Israel, convert them, and declare that they are Jews." In Nigeria alone, there are at least twenty-five million Igbos—more than four times the number of Israeli Jews. For sure, only a tiny percentage of Igbos currently affirm a Jewish ancestry; the twenty or so synagogues, mostly in the southeastern part of the country, account for only between three and thirty thousand Jubos.[3] But if a rabbinic decision obligated the Jewish state to confer the Right of Return upon all Jubos? Economic incentives to immigrate, it is feared, would drive millions of Nigerians to convert.

---

[3] Howard Gorin, the Conservative rabbi, provides the more conservative estimate, his criterion based on practice of normative Judaism. Edith Bruder, the scholar of black Judaism, estimates that thirty thousand Igbos practice "a form of Judaism." Yet even her enumerated list of eighteen Nigerian synagogues (Bruder 2012:35) accounts for barely five hundred "regular participants." I channel a strong Jubo stance in asserting that "a form of Judaism" does not Judaism

But none of the Jubos I met spoke of moving to Israel. To visit Zion, yes, but not to live. "I don't want to go there and trouble anybody," Dr. Lawrence Okah tells me, expressing a common sentiment. "From here in Nigeria, we can help Israel. [This is where] Ha-Shem started us to establish ourselves."[4] And here's the rub: because theirs is not recognized by the Nigerian authorities as a bona fide religious community, Jubos do not receive the kinds of subsidies that Muslims do to go to Mecca and Christians do for Jerusalem. So, in order to go on pilgrimage to Israel, Jubos have to "pass" as Christians.

If adoption of rabbininc Judaism *is* a kind of anti-colonial stance, at least for some Jubos at some level, then perhaps its appeal, paradoxically, lies partially in the fact that there are no rabbis around. In the colonial era, Christianity came to Nigeria in the guise of white missionaries. They trained local proselytizers, whose successors remain very much in evidence today. But there is no gain-

---

make. To be counted among "Christian Jews" or a "black Hebrew" global community or those practicing "a kind of Judaic-looking faith" or "a kind of Israelite-type precolonial religion" (terms that Tudor Parfitt employs in the context of Black African Jewry more widely) would vex them mightily. That is why the works of Charles Ujah and O. Alaezi (who, by conflating Igbos with Jews, also inflate their numeric importance) should not be read as representing the beliefs of the Jubos. As for the widely circulated attribution to Noam Katz, as Israel's ambassador to Nigeria, that "I'm sure, Igbos are descendants of the Jews": in conversation with me, Katz has denied making this statement. Indeed, "it is doubtful that any ambassador officially confirmed the Igbo as a lost tribe of Israel" (Lis 2012:105, 116, n. 113). This is not to gainsay the sympathy that some Israeli ambassadors have expressed to the community, including a 2013 visit to the Gihon synagogue.

[4] Chima Edwards Onyeulo, described by Lis (2012), is a rare Igbo who moved to Israel to strive (unsuccessfully) for Israeli citizenship on the grounds of Lost Tribe status of Igbo Judaism. Other Jubos, such as Hi Ben Daniel (Lis 2009:30), have successfully converted to Judaism in Israel. However, according to Ben Daniel (whom I met at the Shevet Achim synagogue near the Tel Aviv bus station in 2013), most have been deported by Israeli officials dismissive of the authenticity of their motives for becoming Jewish.

saying that Christianity is a foreign import. Postcolonial Nigerian Judaism, on the other hand, is not a foreign innovation: Jubos have voluntarily adopted it, absent external imposition or pressure. Jubos consequently control its expansion. Juboization is much more democratic than was Christianization of the Igbos. *They* decide which rabbis from abroad they wish to accept and follow. It is recounted that a Reconstructionst rabbi from America came and expostulated on the advantage of Reconstructionist Judaism in universalizing Judaism. Some Jubos walked out on him. "We did not leave one idolatry to enter another," it was said.

Last Night of Hanukkah

Earlier, I posed the question, "To whom does Judaism belong?" This is different from the more common—but no more contentious—issue, "Who is a Jew?"

Boundaries deployed to determine "Who is a Jew?" divide the Jewish community itself. According to halacha, Jewish law, anyone born of a Jewish mother is automatically Jewish, regardless of faith or practice. (One can be excommunicated for "opting out" of Judaism by converting to another religion, but in the absence of a centralized ecclesiarchy, Jewish excommunication is, in practice, extremely rare.) Indeed, it is neither necessary nor sufficient to practice Judaism, according to Orthodox Judaism (and, by extension, the Rabbinate of Israel), to be considered a Jew: a non-practicing Jew is still Jewish, but a practitioner of Judaism without a Jewish mother or an Orthodox conversion is not. Reform Judaism introduced paternity as a condition of inherited Jewishness, an innovation vehemently rejected by the Orthodox as tantamount to heresy. Similarly, through its monopoly claim on legitimate conversion, Orthodoxy rejects as Jewish anyone who has been converted by Reform or Conservative rabbis.

The Jewish State—that is, the government of Israel—does accept, however, for the purposes of granting citizenship, the Jewish status of a convert from abroad. This infuriates the Orthodox rabbinate and, on more than one occasion, has threatened to lead to the break-up of Israeli governments dependent on coalition with religious political parties. Accordingly, the "Who is a Jew?" issue has also created serious rifts between the American Jewish community and the State of Israel, whenever the latter comes close to acceding to Orthodox demands to change the law regarding recognition.

But the question, "To Whom Does Judaism Belong?" transcends the bounds of the Jewish community itself, however that community is defined. For it is not only Jews who control, much less define, Judaism. To the extent that Judaism is a world religion, it belongs to the entire world. And it is a world that has done many different things with and to Judaism.

For much of Western history, Christendom has claimed Judaism as a precursor to the One, True Faith. That is why it so valued Jews who freely converted to Christianity, and so resented those who refused. In the twentieth century, a depraved part of the world, in power in Germany, decided that Judaism was its own to destroy outright. In post-Holocaust Europe, some penitent governments have made rehabilitation of Judaism part of their national destiny. Others, while acknowledging Judaism as part of their national fabric, simultaneously insist on jurisdictional control over its activities. (Hence, the British courts' decision prohibiting state-funded Jewish schools from excluding pupils who are not Jewish according to Orthodox, matrilineal criteria.) By virtue of its embeddedness within the nations of the world, Judaism cannot belong to Jews alone.

Putting aside for the moment the Jubos' genealogical claim of Hebraic origins to the Igbo people, what is there to stop them from claiming Judaism as their own? Nothing. While the two are related, the practice of Judaism is not identical to Jewish identity. And that is the challenge for most North American Jews—the second most populous Jewish population in the world—for whom "true Jewry" is practically synonymous with Yiddishkeit, a cultural affiliation derived from European Jewish roots. Pride in being Jewish is hardly restricted to those who practice the religion. Many secular

Jews are proud to identify as such, even if they couldn't care less about the *mitzvot* (commandments) or rituals. "Ethical Jews" abound—the late Tony Judt, was an examplar, as is Tony Kushner, co-editor of *Progressive Jewish-American Responses to the Israeli-Palestinian Conflict*.

So why don't we automatically embrace the Jubos as our own? What justifies the sense—especially among the non-observant cultural or ethnic Jews, not to mention the agnostic or atheistic—that they are "real" Jews, and the Jubos are not? Ethnic Jews take their Jewishness for granted; but in discounting the religious element, are they not willy-nilly discounting non-ethnic Jews who do assume the mantle of Judaism? Does Judaism not belong to whoever takes it upon him or herself? Why should Ashkenazic intellectuals who reject Judaism be considered more authentic Jews than Igbos who embrace it?

We Jews need to overcome an assumption that we are the "real" Jews, regardless of our actual degree of faith, observance of ritual, knowledge of Torah, familiarity with Hebrew. We must resist the temptation to see Nigerians who follow Halacha as a curiosity, an eccentricity, exoticism. We must overcome the instinct to reject Jubos, and other judaizing Others, as a collective impersonation of ourselves. They are quite distinct from the odious impersonators of the Jews, who range from neo-Nazi Christian Identity types to certain fundamentalist Black Hebrews, both of whom assume the identity of "true" Jews chosen by God while rejecting normative Jews as pretenders and usurpers.

If it is the non-religious Jews who reject the Jubos as fellow Jews, because they themselves don't see religious faith as sufficient to make the bond, are they not the ones being xenophobic or racist for want of genealogical relationship? Genetic lineage is hardly a basis of Jewishness; there are no "DNA Jews" (an expression I first heard in Nigeria). Millions of people on this planet carry chromosomes that prove descent from Ur-Jews. So what? Assimilation and conversion (forced and not) de-judaized countless Jews of yore. To impose upon their descendants—many of them contentedly following some other faith—an unrequested, retroactive Jewish identity is presumptuous, insulting, or worse. Conversely, what difference should the validity of Igbos' putative descent from ancient Hebrews be?

Compared to most Jews, are the Jubos not the truly yearning ones, the real Hasidim, struggling to come ever closer to Ha-Shem, the Name (of God)?

If the Jubos aren't Jewish, then what about those of us who call ourselves Jews, without anywhere near their level of practice and observance?

Final Day of Hanukkah: Congregation Tikvat Israel, Kubwa, Abuja

In *Things Fall Apart*, Chinua Achebe lamented the deterioration of traditional Igbo culture that accompanied the advent of colonialism and Christianization. Reclaiming Jewish ancestry and identity, according to Remy Ilona, the most prolific Jubo writer today, is part of the contemporary Igbo struggle against those colonial and missionizing legacies. One of the aims of the British, claims Ilona in *Introduction to the Chronicles of Igbo-Israel* and *The Igbos: Jews in Africa*, was to alienate them from their real roots, contemporary and historic. For Remy, part of the work of cultural decolonization is to reclaim Judaism as the true religious heritage of the Igbo. Whether world Jewry itself is prepared to embrace this or any type of African Judaism as a reaction against religious colonization is another matter altogether. Anti-semitism is the scourge that incenses and unites global Jewry. But colonialism?

For decades I had periodically immersed myself in (escaped to?) Nigeria and Niger precisely because it was so alien, so other from the suburban New York Jewish world in which I had grown up. Hausaland—my corner of Muslim West Africa—represented a parallel universe in which I could define myself as Jewish and shape my hosts' understanding of Judaism.[5] My friendships with southern Nigériens and northern Nigerians transcended, to my mind, the global fray between Palestinian and Israeli, Muslim and Jew. It was a privileged position from which to resist meta-polarization, to somehow reconcile the anti-Zionism and Judeophobia expressed by some northern Nigerian elites with my own Hausaphilia at the village level.

Now, more than three decades after first befriending Muslims and witnessing Islam up close as a Peace Corps Volunteer, this encounter with fervent Nigerian Jews represents a fundamental challenge to all that. Not because it jeopardizes my relationship with Nigerian Muslims in any way: in some respects, those ties are stronger than ever, even if newly perplexing. But Nigeria has its own Jews to define Judaism now. It is up to them to shape the image of Jews and Judaism in the mind of their Nigerian compatriots.

Still, I cannot remain indifferent to the images they project, and the perceptions they create. There is no escape from being a Jew. Certainly not on Long Island. Not even in Nigeria.

Time has come to bid *shalom* to the Jubos. Taking leave of Hezekiah is hardest of all. I see it is difficult for him, too. He is a prodigy, this eleven-year-old, who chants for the community in soulful Hebrew. Quiet and soft-spoken as a boy, as future prayer leader, his beautiful and full-throated chanting sails far beyond the unfinished rafters of this Nigerian shul.

With the deep eyes of a Hasid-in-the-making, this African boy looks up to me and asks, in a mixture of sadness and hope, "Will you come to my bar mitzvah?"[6]

---

[5] Dierk Lange (2012:139) is now taking these two identities in a radical new direction by advancing "the possibility that Israelites played a leading role among the ancient Near Eastern state builders in Hausaland."

[6] Two years later, I did. My account of that experience appears as "A Bar Mitzvah in Abuja" in *Jews of Nigeria: An Afro-Judaic Odyssey* (Princeton: Markus Wiener Publishers, 2013).

With Hezekiah (front), the budding cantor

Hezekiah's sisters (and little kid)

PART TWO

Beyond West Africa

FIFTEEN

African Judaism, Race, Romance, and My Mother: A Review of Edith Bruder's *The Black Jews of Africa* and Richard Hull's *Jews and Judaism in African History*[1]

Hath writing ere such
A double book review

Ever had such impact on
An Africanist Jew?

Were it not for the books offered for this review, I would not be spending this Hanukkah in Abuja, Nigeria. Yet so compelling are the historical and contemporary accounts of Jews in Africa, and of African Jews, in these volumes by Edith Bruder (2008) and Richard Hull (2009) that I could not resist (admittedly in a "use it or lose it" university research grant environment) travelling during final exam week to arrive in time for the first candle lighting in one of the two (yes, two) synagogues of *Jubos* (my term for ethnic Igbo Jews) in Nigeria's Federal Capital Territory.

Originally, I had intended to begin this review by relaying my early Hebrew School discovery of "Falashas," and the consternation it gave my Ashkenazic mother when I announced (before bar mitzvah age, no less) that I would marry an Ethiopian Jewish girl.

[1] Originally published in the book review section of *African Studies Quarterly* 11:2-3 (2010).

But enough about me: it is Hull and Bruder who are true experts on the subjects, and need to be given just due.

Despite the similarly-sounding titles and themes, these are very different books. Hull, an American at New York University, is a veteran historian who brings several decades' worth of research, publication, and teaching experience to the (writing) table. Bruder, a Francophone research associate at the School of Oriental and African Studies, turned her 2006 SOAS doctoral dissertation into *The Black Jews of Africa*. Both books strongly bear the hallmarks of their authors' backgrounds, and their associated virtues.

For university undergraduates—presumably a target audience for *Jews and Judaism in African History*—Hull's book is the more accessible of the two books. Hull writes in short, clear sentences, with nary a footnote. (His comprehensive referencing is in MLA style—perhaps as a model for students to adopt in their papers?) His approach—as befits a classical historian—is basically chronological.

Launching his account from classical antiquity (Elephantine, Ptolemic, and Alexandrian Egypt), Hull takes us up until the seventeenth century in North Africa, relating how Jews fared under successive Muslim regimes (Fatimid, Mamluk, Almoravid, Ottoman, etc.). He then deviates slightly from his dateline, bringing us back to the fifteenth century and the beginnings of the Atlantic Slave Trade. Hull deals with the potentially provocative topic of Jews' involvement in African slavery in a non-polemical, "just the facts" manner. Jewish participation in the construction of South Africa is the next theme, followed by Jewish immigration to eastern, central, and southern Africa. In his concluding chapter, Hull returns to the north to assess how Jews of the Maghreb and Egypt have fared from the seventeenth century until after the establishment of Israel. There is no concluding chapter as such, something which this reviewer missed. The half dozen maps, and as many illustrations, greatly enhance the reader's ability to follow spatially and visually the Jewish thread in Africa.

In contrast with Hull's non-interpretative historiography, Edith Bruder's work is infused with theoretical perspectives that invoke sociology, theology, psychology and anthropology at a level more appropriate for graduate students and beyond. It is helpful, for instance, to be already familiar with Mircea Eliade, Michel Foucault, Rollo May, and Edward Said. This more eclectic approach lends itself to a structure that is at least as thematic as it is historical. In Part I, Bruder grapples with the mythic dimension of African Jewry: Lost Tribes of Israel, King Solomon, and Queen of Sheba, etc. Part II explores colonial (most prejudicial) framing of Jewish and African peoples and religion and the relationship between them. The concluding section describes various Black African ethnicities and communities who, either through descent or conviction, stake their claim to Judaism. A nicely rounded Epilogue synthesizes the whole with respect to the otherwise paradoxical finding of "Judaism as a source of black identity."

Perhaps the most important difference between the works relates to their respective ethnic foci. Whereas Hull emphasizes Sephardi and Ashkenazi migrations throughout what used to be caricatured as the "Dark Continent," Bruder's interest lies more with sub-Saharan peoples with an abiding identification with Israelite origins, Judaism, or both. For some groups, such as the Ethiopians, the identification is longstanding and descent-based; for others, such as the Abayudaya of Uganda, it is relatively recent, and entirely faith-based; and for yet others, such as the Igbos of Nigeria, the Hebraic faith and descent are being (re)discovered. The Jewish credentials of Hull's subjects are rarely in doubt; but even Bruder feels bound to place cautionary quotation marks around some of them, as indicated in her section heading "Africa, Judaism, and African 'Jews.'" For sure, Hull does provide a comprehensive section on Ethiopian Jewish history; his treatment of the Lemba, in southern Africa, is cursory. (Professor Tudor Parfitt, Bruder's doctoral supervisor, has written extensively about the Lemba, and the attention they receive in her book is not surprising.)

Or perhaps the difference in emphasis is less one of ethnicity than historicity: whereas Hull is intent on providing a comprehensive historical account of the Jewish presence on the African continent, Bruder is more concerned with explaining contemporary dynamics in the formation of Jewish identity in Africa. "Why is it," she asks on page 187, "that this particular period of African history should witness the rise of Judaizing movements?" If Hull provides the foundation for appreciating the longstanding presence and contradictory roles of Jews in African society, Bruder gives us the springboard for assessing the revitalization of, and attraction to, Judaism in Africa today.

Both books constitute important additions to the growing literature on the historical and contemporary interstices between Africana and Judaica, be it in Israel, Africa, or their respective diasporas. Neither author sufficiently addresses the question of *why* s/he has been drawn to this particular comparative venture, although intimations of interest in shared status as minority groups at the global level seem to undergird both works. Speaking to different audiences, with different thematic emphases and heuristic aims, Bruder and Hall nevertheless converge in successfully binding between their respective covers two peoples whose destinies have overlapped in ways that neither Hebraicists nor Africanists have generally appreciated.

To return to my mother, and matrimony: in the end, I did not wind up marrying a woman from Africa, Ethiopian or otherwise. But my West Indian bride does have some African ancestry—as well as a certificate of Jewishness—and became as close to my mother as a daughter-in-law can possibly be. Evolution in Mother's tribalistic feelings mirrors somewhat the expanded notion of Jewishness within North American and Western European Jewry. These fine books by Edith Bruder and Richard Hull are reflections of, and important contributions to, this heightened consciousness.

For their follow-up research, perhaps Bruder or Hull might wish to consider investigating Jews of the African diaspora, including the perception of their romances with other Jewish diasporics. If so, they may begin by interviewing Mom: telephone number upon request.

Abuja, 25 Kislev, 5770

SIXTEEN

Notes from a Haunting Conference: Rwanda[1]

From the edge of the forest, a half hour's hike though maize and bean fields from the park rangers' base camp, it is only another thirty minutes of steep, pant-provoking climb through dense bamboo woods. At the guide's signal, we hand our backpacks to the trackers who remain behind with the jungle-fatigued soldiers lugging automatic weapons. Anti-government guerillas have been hiding out in these parts, and so I, the sole American of the group, am contravening a State Department advisory in coming here. Still, our leader insists the guns are necessary to protect us only from "wild buffalo."

Slowly, we follow François, our French-speaking guide, as we try to respect all the instructions he has given us: *Do not point.* If stung by ants, *Do not shout.* If attacked, *Do not flee.* We are quiet, watching François lope ahead, listening to the strange guttural sounds he is emitting.

In no time at all we come upon our touristic grail: the Amohoro ("Peace") family, one of seven inhabiting this Virungu Forest in the Great Lakes region of Central Africa. There are only about four hundred individuals left, and UNESCO has declared them deserving of international recognition and special protection.

I am paralyzed between ecstasy and disbelief, standing within spitting distance, in the wild, of a dozen mountain gorillas. One of the two Amohoro "babies," a rather hairy and curious eight-month-old, begins creeping forward, to touch us. Following François'

[1] A much-abridged version of this essay was first published as "The Forgotten Holocaust" in *Moment Magazine* 28:3 (June 2003), pp. 36-40.

lead, we withdraw. At these close quarters, we need to keep our germs to ourselves. The youngster turns back and, under the protective gaze of silverback dad and grooming mom, wrestles with his brother.

An hour later, still feeling high from the me-ape encounter, the contradiction begins to gnaw at me. We have just had this unique and unforgettable primate experience in the jungle, a testimony to the rapture of life and creation, in the Republic of Rwanda, better known to the world for its savage genocide of just a decade prior. Indeed, it was a conference on the aftermath of the genocide—"Life after Death"—that has brought me to Rwanda in the first place.

The conference, and succeeding week of interviews and official visits, not only has taken a severe emotional toll; as a student of the Holocaust, it has forced me to reevaluate long-held views about justice and punishment in a post-genocidal world order. The ambivalence hovers over the euphoric buzz occasioned by the close encounter of a gorilla kind.

Jewish representation in the conference on Rwandan genocide was significant. Indeed, the international committee for "Life after Death" was headed by Yael Danieli, originally from Israel, the daughter of Shoah survivors and now a psychologist specializing in trauma therapy for Holocaust victims and families. Also in attendance were Shimon Samuels of the Simon Wiesenthal (the Nazi hunter) Center in Paris; Bob Melson, the Purdue political scientist whose acclaimed autobiography *False Papers* recounts his years hiding his Jewish identity as a child during the Second World War; Lea Balant, another child survivor, director at the ghetto and Shoah survivors' kibbutz museum in northern Israel; and Hedi Fried, the aging but elegant survivor of the Auschwitz death camp, a psychologist and therapist living in Sweden.

For sure, the international delegation was not composed uniquely of Jews—there was also an Australian aborigine, a native

American Lakota, a Bosnian survivor of "ethnic cleansing," a French psychotherapist, a British Holocaust center sponsor, a Protestant religious studies professor from the Midwest, and the head of Denmark's genocide research institute. But Jewish or not, none of the international participants risked what members of Ibuka, the association of genocide organizers who organized the "Life after Death" conference, did. For Ibuka is under continuous pressure—including threats—to desist from their campaign of perpetual commemoration. In Kinyarwanda, the national language spoken by victimized Tutsis, pygmy Twas, and majoritarian Hutu alike, Ibuka means "Remember!" I heard it as the African equivalent of the post-Holocaust battle cry, "Never Again!"

The relationship between Jews and Tutsis is complex. In the nineteenth century, German and Belgian anthropologists hypothesized that the Tutsis—stereotypically tall, noble, pensive—originated from far away, in northeast Africa, perhaps from the same "stock" as the ancient Hebrews. This, theory known as the Hamitic Hypothesis (from Ham, son of Noah), both elevated the Tutsis in the minds of the colonists and incited jealousy among the Hutu, the supposedly "indigenous" but "inferior" group of Bantu origin.[2] With independence and majoritarian rule, the Hutu turned the historical tide against the minoritarian Tutsi. Tutsis in the 1990s were slated, as were the Jews of the 1940s, for extermination. Both groups carry the scars—although in Rwanda, the wounds are fresher, much rawer, than that of the Holocaust survivor.

Even among genocide survivors, some of the stereotypes persevere:

---

[2] My elaboration of the application of the Hamitic Hypthosis in Rwanda can be found in my 2000 article in the *Journal of Genocide Research,* "Hamites and Hebrews: problems in 'Judaizing' the Rwandan Genocide." For an excellent treatment of the broader uses and abuses of the Hamitic Hypothesis by Europeans, Americans, and Africans over the ages, see Tudor Parfitt's *Black Jews in Africa and the Americas* (reviewed in chapter 24).

"You cannot tell by looking at a Tutsi what he is thinking or feeling," says Dieudonné, a Tutsi schoolteacher whose name means "God Given." "He is reserved, reflective—like the Jews. A Bantu is so much more expressive—you can tell by his face if he is happy, or sad, or angry."

You are introduced to a member of Ibuka—well-educated, articulate, French-speaking—and within minutes learn that he or she is the only surviving member of the family. The lonely pain of the Holocaust survivor is relived. "Mother, father, children, brothers, sisters—all are gone." Another appends his status as lone family survivor with a fatalistic "*C'est l'histoire*" and a forced guffaw. In a society in which the extended family reigns supreme, being the only family survivor is all the more devastating. To compensate, survivors "adopt" each other as cousin, sister, mother. Age is no object.

At a conference dinner, I am seated in the "Francophone corner," across from a young, pretty, shy woman. She tells me she works for Avega. Trying to make small talk, I blithely query, "Oh, what does Avega stand for?"

"Association of Widows of the Genocide," she replies, matter-of-factly. All I can do in response is take her hand, which I hold for several minutes.

Our conference site is the four star Mille Collines in Kigali, a hotel whose singular role as haven from murder is rivetingly described in Philip Gourevitch's acclaimed *We Regret to Inform You That Tomorrow We Will Be Killed With Our Families*. In the hotel lobby, a VCR in loop mode has been set up so that, even between sessions, one can watch at any moment a documentary about the genocide. But in the background, the hotel acoustical system is also piping in a Muzak version of "Bridge over Troubled Water."

Conference survivors are in their element at the Mille Collines. In impeccable French, an elegant, bejeweled, statuesque woman recounts in the hotel conference hall the harrowing details of how she was widowed by ethnic murder, and then rendered childless through mindless torture. It was not only ill-educated, impoverished peasants who were massacred in Rwanda: those with higher degrees were killed—and did the killing.

On our official conference outing we are brought to the National University of Rwanda. Not even this university in Butare, the southern province which for long had resisted the Interahamwe madness, escaped the nightmare: eventually, Hutu professors killed Tutsi students, a university administrator informs us; students who were Hutu killed professors because they were Tutsi.

But it is impossible, I tell myself. How could genocide have spread to a college campus? Then I recall that the German university was hardly a haven from Nazism. How can we be sure that *any* university community is totally immune from the genocidal virus?

It takes months before I get over this tormenting thought on my rounds to class in Boston.

An assistant to the attorney general of the Republic of Rwanda takes me to visit one of the mass, open-air prisons housing thousands upon thousands of accused genocidal murderers.

"How do you look them in the eye?" I ask.

"When I deal with them now," the prosecutor replies, "I no longer have any emotions."

(But the president of Ibuka, himself a survivor, will later seize upon this same question. "It is we who lower our eyes when we encounter a *genocidaire*. They should be the ones ashamed to look at us. But it is the other way around—we are the ones who avoid eye contact. That is what we are living with.")

"The Hutu lead a life of denial," the assistant attorney general admits. According to Gerald Gahima, then the attorney general,

"Many of the [prisoners] have forgotten why they are in there."

"But remorse is growing," claims the assistant. "Privately, many are thinking, 'Why did we think we would become rich if we killed Tutsis? Why did we think this would lead to a better life?'"

"In real life," he reflects, "if you take my eye—if you've killed my son—and I forgive you, I've given you the biggest challenge of your life." Indeed, revenge killings are extremely rare in Rwanda—limited, it appears, to those few genocidaires who have been released without punishment, either on a technicality or because no witnesses have come forth.

Our "tour guide"—dressed, as are all prisoners in Rwanda, in shocking pink shorts and short sleeves—is an amiable, well-spoken, bespectacled Francophone of about my own diminutive height. He shows us the prison infirmary, the soccer field, the barber shop. He takes us to see a basketball game, to listen to a choral group, to overhear church services. We swing by the school for genocidaires-in-detention: classes are being simultaneously conducted in basic literacy, automotive mechanics, and Swahili as a foreign language. "Our greatest need," the Rwandan warden pointedly informs me, "is books. If you could send us some texts, it would be very helpful."

"They are very well organized," the prison director informs me in the debriefing, referring to his wards. "They are better organized than is society outside the prison. It is also safer inside than the outside—in here, there is no crime."

As I prepare to say goodbye to my prison hosts (not guards—not a single armed guard patrols within the prison itself), curiosity about our prisoner-guide gets the better of me. It would be tactless, I think, to ask pointblank with what crime he has been charged. But there is something about him that emits familiarity, urging me to determine his former occupation. *"J'étais professeur,"* he informs me, in a collegial tone of voice, *"de langue."* Our host of this inferno, undoubtedly indicted for some genocidal crime himself, is ordinarily a high school teacher of French.

One morning I attend a trial of some ordinary, run-of-the-mill genocidaires. In the run-down makeshift courtroom next to the main prison—buckling ceiling, water-stained walls, bare cement floor, pane-less windows and bulb-less fixtures—a group of six men are standing trial for multiple murder and rape. (In Rwanda, as well as former Yugoslavia, sexual crimes committed against women because of their ethnicity can be considered acts of genocide.) They stand before three black gowned magistrates—two men, one woman—with gold sashes. On the wall behind the magistrates is a fresco with the judicial seal: within the shape of Rwanda, a scale intersecting a thermometer. I am in the so-called "visitors' gallery" next to the accused—a backless, wooden bench dragged to the faded yellow side wall from a spectators' row for my benefit. Gowned prosecutors and defense lawyers (most of them hired by international non-governmental organizations) also sit on hard wooden benches. There are about thirty men-in-pink in the audience—old and young, rough and refined, peasant and intellectual. A few women-in-pink also wander in. One bespectacled, intelligent-looking man-in-pink wearing black shoes (unlike his brethren in thongs and sneakers) conspicuously sports a wooden crucifix around his neck. (United Nations and Belgian courts have already condemned pastors and nuns to prison for genocidal collaboration.) Spectator prisoners get up and walk in and out of the courtroom at will. There are no guards or policemen. The smell of wood smoke wafts through; an occasional mosquito, an errant fly, drift in.

One of the accused—the group leader, from what I can infer—is changing his testimony. He is about thirty, short and modest in build, mustached and spry. Except for his heavy eyelids, he resembles in these respects the chief magistrate.

Despite what he signed after the police investigation, and despite the other evidence already submitted in court, the prisoner now claims that he possessed a uniform and firearm only to *pretend* he was one of the Interahamwe, the murderous Hutu militia. His wife was herself Tutsi, he explained; he did all this pretending to protect her. He implicates different people—none of them present or whereabouts known.

The chief magistrate—a slight man with fine features and groomed hair over his lip, in his early thirties—is visibly exasperated by this change in testimony. He challenges the defendant, refers to the original confession, remarks on holes in the new story. Still, the magistrate lets the accused have his full say. Each lawyer (including the one representing the victims, seeking civil damages) also is given free reign to plead. (The alleged rape victim, however, is long dead.) The proceedings drag on for two and a half hours until the court finally moves on to the second man accused among this same group.

There are only thirteen such court sessions being held simultaneously around the country. At this rate, it is estimated it will take one hundred years to clear the court dockets of genocide crimes.

This is not summary justice. It is an arduous process—mentally arduous for the magistrates forced to retain concentration, physically arduous for all of us sitting on these hard and uncomfortable benches.

"In the early trials," the prosecutor explains to me afterwards, "cases like these would be routine, uncontested. But now the prisoners are very well organized. They are aided by the NGOs, who provide free advice. They strategize. They construct new alibis. They realize they have nothing to lose. Many of them are temporizing, hoping to delay until *gacaca* takes over."

Gacaca (pronounced ga-CHA-cha) is an experiment in genocidal justice, empowering local communities to mete out mitigated sentences in exchange for confessions of guilt and expressions of remorse. Literally, gacaca means "flattened grass," referring to the physical space in the village green where, in precolonial days, disputes were resolved on the local level.

From a legal standpoint, the notion of resurrecting a pre-modern consensus-building mechanism to deal with crimes against humanity is nothing less than audacious. Some survivors view gacaca as a disingenuous means of granting amnesty. Even if the most culpable planners and gruesome perpetrators are still liable to prosecution by the normal criminal justice system, tens of thousands of "lesser" killers and accomplices will be released after undergoing gacaca.

"Your mission is indispensable to prepare the future of the country," reads the instruction manual for those elected gacaca judges. "Your mission is crucial to make the truth come out, so that justice is done to the victims, so that those who participated in the genocide and related-massacres are punished with justice." While gacaca courts can impose prison terms, the greatest punishment they are expected to impart is community shaming. And shaming is a precursor to reconciliation.

It is a stupendous expectation. Nobody envisioned a reconciliation process, for example, between Jewish survivors of the Holocaust and their Nazi tormenters. Yes, Germany continues to pay reparations to victims of the Shoah. Programs still bring German youth together with both their Jewish age-peers and even with actual survivors. But none of these efforts is tantamount to getting former Nazis to sit down with, or to make public confessions of guilt to, the targets of their crimes. For the sake of national healing, Tutsi survivors are asked to display a superhuman capacity for forgiveness.

How do you tour Rwanda ethically? This is how the official tourist pamphlet, in its suggestion for those with four days to spend, awkwardly concludes:

> The fourth day wakes you up at the tea plantations which [are part of] the forest that you cross for coming back to Kigali. You leave [them] with one thing in the memory helas to visit the atrocities of Gikongoro which means the unspeakable site of genocide of MURAMBI where you leave unfortunately sad to Kigali. (Extract from Rwandan tourist brochure)

Once a regional high school, in the spring of 1994 Murambi became a gathering point for refugees. Today, it is a grisly memorial.

In room after room, stacked upon one another on beds, are the cadavers. Many are contorted, their mouths still rounded in terror of the violent death befalling them. Although chemically treated and sprinkled with lime, they slowly continue to decompose. And to putrify. The slender arm of one of them is uplifted in perpetuity, as if still trying to deflect the blow of the machete. It is the arm of a small child. There are remains of many other small children.

Thousands upon thousands of these half-corpse, half-skeleton bodies are on display. A narrow passage is left clear in the center of the room. But there is no partition between visitor and murder victim. So be careful, if you decide to enter, not to brush against a dangling limb.

Elsewhere throughout Rwanda one can find similar museumeteries. On a hill overlooking Kigali, skulls are neatly lined up on one side of a catacomb; on the other side lie the bones. But no memorial site is as large or overpowering as that of Murambi which bears gruesome witness—for mourners and tourists alike—to the horrors that went on in that valley.

To what can Murambi be compared? To the forensic displays at Auschwitz-Birkenau? To the evocative piles of half-century old shoes and hair, respectfully preserved behind glass? At Murambi you are faced, in almost unbearable intimacy, with the murdered masses themselves.

As you travel across the lush and rolling hills of banana-leafed Rwanda, you periodically come across scores, if not hundreds, of the pink-clad prisoners ambling down the road. Released during the day on work assignment, they travel under only symbolic guard. Escapes are extremely unusual. Some say the prisoners' docility lies in the same cultural trait that made the genocide itself possible: deference to hierarchy and obedience to authority. Others are more prosaic in their explanation: Where would they hide, these men-in-pink? Easily identifiable by their shocking pink outfits, known back home for their alleged crimes, they would soon be back in custody, anyway. "Outside is one large prison called Rwanda," says the assistant attorney general. At Kabuye in western Rwanda, the genocidaires are "imprisoned" by a piece of string that symbolically marks the entrance to the prison. It is from the store stocked and run by this prison for genocidaires that I purchase a fine woven basket, specialty item of Rwandan handicraft. This dubious testimony to post-genocidal commerce exudes moral ambivalence in my university office back home, an esthetic but tainted souvenir from the most haunting conference trip of my life.

And the price of the optional tours? To spend a few hours with gorillas in the forest cost 250 dollars. To view the 40,000 cadavers was absolutely free—but you pay for it all your life.

Genocide museum

Victims' clothing

Survivors of genocide: Rwandan and Nazi

SEVENTEEN

Israelite in Kenya: Father-Daughter Ruminations

(with Arielle P. Miles)

Father

I walk into a "hotel" (barebones restaurant) in Kakoneni, a nondescript village seventeen miles west of the Indian Ocean in East Africa. A tall, muscular man introduces himself. He teaches at the local primary school. Pleasant enough. Within three minutes of our chatting, the man informs me that he is "saved" (i.e., a Christian) and asks what I think about God. Hearing the turn the conversation has taken, my host and companion Karembo darts out of the "hotel."

"It is a lifelong question," I respond. "As long as God gives us breath, it is a question we ought to be asking." My "saved" teacher inverses my adjectival compound.

"Yes," he agrees, "it is a long life issue."

I'm not sure if his is a grammatical slip, or a subtle suggestion that my life expectancy is tied to finding Jesus Christ. I join she who is the reason I have come to this out-of-the way rural community in Kenya in the first place—my daughter Arielle, who has been rechristened The Beautiful One (Karembo) in the local Giriama language.

Navigating my Jewishness in Africa is hardly new. But it is a change of pace to do so among evangelical Christians in eastern Africa. Finding commonalities among Muslim Africans has always come easily. In thirty years of working, traveling and residing in West Africa, no one there has ever pushed me to "accept Muhammed." But around here, you can't get around Jesus or the suggestion that you either accept him as Savior or suffer dire consequences in the afterlife.

Arielle has been teaching math and chemistry as a Peace Corps Volunteer for seven months at this point. Her mother and I had dispatched her with the bare essentials of Judaica—Shabbat candlesticks, a *siddur* (prayer book), some dreidels for Hanukkah. Certainly not to proselytize but to have some tangible reminders of home. We all thought that, given her familiarity with Arabic (having studied it in Montreal in college and with a grant in Morocco), Peace Corps would assign her to a Muslim community on the east coast of Kenya. That assumption was reinforced by preservice language training that focused exclusively on Swahili, which only Kenyan Muslims along the coast claim as their sole African language. As it turns out, although Zahara (her Arabic name) was indeed posted to a site in Coast Province, her school assignment (to a girls-only government boarding school) was in a thoroughly Christian area.

So Christian, in fact, that the full-time assignment of one of my daughter's colleagues—Mr. Maitha—is teaching Christian Religious Education (C.R.E.). There is not sufficient demand for an I.R.E. (Islamic Religious Education) teacher in Kakoneni Girls' Secondary School. I have long discussions with Mr. Maitha in the staff room when Karembo/Zahara/Arielle is teaching or proctoring exams. But Mr. Maitha himself never broaches religion with me: imparting Christianity is his day job, confined to his work with students. With me, he prefers to discuss local history, politics, and culture.

Rather, it is Mr. Kioko, the young and charismatic teacher of biology and chemistry, who feels the need to convert me in the staff room. My daughter has proven to be a conundrum at best, stubborn at worst: what kind of Mzungu (white person) rejects Christianity? He must know that I am the source of her theological obduracy.

"Do you go to Church?" asks the science teacher who, on his own time, is a pastor.

"I go to synagogue," I reply.

"So you are an Israelite?"

I am going to have some definitional issues with Mr. Kioko.

I explain the importance of respect in religion—starting with the respect I show my late father in preserving the Judaism he imparted to me.

"Being a Christian is a matter of choice," he tells me —not a matter of inheritance, or of ceremony, or of habit. "It is about deciding to consecrate your life to Jesus Chris as Lord and Savior." For my part, I decide that the best way to explain what it means to be Jewish is to go tribal on him.

"Are you a Giriama?" I ask.

"No, I am Kamba."

"What does it mean to be Kamba?"

"Well, it is a way that we are born and grow up. With traditions, with language. But I do not believe, or need to believe, everything that the elders do or believe."

"That is what it is to be Jewish," I explain. "You are born in it, you are raised in it, you are educated in it. You do not choose it. You *are* it."

"So it is not a religion."

"It is both." Mr. Kioko ponders this idea.

We switch from theology to religious politics, but in a vocabulary I am not used to.

"Why," he asks, "is there such fighting 'til now, in Gaza, between the Israelites and the Philistines?"

I do not correct Mr. Kioko that the people of Gaza, be they of Hamas or of Fatah or neither, hardly think of themselves as Philistines. Nor do I attempt to nuance the distinction between the Israelites of the Bible and Israelis of today. "The fighting is not good," I reply, evading the challenge of explaining contemporary Middle Eastern politics in Old Testament terms. Then Mr. Kioko relates a conversation I doubt I would be privy to in any other context.

"I saw my former landlord recently. He is a Muslim. 'I know you are a friend of Jesus,' he said, 'because you are a Christian. But I, if I knew that there were ten Israelites around, or even five, I would strap on a bomb and go blow them up. Better to die like that and go to paradise than die in a hospital one day, like a cow.'" Mr. Kioko turns to me, in a purely conversational tone, and adds, "So, I wanted to ask you, and hear the other side."

The other side to suicide bombers?

I do my best to convey Jewish preoccupation with survival, with modern Israel's resurrection after the Holocaust, with the need to have one secure homeland in the world.

"Are there Israelites who say," the inquisitive teacher wants to know, "that God has given them all that land, and so they must keep it? Is that what Yitzhak Rabin said?"

I try to explain the difference between religious Zionists, like Gush Emunim, and security Zionists, as Rabin had been—and why, in moderating his stance on the land, he came to be killed by a fellow Jew, a religious extremist.

"Do Jewish extremists commit suicide bombing?" I am startled less by the question itself than by the sheer ingenuousness behind it. Only in the interior of Kenya's Coast Province have I ever been asked to imagine such an equivalency.

Daughter

I joined the Peace Corps for an adventure, to gain some professional and life experience, and to do, as it is said in Hebrew, tikkun olam. My father being a Returned Peace Corps Volunteer (he served in Niger in the late seventies), I've always known that I would follow in his footsteps.

What is tikkun olam? Literally, it means "repairing the world." It's a *mitzvah* (commandment/good deed) to give *tsadaka* (charity), but what can a person do to make an impact that lasts? Developing personal relationships and leading by example are first steps in effecting a positive influence and trying to improve the world. I hope to leave a mark by doing this with "my" girls.

We remember our teachers. We are shaped by them. Maybe we don't recall the specific products that our chemistry teachers taught us are formed when zinc reacts with hydrochloric acid (zinc chloride and hydrogen gas), but we are shaped by *how* they taught us such things. Most of my students won't get the C+ minimum necessary on the Kenya Certificate of Secondary Education exam to go to a public university. Still, I hope I influence them enough to become the next generation of confident, helpful, capable women necessary to make this country advance.

People are intrigued by me, as I'm often the first "Hebrew" they've met, a descendant of the Israelites they learned about in school in C.R.E. (Christian Religious Education). Depending on the faith of my interlocutor, when the conversation eventually rolls around to religion, as it inevitably does, I usually say one of two things: a) "I am of the same religion that Jesus followed" or b) "I'm not Muslim, I'm not Christian, but my people are in the Qur'an. Your hint is *Ahl al-Kitab* (People of the Book)."

I'm reasonably sure I was the only Jew living in Malindi district until a new volunteer joined the dispensary in the neighboring village during my second year. The nearest "Jewish" community is a shul in Mombasa, three and a half hours away. Attendees are "Messianic Jews." I haven't visited it, but my friend and fellow Peace Corps Volunteer Ari—who grew up in an Orthodox household in Brooklyn—assures me that it is weird. For a time, to become integrated into the local community, I went to a different church service every Sunday.

Kenyan Christians hold very firm convictions about their faith. In cities, signs advertising various pastors' churches are pasted to poles; on Sundays, preachers fill your ears with shouted sermons over loud speaker systems; on TV, men of G-d perform such miracles as making the lame walk, and shrinking cancerous tumors. As we concluded a get-together in Kakoneni to discuss our respective faiths, the pastors of various churches said they trust that G-d will show me the Truth—I'll come to accept it by hearing it. (I responded that they should feel free to pray for me but that I'm a stubborn person.) Lay Kenyans in my community are not extremely forceful about converting non-Christians; they just hope one day I'll be saved. Some of my Peace Corps friends who are posted in other parts of the country have had different experiences, however. Some of them may have a harder time dealing with those encounters because they don't have "but I do believe in G-d" to fall back on as a common bond.

Before coming to Kenya, I thought I wouldn't have much opportunity to practice the rituals I do at home. Even though I packed a pair of Shabbos candlesticks, I didn't light candles every week; but Dad and I did Kiddush together when he came to visit. I'm glad I had Chabad *hanukkiah* (candelabra provided by the ultra-Orthodox Lubavitchers), a set of candles, and a handful of dreidels. Though you can get matzah in Nairobi for *Pesach* (Passover), acquiring some would mean a three-day operation, starting with a van ride to Malindi two hours away, another one to Mombasa three hours away, an overnight in Mombasa, then an eight- or nine-hour bus ride to Nairobi, and then an another overnight.

A Jew is a Jew no matter where s/he is. But a big part of being Jewish, one that should not be taken for granted, is having a Jewish community nearby. That is obviously not the case for me now. Peace Corps Kenya is not a place to find a *minyan* (Hebrew: prayer quorum) but I, Karembo Zahara, still strongly feel Jewish. Even in—especially in—Kakoneni.

EIGHTEEN

Holocaust Education in an African Museum: Reflections Following a 2002 Visit to South Africa

Should the Shoah be taught in societies far distant from the theater of Second World War genocide? Does Holocaust commemoration make sense in the Third World? Can the lessons of genocide and racism be successfully transferred from one cultural and historical context to another?

Established in 1999 with private funds from the Jewish community of South Africa, evolution of the Cape Town Holocaust Centre mirrors many of the tensions that have pitted the "uniqueness" against the "universalist" schools of Holocaust historiography. (The former school takes the position that the Shoah is incomparable to other genocides; the latter argues that it needs to be situated within the greater history of evil.) As an educational institution open to the general African public, however, the Cape Town Holocaust Centre transcends the purely academic nature of this debate. Memorializing the victims of the Shoah in a nation still emerging from the injustices of apartheid poses particular challenges to world history, communal memory, and civic education.

Despite initial (and some lingering) reluctance by Holocaust survivors who spearheaded the Cape Town Holocaust Centre, references to official South African discrimination by race—apartheid—were included in the Museum's permanent exhibit. Less expected was the extent to which the educational wing of the Centre would evolve into a space for resolution of more recent, and even contemporary, conflict.

From hosting Cape Town-area school visits, the educational wing of the Cape Town Holocaust Centre regularly receives school groups from throughout South Africa and neighboring countries. It has also come to tailor visits for professional development purposes—including the police force and prison department. Using absolute evil (as represented by the Shoah) as a point of departure greatly facilitates state agents' acknowledging their previous participation in the "lesser evil" of apartheid. In the absence of a veritable apartheid museum in South Africa, the Cape Town Holocaust Centre serves as neutral space for groups wishing to deal with the aftermath of apartheid in a less confrontational setting than that afforded by the official Truth and Reconciliation Commission. At the suggestion of the police force, the Cape Town Holocaust Centre has also brought together rival township gang members in a similar reconciliation process.

Unfortunately, no systematic study of the content and impact of the educational programs at the Cape Town Holocaust Centre has yet to appear in the scholarly literature. Indeed, none of the otherwise exemplary treatments of Holocaust education in North America, Great Britain, Israel, and Central Europe examines extra-academic programming.

Two related issues ought to be considered. These are: the current status of the Muslim community in South Africa (including Muslim-Jewish relations); and the various positions taken by the organized Jewish community, and by prominent South African Jews, during the apartheid era. Contemporary responses to the educational programming of the Cape Town Holocaust Centre are, in part, affected by the perceptions of South African Muslims of Jewish institutions; and of indigenous Africans vis-à-vis the South African Jewish community. The Cape Town Holocaust Centre raises wider questions beyond the concerns of these local communities.

Advocates of the "uniqueness" school invoke the pseudo-scientific genocidal intentionality of the Nazis, their use of high technology to murder civilians *en masse*, the creation of death factories, and the unprecedented mobilization of a modern state bureaucracy to destroy an entire people. "Universalists," without minimizing the horrors of the Holocaust (or denying its specific features), nevertheless feel compelled to situate the Shoah within a broader history of genocide. An event that is "out of ordinary history," they claim, becomes fundamentally incomprehensible, providing few insights into the past and no lessons for the future. The Holocaust, therefore, must be studied alongside other genocides. Yet such a comparative approach, according to uniqueness advocates (who are joined by most survivors), tends to diminish the significance and specificity of the Shoah. Implicitly, the specific suffering and experience of the Holocaust survivor is deemed relativized (if not trivialized) by the "universalists."

Transposed to southern Africa, the Holocaust uniqueness-universalist debate resonates with especial intensity. Both Jews in Germany and Blacks in South Africa suffered official racism, state-organized deportation, and institutionalized violence. Both communities currently pursue processes of reparation (the latter in the guise of "truth and reconciliation") for the ensuing deaths and appropriation of property. However, only hyperbolically can one equate the unjust "parallel development" foisted by the white minority regime upon Black Africans with the genocidal "final solution" organized by Nazi authorities against European Jewry. While Holocaust universalists identify commonalities in racism, uniqueness advocates reject the analogy on account of ostensibly differing outcomes.

In South Africa, then, how does one manage to integrate the history of apartheid in a Holocaust center? How does one do so without, on the one hand, alienating the advocates of Holocaust uniqueness (and the survivors themselves) and ceding paradigmatic authority to the universalists, on the other?

Holocaust Education has become an integral component of social studies curricula throughout the United States, with state education guidelines for over fifteen states. Private foundations such as Facing History and Ourselves, based outside of Boston, as well the educational departments of the Museum of Tolerance in Los Angeles and the United States Holocaust Memorial Museum in Washington, D.C., also engage in school outreach to help teachers apply the lessons of the Shoah to contemporary American society.

What ought to be added is a comparative basis, using an Africa context, to assess the utility of Holocaust studies for civic education in societies historically divided by race and an assessment of the impact of Holocaust education upon young adult professionals working in law enforcement and correctional capacities.

NINETEEN

Jewish in Mauritius: From Hebrew to Hindi

At first blush, there is little similarity between multilingualism in Mauritius and assimilationism in America. Yet it is only as a Jew that I fully came to grasp the key dilemma facing the various Asian communities on that remote Indian Ocean island: how to build a prosperous and progressive society without losing one's identity and soul.

My family and I arrived in Mauritius shortly before Rosh Hashanah of 5757 so that I could begin nearly one year of Fulbright-sponsored research into language and development. Background reading had revealed that two-thirds of the islanders originally hail from India and are struggling to preserve their ancestral languages: Hindi, Tamil, etc. Another one-third of Mauritians are, like American Blacks, descendants of slaves from Africa. All use a Louisiana-like Creole—a simplified French with some African words—as their mother tongue. The official language is English, but French is the language of prestige. In the Mauritian countryside Bhojpuri—an indigenized version of a northern Indian dialect—long held sway.

By sheer chance, we had learned that there were also a few dozen Jews whose unofficial leader, Owen Griffiths, was an Australian-born crocodile farmer. It is thanks to Owen that, even in these tropics, the shofar is blown on Rosh Hashanah and matzah is eaten on Passover.

Yet the Jewish connection to Mauritius is much longer, and

more somber, than this Ashkenazic answer to Crocodile Dundee. During World War II, Mauritius served as a British detention center for well over a thousand would-be immigrants to Palestine. One-hundred twenty-four of them never left Mauritius: they died in detention and are buried on the island. Over the gate of the immaculately tended Jewish cemetery outside Rose Hill hangs a Star of David and the inscription "Blessed be the True Judge 1940-1945." Tombstones are engraved in both Hebrew and English.

Yet even if Jews are few, Zionists are numerous in today's Mauritius. Hundreds are members of the *Mauritius-Israel Amicale* (Friendship Society), whose Tamil president, Suppaya Curpen, also serves as Israeli honorary consul. The Amicale, composed mostly of Mauritians who have trained or studied in Israel, meets regularly, hosts visiting Jewish and Israeli dignitaries, publishes *Mauritius Shalom Magazine*, and, as we learned in the days following

Gate to Jewish cemetery in Beau Bassin, Mauritius

Adult's tombstone

Child's tombstone

our arrival, puts on a lively Rosh Hashanah party complete with Mauritian musicians playing Israeli folk tunes to a calypso-like beat. Plans are afoot for the Amicale to enlarge their facilities and include a prayer site for their Jewish friends. If these plans materialize, Mauritius will be the only country in the world where a synagogue will have been conceived and built by non-Jews.

With a significant Muslim population that includes a small fundamentalist faction, Mauritius has not been entirely immune from anti-Israeli and anti-Semitic outbursts. But the majority religion is Hinduism (Catholics are about one-third the population) and toleration of religious minorities is an abiding feature of Hindu culture. Mauritius is a parliamentary democracy, and its titular president, Cassim Uteem, is a progressive Muslim who would not tolerate any state- or imamic-sponsored anti-Jewish prejudice.

In America, multiculturalism is a buzz word. In Mauritius, it is a reality. In addition to the Indo-Mauritians, Afro-Mauritians, and Muslim Mauritians, there are also Sino-Mauritians and Franco-Mauritians, each group tending to stick together and promote its own. One of the most tendentious issues—and the one I came to study—is how the languages of these diverse groups serves as facilitator or hindrance to economic and political progress.

Both Mauritius and America are immigrant societies which pride themselves in their development and democracy. Both have harnessed the work ethic to achieve spectacular results. Mauritius, with its three-pronged strategy of sugar cane-based agriculture, textile export processing, and high-class tourism is, of course, a relative newcomer within the community of middle-income nations.

In the United States, it took several generations before a sense of nationhood took root, "melting" the different immigrant communities—English, Irish, Dutch, German, Italian—into a similar national "pot." Forging a single nation out of formerly separate cultures has been a prerequisite for American success. One of the costs of this strategy of assimilation—a price that Mauritians are seemingly reluctant to pay—is the loss of ancestral cultures and languages. In its march towards economic development, however, even Mauritius has begun to exchange essential traditions for the fruits of modernity.

It is as the grandson of European (Polish and Lithuanian) Jewish immigrants to America that I have been most able to identify with the predicament of Mauritians of Asian and Oriental background wanting to preserve their respective religions, cultures, and languages against the pressures of a rapidly evolving, increasingly competitive and individualistic society. Hyphenated Mauritians have created a plethora of fraternal organizations and interest groups to promulgate their respective faiths and/or ancestral languages and to ensure their acceptance by the government. As a result, as a third language in the public schools (after English and French), Mauritian schoolchildren may elect to take Arabic, Chinese (Mandarin), Hindi, Marathi, Tamil, Telugu, or Urdu. Television and radio stations (all state-run) also must include all these languages in their programming.

My immigrant grandparents arrived in New York speaking barely a word of America's "official" language—English—and conversing rather in Yiddish, the German-based "creole" of European Jewry. They were Orthodox Jews who prayed in Hebrew—the "ancestral" language of the Jewish people—and who sent their own children to after-school *heder* (whose Hindu equivalent is the *baitka*) so that the ancient tongue and rituals would not be lost. Given the pressures to assimilate the American way of life, however, they only partly succeeded.

Although one can find pockets of ultra-Orthodox Jews in America who still cling to Yiddish, this creolized mixture of German, Hebrew, and English has virtually disappeared as a Jewish lingua franca. *The Forward*, the newspaper that my grandfather used to read, folded its Yiddish version,[1] and even my own parents, who spoke the language as children at home, lost fluency as adults. Census figures in Mauritius demonstrate that Bhojpuri is rapidly losing ground to Creole, much as Yiddish has ceded to English in America. The reasons are similar. Neither Bhojpuri nor Yiddish was ever regarded as a "high culture" idiom, nor fundamental to the religion—Hindu, Jewish—of its practitioners. Linguists predict within

---

[1] An excellent English edition has replaced it.

a generation or two for the children of today's Bhojpuri speakers in Mauritius a fate similar to that of Yiddish.

Jewish educators in America place their hope in transmitting to their youth the Hebrew language as the ancestral and sacred tongue of the Jews. Hebrew is also, of course, the vernacular tongue in Israel; but it is the Biblical and liturgical versions, rather than the modern form, which is privileged in most Hebrew schools in America. Hebrew is thus learned not to be spoken but so as to maintain tradition, religion, and sense of community. Similarly, Mauritian Muslims cling to Urdu or Arabic as a means of preserving their own distinctive identity.

Is this not also the case with Hindi, Tamil, Marathi, Telugu and Mandarin in Mauritius today? None of these languages, I was surprised to discover during my research, is actually spoken in the homes of Mauritians professing to belong to these respective linguistic and religious groups. Even Hindi, the most widely studied and known of the so-called ancestral or Oriental languages, thrives more as a group identity marker than as any Mauritian's maternal tongue. Great efforts are made in the nation's schools and media to maintain these Asian and Oriental languages, but it is much more a matter of cultural than linguistic survival *per se*. There is also a strong political dimension to the ancestral language issue: when the government in 1995 proposed plans to introduce Asian languages for ranking in secondary school entrance examinations, the move precipitated a constitutional crisis and early elections and led to the government's downfall.

Sadly, relatively few children emerge from Hebrew school in America with more than a rudimentary, and often simply phonetic, command of the language of their forefathers. How many Jews with a religious education complain of reciting verses or prayers whose meaning totally escapes them? Hebrew education in America for most Jews ends with the bar/bat mitzvah.

This is similar to Mauritius, where few pupils elect to continue their Oriental language studies beyond primary school. Of course, there are some Mauritians for whom knowledge of Hindi (and, to a lesser extent, Tamil) has facilitated studies and careers in India, just as some American Jews have parlayed their Hebrew into successful integration in Israel. But, by and large, upwardly mobile Indo-Mauritians are now, no less than American Jews once did, shunting off the languages of the "old country" in favor of subjects pursued more usually in the English language.

And what of Creole? What of the Creoles (Afro-Mauritians)? Descendants of the "involuntary immigrants" to both Mauritius and America—African slaves—constitute a significant minority in both countries. As a previously discriminated against minority in America, Jews have long extended a sympathetic hand in the struggle for American Blacks to achieve civil rights. Only latterly have the contributions of "America's Creoles" begun to be acknowledged within the wider society. In Mauritius, perhaps the most important legacy that the Creoles have bequeathed to the nation as a whole is the Creole language itself. Indeed, Creole is the most unifying factor throughout Mauritian society.

Though my research project originally began with a focus on English and French bilingualism in Mauritius, it came to encompass the role of other languages on the island. My own experience in Hebrew school, together with dim family memories of Yiddish, undoubtedly afforded me greater insight into the stakes and passions surrounding the issue of "ancestral languages" in Mauritius than otherwise would have been the case. For sure, one does not have to be Jewish to appreciate the nuances of assimilation in other cultures and lands; but it surely can help.

TWENTY

Jews in Paradise: Indian Ocean Encounters on Réunion and Île Maurice[1]

"The Hasidim don't have such a good reputation over here, you know," confided long-haired Bernard in Parisian-accented French.

"Here" was one of the most unlikely spots on earth to be considering the merits of the Jews, regardless of their degree or type of religiosity. We were on Réunion, a tropical island in the Indian Ocean that, two decades into the twenty-first century, still belongs to France. Bernard Benyamoun had come from Paris seven years before I encountered him there in the late 1990s, but his parents had been born in North Africa.

Réunion and Mauritius are part of a chain of islands off the coast of Madagascar known as the Mascarenes. Small and remote, with just over 1.5 million inhabitants between them, the *îles soeurs* (sister islands) tend to attract wealthy expatriates from Europe and America. The Mascarene Islands are hardly bastions of Jewish life, of course, but Jews continue to wander, even to the most unlikely parts of the globe. Somehow, we always manage to find each other. And then we *kvetch* about other Members of the Tribe.

"They think that all the Jews in the overseas departments are rich," continued Bernard, referring to France's far-flung provinces in the Caribbean, South America, and the Indian Ocean. "That may be the case in Guadeloupe and Martinique, but here in Réunion,

[1] A version of this essay was originally published in *Transition* 77 (1999), pp. 56-68. Reproduced with permission of Indiana University Press.

we're just trying to get by. You've seen our synagogue. It's hardly the synagogue of a prosperous Jewish community."

Indeed. Without an exact address, you'd never find the shul in St. Denis, Réunion's capital. Nothing about the building itself suggests that this is the center of Jewish life in the Indian Ocean. And although there's a balcony with a nice view of the ocean, the interior of the *syno* is somewhat shabby. The decorations and wall hangings in the walk-up prayer room are a bit amateurish. And there is the floor: when the faithful become especially numerous or fervent on their feet, as during the High Holy Days, it begins to buckle. They've been discussing reinforcing that floor for so many years that it has become a "standing" joke.

Bernard originally came to Réunion as a draftsman for the local government, courtesy of the French army. He was fulfilling his military service in a civilian capacity, an option available to those lucky few who can secure a place in the French equivalent of the Peace Corps. When his tour of duty was up, he stayed on, working as a furniture maker and commercial interior designer. Bernard had a passion for hang gliding; although he had sworn off the sport after a premonitory encounter with his Maker, he still had his kite. Bernard was also a hell of a baker: he spent most Friday afternoons making the most delicious challah this side of the Mozambique Channel.

Bernard was living with Lolita, a young Réunionnaise. Most natives of Réunion are dark-skinned, and their features recall involuntary immigrants from continental Africa—slavery was abolished in 1848—or slightly more voluntary (but no less desperate) migrants from southern India. But Lolita was light-skinned and broad-boned, as aristocratic islanders from Madagascar are wont to be. If there was any hint of *métissage* in Lolita's family history—and race mixing is part and parcel of Mascarene culture—it would have been a splash of Chinese. She worked, quite appropriately, in a boutique, selling beauty supplies. Poor Bernard, good Jewish boy and fervent *davener* that he was, had no choice—Lolita was voluptuous.

Most of the other Jews here on Réunion, whether Orthodox or secular, Conservative or Reform, Ashkenazic or Sephardic, had landed on the island under similarly haphazard circumstances. Some had made a small fortune and then lost it; they stayed on to wait for a more favorable turn of *beshert* (Yiddish: fate). The Jews were now scattered over the Mascarenes, but assembled as a single congregation they would number 150, perhaps 200 souls.

"A number of these Hasidim have come all the way to Réunion to ask for money," Bernard went on to complain. "They make no bones about it: 'How much are you going to give?' They say they are collecting funds for good causes: a sick cousin, a family in distress. But they have this way about them that really rubs me wrong . . . "

I try explaining that these bearded, black-hatted, sidelock-wearing, jet-setting *schnorrers* probably weren't actually Hasidim. Hasidim ("pious ones") are a mystical branch of ultra-Orthodox Haredim ("those who tremble"). The traveling Jews were probably simply Haredim. It's a distinction I couldn't help making, having spent seven months in Jerusalem—where the Haredim are said to be "taking over the neighborhood"—and having grown up near Brooklyn, where turf wars between equally orthodox Satmars and Lubavitchers are legendary. But for Bernard, it was *bonnet blanc et blanc bonnet:* six of one, half a dozen of another.

"Well, whatever he was, he stayed at my house for several days. This was when I was still a volunteer, doing my military service. One morning at breakfast, he came out with it point blank: 'What are you going to give?' It was embarrassing. I was barely making ends meet on my living allowance, but I told myself, 'Well, he must be here for good reasons, doing charitable deeds.' So I gave him what I could, maybe 250 francs. The guy flew into a rage. '*Tu te fous de moi?*' he yelled. 'Are you jerking me around? 250 francs?! I've taken an airplane all the way from France, and you're offering 250 francs?' This Hasid—okay, Hared—just kept abusing me. He hit on the others just as hard.

"You can imagine the rather bad taste these people left in our mouth. So when we heard that the *rebbe* was arriving for the holiday, we were not overjoyed."

It was Hanukkah 5757 (1996), and the visiting rebbe, David Portiche, was a Lubavitcher on assignment from Paris. Rabbi Portiche had also spent several years in London, New York, and Israel; I couldn't quite figure out where he was from. When I asked him, he became visibly annoyed and brushed the question aside. "I am a Jew," he seemed to be saying. "This is my identity. Whatever my birthplace, wherever I happen to live, my identity remains unaltered. So it should be with *you* and every other Jew."

I have not described the rebbe physically. Why bother? All ultra-Orthodox Jews dress the same, whether the climate is northern or tropical: white shirts, baggy black trousers and overcoats, beards, black hats that reveal black skullcaps when doffed. White fringes *(tsitsit)* from an undershirt jut out from their waists. Side-locks *(payot)* dangle down both cheeks, or are discretely twirled and tucked behind each ear. Of course, within the world of the ultra-Orthodox there are subtle distinctions of dress, invisible to the outsider, which mark off one circle of believers from another. But that is irrelevant here. Any kind of ultra-Orthodox Jew alighting on any of the Mascarene islands is out of the ordinary. Hindu swamis come and go, as do Muslim muezzins. But a Lubavitcher in Réunion? It made the nightly news on TV.

The French names used to describe Jews are emblematic of the distinctive way that the descendants of Abraham, Isaac, and Jacob are perceived in the land of Molière, Napoléon, and de Gaulle. As a community, Jews—*les juifs*—are commonly referred to as *Israélites* or the even more ancient-sounding *Hébreux*. Thus, the synagogue in St. Denis is officially known as the *Centre Hébraïque de la Réunion*. If the French have a harder time than Americans do distinguishing between the Jewish people and the modern nation of Israel, it is perhaps because the difference between *Israélien* and *Israélite* is more subtle than the difference between "Jew" and "Israeli." But calling yourself an Israelite sounds rather anachronistic in twenty-first-century English.

I had arrived at the synagogue for Friday night services, early and unannounced. There were only three people there: an adolescent, who was tending to the enormous menorah, and two middle-aged men. They were joking with each other, and they quickly included me in their conversation without pausing for an introduction. Such spontaneity of reception was disarming, even for a synagogue. In Paris, when I arrived at the one on Rue Copernic for Friday night services, I had been interrogated before being let into the sanctuary: Jew or not, I was obviously a foreigner. (In 1980, terrorists had infiltrated the building, killing four and wounding twenty worshippers, and suspicion still was in the air.) Even in Israel, particularly in Sephardic synagogues, I sensed a certain reserve toward Ashkenazic strangers. But here in Réunion, the two men acted as if they had been expecting me.

The taller of the two men, slim and handsome, was Léon, the president of the Centre Hébraïque de la Réunion. His partner, Georges, perhaps ten years older and a great kibitzer, was an Ashkenazi. More surprising than his ethnic background was the tattoo on his right arm. One thinks, automatically: "European Jew, tattoo, concentration camp." But no, this was a secular tattoo, a cartoon heart. What kind of Jew tattoos his arm on purpose, vulgarly like that? And against the one Jewish law that even the least observant Jew honors! Georges was obviously fond of cutting his fellows down to size, regardless of race, religion, or post-exilic denomination.

"Yes," he pronounces in deadpan irony, "Léon is our esteemed president. Elected unanimously—after all, who else would take the job? I had it before him. He may be a president, but you know his nickname? '*Le Boucher*. The Butcher.' *C'est vrai,* that's what he's known as around here, *n'est-ce pas, monsieur le Président*?"

Léon grinned at Georges' ribbing. It turns out that Léon was a doctor, head of the surgical unit at the island's main hospital. Calling him "The Butcher" was a way that friends and fellow congregants reminded him that he was, for all his professional status, just another Jew. That's something I remind myself, when beginning to succumb to swelling of the ego: no matter how accomplished you may think you are, in order to form a minyan, you still need nine other Jews, regardless of their profession, celebrity, income, or social status.[2]

The services began at sunset. The opening Sabbath eve prayer, *l'cha dodi,* is a metaphorical welcoming of a bride. The verses of l'cha dodi can be sung in a number of ways, some of them pacifying, some of them invigorating. To an Ashkenazic ear, though,

---

[2]Jewish wisdom, to be sure, also guards against false modesty. I admitted as much in my inaugural lecture as the Stotsky Professor of Jewish Historical and Cultural Studies at Northeastern University:

> In a suburban synagogue outside Boston, the rabbi made a particularly compelling sermon about the insignificance of mankind before the Almighty. At its conclusion, a prominent member of the community, a very prosperous lawyer, stood up from the front dais where he had his seat of honor, and spoke up:
>
> "Rabbi, for fifty years I have been coming to Yom Kippur services. But never before have the words uttered here so shaken me. They have struck me as a dagger in the heart. I realize now that my success as an attorney—the renown, the prestige, the accolades—they are all sheer conceit. All the fancy works I have ever uttered in a courtroom are empty compared with the humbling wisdom you have now imparted. Before the Lord, I am a worm. I am nothing."
>
> There was silence, absolute silence in the synagogue. Nothing of the sort had ever happened before. Then, from the opposite side of the pulpit, a woman stood up: Brookline's most prominent businesswoman, president of the city's Chamber of Commerce, a known tycoon and reputedly a multi-millionaire.
>
> "Rabbi," she began. "I, too, have heard your words. Also, those of our brother from the bench. But he cannot possibly feel the degree of shame that I do now. My 'fortune,' my 'riches'—I now realize, as you say, that they are mere mirages. Your message cuts me to the quick. Before the Lord, I am lower than a worm. I am an insect. I am *nothing*!"
>
> Stunned was the congregation. Never before had a Yom Kippur sermon had such an impact, and this on the community's most respected, powerful, wealthy members. Nobody knew what to do or say next, including the rabbi.
>
> Then, from the back of the sanctuary, stood Professor Poverty, the congregational gadfly.
>
> "Rabbi," moaned the shabbily dressed man, I have been spiritually pierced by your words. All my invited lectures, all my grants and awards, all my publications are naught compared to the creations of God. My contrition is greater than of all others assembled here on this night of penitence. I am less than a worm, less than an insect. I am no more than a single-celled micro-organism floating in the mud of the gutter. I AM NOTHING!"
>
> At this culminating confession, a regular member of the daily minyan (as the three previous speakers are certainly not) turns to his neighbor and utters in a Temple stage whisper:
>
> "Hey, Bernie, look who's sayin' *he's* a nuthin'!" (Loosely adapted and greatly embellished from Telushkin [1992:155], with thanks to Professor Michael Horowitz of Binghamton University whose oral rendition of it greatly impressed me.)

Sephardic renditions of these familiar prayers are atonal, jarring. Jews share the same prayers, but the music is a reminder of differences between the Jews of the East and the Jews of the West.

Jewish musical chauvinism works in both directions, of course. A Sephardic sociologist in Israel once admitted to me that he simply can't stand the music at his wife's hometown synagogue in New Jersey. For someone whose religious roots are in the Maghreb, in North Africa, the American songs are "not quite Jewish-sounding." Whenever he is in the United States for High Holidays, he and his wife go to different synagogues. That women and men cannot sit together in orthodox Jewish congregations I can understand; that a man and wife would attend services at separate synagogues is somehow shocking to me.

"It's something fundamental," Maurice explained. "What you hear as a child growing up, that's what you yearn to hear as an adult. I'm sorry, but your syrupy Ashkenazic singing doesn't quite do it for me."

In the Indian Ocean synagogue, Sephardic tunes hold sway, although the congregation in Réunion is ethnically mixed. Some members of the minyan were outright Creole in appearance. A few davened fluently, while others just hummed the prayers. "Some Réunion islanders who are not even Jewish are drawn to the synagogue," Léon later explained. "They feel that they have some Jewishness in their family backgrounds, however remote, and they want to reconnect. It's difficult, of course—there is no permanent rabbi to instruct them. But they come." None of the Creoles stayed for the meal after services, but the spouses came, and the ambiance combined warmth, familyhood, and métissage.

Georges seemed to revel in his minority Ashkenazic status; his acerbic humor was given free rein. Often, it was Rabbi Portiche himself, seated next to Georges near the head of the table, who was the butt of his irreverent joking.

"What religious group is closest to the Jews?" Georges asked meaningfully.

"Jehovah's Witnesses?" one person asked, on account of the sect's ardent use of the Jewish God's name.

"Nope."

"Seventh Day Adventists?" came another response, based on that Christian sect's observance of Saturday Sabbath.

"No, no, no. What religious group is closest to the Jews? It's easy. Why, the Lubavitchers, *bien sûr!"*

I felt a strange rapport with the ribbed rebbe. His outfit and demeanor were more suited to Borough Park than the Indian Ocean, more suited to the diamond district of New York than to the *mellah*—the ghetto—of North Africa. I prayed extra loudly in his presence, to demonstrate that this Jewish wastrel was not necessarily ignorant of Hebrew. He was hardly in his element, and I thought I represented the kind of Jew he was more used to seeing—though not necessarily dealing with. Later, I imagined the conversations that the rebbe would have back at Chabad headquarters:

"These overseas Jews. They're becoming like the *goyim* around them and they don't even know it. *Shiksas* (Yiddish: female Gentiles) flock to them and they have no defenses. They try to remain Jewish but, *gevalt,* what a strange kind of life they make for themselves!"

What the rebbe was seeing here must have made his head spin. For all their idiosyncrasies, the Indian Ocean Jews seemed to be doing quite well and to be fully conscious of what they were doing. They were living—indeed, creating—a new kind of Jewish community, one which was as indigenous to the local environment as it was heretical in the eyes of the shtetl rabbinate.

Strangely, no one asked me how I had managed to find the Centre Hébraïque de la Réunion. For that precious information I was beholden to the unofficial head of the Jewish community on Mauritius, an Australian Ashkenazic crocodile farmer by the name of Owen Griffiths.

The island of Mauritius has twice the population of Réunion but a fraction of the Jews, a few dozen. Two-thirds of the island's population descend from East Indian sugarcane cutters; most of these are Hindu, but there is also a sizable Muslim minority. The other third of Mauritians are descended from African slaves: they are invariably Christian, predominantly Roman Catholic. There are a smattering of Chinese, and some white holdovers from early plantation days. None of the tourist guides or reference texts mentions that there are any Jews.

Perhaps they shouldn't. There is no synagogue, no Jewish community or cultural center, no prominent Jew of Mauritian nationality. In Mauritian consciousness, Jews exist more as metaphor than reality. When you visit the museum of Indian settlement at the Gandhi Institute, there is only one quote from the Mahatma framed on the wall:

> *I am a Hindu, a Muslim, a Christian, and a Jew.*
> *So are all of you.*

A Creole teacher, speaking about the ubiquity of his countrymen abroad, told me, "Mauritians are like Jews. They go everywhere in this world." Jews are comparable to the Chinese, a Catholic priest told me, because they assimilate into every culture in the world but still manage to retain their own specificities. At a youth gathering following the weekly *Dîner des Clochards* (Supper of the Hobos) outside the diocese church of Port Louis a few months later, that same priest asked me—following benedictions in French, Hindi, and Arabic—to offer a prayer in Hebrew.

Virtually all the Jews on the island have drifted in from Ashkenazic communities in South Africa, Australia, and America. As in Réunion, many of them have married out. Owen himself, the croc farmer, took a stately, regal Creole woman for a wife. Yet it is in their homestead, overlooking the pounding sea on the southern coast, that Rosh Hashanah is celebrated, in grand tropical Jewish style, for any Jew and companion on the island.

Owen is not unaware of the contradictions of his life. He would often mull over the state of Israel, the assimilation of the Jews, and the seeming dilution of Jewish consciousness in the Jewish state and in the diaspora. *"Enfin,"* he would begin, reflexively interlacing some French and Creole into his English, "I must admit I'm contributing to it, too, in my own way." Poignant is the plight of the Jew who wishes to dwell, as a Jew, in earthly paradise. Owen subscribes to the left-leaning *Jerusalem Report* as well as the more conservative *Jerusalem Post,* studies Hebrew, and has a reference library on matters relating to Judaism and Israel. He uses the Yiddish word *kinder* to call his Creole children. Folk or liturgical music is always playing in his car: one drives to the Vanilla Crocodile Farm to the tune of "Draw Thy Water, Joyfully" or some other Hebraic ditty.

Yet even Owen has problems with the "missionaries": "They keep sending me their literature-glossy flyers with all the latest news from the London Lubavitch House. I feel guilty when I chuck their mailings in the rubbish bin—all that postage going to waste. I've written them to say not to bother, but they keep on sending the stuff, month after month.

"Then they write to say that they want to send someone to visit. How do I tell them that it's not worth it? I can't tell them not to come, but what would be the point?" He concluded philosophically. "We are what we are."

The most ardent Zionists of the Indian Ocean are not even Jewish. They are the two hundred members of the *Amicale Maurice Israel*, the Mauritian-Israeli Friendship League, also known as the Shalom Club. The Amicale, founded in 1966, is made up mostly of Mauritians who have gone to Israel for schooling and wish to remain in contact with the Jewish state. Even during the suspension of diplomatic relations between 1976 and 1993, hundreds of Mauritians managed to receive scholarships for study in Israel.

The Amicale is headed by Baby S. Curpen, honorary consul of Israel in Mauritius. Baby is a warm and outgoing diplomat, happy to sprinkle a little Hebrew into his French, English, and Creole. Among the many papers and certificates in his cramped study, Baby particularly cherishes a letter from the late Israeli prime minister Yitzhak Rabin, acknowledging Baby's congratulations for winning the Nobel Peace Prize. It is largely thanks to Baby that Purim and Passover are celebrated in Mauritius, even if few of the celebrants are actually Jewish.

Only in Mauritius can one hear *sega*—a kind of calypso—and the Jewish shofar within a few beats of one another. This occurred on Rosh Hashanah at the Amicale's headquarters in Beau Bassin, not far from the island's Jewish cemetery.[3] After introductory speeches on the activities of the Amicale and the rituals of the Jewish New Year, Owen Griffiths blew a ram's horn, and a Mauritian band launched into Israeli folk music on guitar, drum, flute, and triangle. *Havenu Shalom Aleichem* was sung to a Mascarene island beat, led by a Mauritian musician whose own notion of paradise was the esplanade in central Tel Aviv.

Yet not everything is perfect for the handful of Jews and Zionists in the Mascarene Islands. Occasionally, an item in the local newspaper inveighs against Israel or some putative Jewish plot. Muammar Qaddafi once tried to incite the Muslim community in Mauritius, and the government had to close down the Libyan People's Bureau. A small but activist Muslim political party—which provocatively calls itself Hezbollah—is known for organizing Muslim protests against Israel. Perhaps the largest was the protest that culminated in the burning of the Israeli flag in November 1996, when the Israeli government opened the passageway to an underground tunnel near the Temple Mount in Jerusalem. Three Mauritian government ministers stood by, turning the Hezbollah action into a minor diplomatic incident.

Still, only a paranoiac would claim that anti-Semitism is a problem in Mauritius. Most people have barely heard of Judaism. It was in India that I first came to savor a liberating nonchalance about telling strangers I was Jewish: no fear of latent anti-Semitism, of being associated with Christ-killing forebears, of being stigmatized for Israel's actions. I just had to get used to the swastikas. In Mauritius, as in India, this ancient Hindu symbol has no malignant connotations. Indeed, it was at the inauguration of the new Swastika Hall in January of 1997 that Dr. Navin Ram-

---

[3]During the Holocaust, Mauritius served as a British detention camp for some fifteen hundred "illegal aliens" to Palestine; over one hundred remain buried there. See Pitot (1998); Zwergbaum (1960).

goolam, the prime minister of Mauritius, spoke of the tolerance and understanding upheld by the charitable Swastika Society.

My favorite interpreter of the Mascarene Jewish experience was a Réunion islander of Tamil extraction, a seventy-year-old retiree named André Marimouttou. Before he knew I was Jewish, he told me something about himself: "India is to us what Jerusalem is to the Jew from New York: a myth." I knew what he was getting at. Here in the French tropics, fourth- or fifth-generation Indian immigrants have assimilated to the local culture. And yet Marimouttou, an outspoken atheist, former Maoist, and one-time math teacher, had been to India several times. He described his attraction to the subcontinent as a kind of slumming: "Why do I keep going? Because it's the only place where I can go into any village and act like a pasha. For 200 francs, I can be treated like royalty."

But there was clearly more to it than that. Well into his retirement, Marimouttou was not only discovering his roots, but learning his forefathers' tongue as well. Not only had he taken up Tamil, but he was creating a Creole-Tamil manual for his adult students at the Open University of Réunion—itself another one of his innovations. "I don't believe in any of this 'back-to-roots' crap," he said, safeguarding his curmudgeonly image, "but some old friends kept asking me to do it. How could I refuse?" Having studied Tamil for well over a year, I was impressed with Marimouttou's post-retirement undertaking.

I felt a bond with him, a sense of belonging not unlike the connection I sometimes feel with other Jews. We are not merely human beings with mythical labels—he, an elderly Indian Ocean islander of East Indian descent; myself, a middle-aged Ashkenazic Jew latterly of Long Island. We are a special breed, each steeped in the distinctive history and culture of our respective peoples, but somehow stretching to find spiritual kindred in the infinite space between our accidental residences and our ancestral homelands.

TWENTY-ONE

Interned and Buried: British Mauritius and the Holocaust[1]

The history of Mauritius is a study in multi-religious migration. Whether in search of territorial and commercial expansion (the French and British), as involuntary labourers (Malagasys and Africans), as contractual workers (East Indians), or as intrepid entrepreneurs (Chinese), Christians, Animists, Muslims, Hindus and Buddhists have all established themselves on Mauritius to create one of the most religiously pluralistic nation on earth. The only major world faith missing from this spiritual kaleidoscope, it would seem, is the Jewish one. And yet Geneviève Pitot's *The Mauritian Shekel* is an important reminder of an oft-neglected episode in the religious history of Mauritius. Subtitled *The Story of the Jewish Detainees in Mauritius, 1940—1945*, it is the first full-length study of the Jews' incarceration by British colonial authorities, as told from a Mauritian perspective. In this vein, it is a valuable addition to the burgeoning literature on Mauritian history by Mauritian writers themselves.

While the diary of Anne Frank has preserved interest in the plight of the Jews during the Second World War, it was the impression left by one Anna Frank on Geneviève Pitot, a native of Moka, Mauritius, that lies at the origin of *The Mauritian Shekel.* Madame Frank was one of over a thousand Jewish refugees who spent nearly five years in the Beau Bassin prison when the British re-

[1] A review of Geneviève Pitot's *The Mauritian Shekel: The Story of the Jewish Detainees in Mauritius, 1940-1945*, originally published in *Mauritius Shalom Magazine* (1999).

fused them entry into Palestine in 1940. Regarded by Great Britain as illegal immigrants for attempting to enter then British-controlled Palestine without visas, Anna Frank and her co-religionists from Austria, Czechoslovakia, Poland, Germany, Russia, and the "free port" of Danzig were imprisoned in Mauritius as a warning to other Jews daring to enter their ancestral homeland without the (grudging) permission of British colonial authorities. During a short-lived period of liberal administration, Anna Frank, an artist, was permitted to leave prison during the day to teach art at young Geneviève Pitot's school. More than half a century later, Mrs. Pitot has unraveled the fascinating story of her teacher's arduous journey from the Danube River to the Indian Ocean and the refugees' detention in Mauritius.

Thirty years after Mauritius' independence and fifty years after Israel's, it can be difficult to imagine how complete was British control over the destinies of Mauritian subjects and Jewish refugees alike. Fearful of Arab reaction to increased Jewish immigration to Palestine, and paranoid that Nazi agents had infiltrated the group of homeless Jews, British authorities insisted that the Jews be under surveillance and far away. Any colony would do: Trinidad almost became the final destination. In the end, out of logistical convenience, Mauritius was settled on: but no Mauritians were consulted as to their desire to "host" on their island these helpless and alien refugees.

Be that as it may, Pitot makes clear that Mauritians, although deprived of any input on the question, demonstrated great sympathy and goodwill to their "guests." For sure, contact between islanders and detainees was limited (especially in the first year), and some defamatory rumors did later circulate (e.g., that detainees were responsible for wartime food shortages; that they harbored enemy agents helping the Germans to torpedo Allied ships). But, all in all, Mauritians regarded and treated the Jews in their midst much more favorably than did the British.

Particularly interesting in the book are details of detention life. Despite the absence of books and teaching materials, a cultural and educational life thrived within prison walls. Two distinct synagogues emerged, catering to the Orthodox and Reform branches of Judaism. Most embarrassing were the tents that—having prohibited families from living together—prison authorities erected on the "Mixed Recreation Ground" for scheduled rendez-vous of married couples. While Beau Bassin was no concentration camp, the book makes clear how oppressive was their lack of freedom, harsh discipline, and denial of basic human rights.

The title of *The Mauritian Shekel* is taken from the membership dues, symbolically disbursed in Biblical coinage, which detainees paid to the World Zionist Organization. At war's end, 1,060 of the 1,300 detained Jews did settle in Palestine/Israel. Even had any desired to remain in Mauritius, a British edict prohibited such a scenario. Only in the St. Martin cemetery have Jewish detainees—127 of them—stayed behind.

Fluid in its writing, generously illustrated with photographs and two helpful maps tracing the Jews' journey from Central Europe to the Mascarenes, *The Mauritian Shekel* is an admirable culmination of one woman's nostalgia-rooted quest to honor a former teacher. As such, it does justice to an imperative common to both Mauritian and Jewish cultures: the obligation to remember.

TWENTY-TWO

French West Indies I: The Jews File[1]

"Your subject is very timely," the young Afro-Caribbean archivist observed as we shook hands and he prepared to hand over a sheaf of half-century-old government files.

He was right. The topic I was researching was suddenly and alarmingly relevant, given the disquieting candidacy of the far-right candidate in the French presidential elections, Jean-Marie Le Pen. Unfortunately, the archivist's words resonate even more powerfully now than they did on that balmy afternoon in May.

I had come to the government archives to do legwork for research on the Jewish history in the Caribbean island of Martinique, which is part of the French States of America (FSA), a place with a checkered history when it comes to Jews (Miles 2005). The FSA is now home to a million, mostly Afro-French, citizens of *la République*. They overwhelmingly rejected Le Pen in the final round of voting—but not before he finished second best France-wide among sixteen candidates in the initial round. Not surprising, given that most Martinicans can count African slaves among their forebears.

The archivist handed me the thick stack of files in brown paper wrapping and tied together by twine. It was "The Jews" file.

As a French colony under the collaborationist Vichy regime during World War II, Martinique was subject to the same anti-Semitic legislation then prevailing in France. In even the sleepiest corners of the empire, government officials were obliged to provide declarations of their "non-belonging to the Jewish race." Ironically,

[1]Originally published in *Moment Magazine* 28:1 (February 2003), pp. 40-41.

many were written on official stationary bearing the lofty motto *Liberté, Egalité, Fraternité.*

How chilling to behold the beautifully scripted declaration of a schoolteacher swearing to the governor that she "does not belong to either the Jewish race or religion." (Under the prevailing legislation, this included having even a single Jewish grandparent.) How strange to peruse the non-Jewish declarations of Catholic nuns working for the welfare bureau. How poignant to read the handwritten "defense" of a suspected high school teacher—providing baptismal and other sacramental evidence—because he bore the suspicious name of Guthmann. While only non-Martinican-born government officials were required to provide such "exonerating" proof, one still reads, with irony, declarations of non-Jewishness appearing under such typical French West Indian names as Théopanie Achéen, Félix-Casimir Fanon, and Joseph Hippolyte Jeanjean.

The more prominent the official, the greater the tendency to go out of the way to exclude even the slightest possibility of Jewishness: "On my honor," wrote a judge assigned to the principal court in the capital on January 11, 1941, "I declare not to be of Jewish origin, neither from the recent nor distant past, be it from a religious or an ethnic standpoint." There is a file of "doubtful agents" —civil servants whose declarations of non-Jewishness required substantiation. When I open the last folder, I come across the stunner—the list of all 23 Jewish families known, as of August 1, 1941, to the government in Martinique.

Whatever happened to Paul Stern, the 31-year-old doctor living in the remote mountain village of Morne-Rouge, who in his spare time taught illiterate peasants how to read? Was Daniel Stern, the 23-year-old army veteran living in Fort-de-France, his younger brother? Did Marguerite Lecoq, Gentile wife of a Jewish man named Bickert and mother of a child therefore listed as a Jew, ever reunite with her husband then in New York? How did Isaac Zion Tueti, father of five and of "Palestinian nationality," wind up in the French Antilles? Could the 36-year-old widow Germaine Gold still work as a photographer? Did math teacher Ilija (Elijah) Salanski ever recover after being fired, simply because he was Jewish, from the high school named, ironically, after the abolitionist Victor Schoelcher, the Abraham Lincoln of France? The archives are silent on the fate of these hapless Jews in the tropics during this era of French fascism. Not even the gendarmerie captain who compiled the list probably knew.

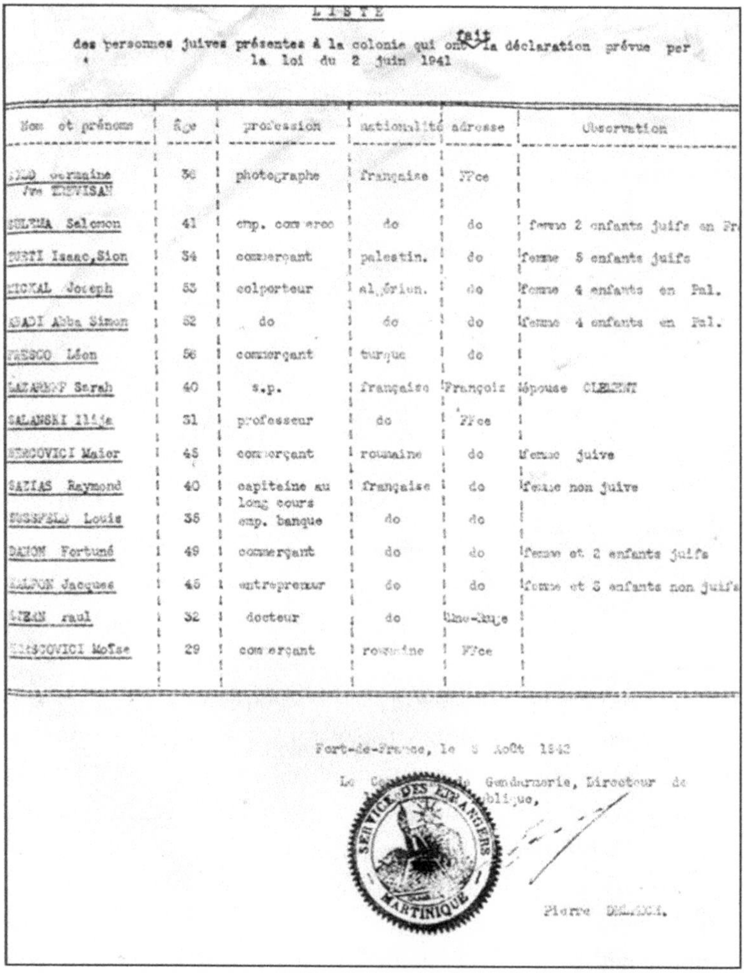

LISTE

des personnes juives présentes à la colonie qui ont fait la déclaration prévue par la loi du 2 juin 1941

Nom et prénoms	âge	profession	nationalité	adresse	Observation
[illegible] Germaine Vve [illegible]VISAN	36	photographe	française	F/Fce	
[illegible]LTMA Salomon	41	emp. commerce	do	do	femme 2 enfants juifs en Fr[illegible]
[illegible]RTI Isaac, Sion	34	commerçant	palestin.	do	femme 5 enfants juifs
[illegible]ICKAL Joseph	53	colporteur	algérien.	do	femme 4 enfants en Pal.
[illegible]ADI Abba Simon	52	do	do	do	femme 4 enfants en Pal.
[illegible]ESCO Léon	56	commerçant	turque	do	
LAZAR[illegible]F Sarah	40	s.p.	française	François	épouse CLE[illegible]
SALANSKI Ilija	31	professeur	do	F/Fce	
[illegible]RCOVICI Maier	45	commerçant	roumaine	do	femme juive
SAZIAS Raymond	40	capitaine au long cours	française	do	femme non juive
[illegible]SSFELD Louis	35	emp. banque	do	do	
DA[illegible]ON Fortuné	49	commerçant	do	do	femme et 2 enfants juifs
[illegible]LFON Jacques	45	entrepreneur	do	do	femme et 3 enfants non juifs
[illegible]ZAN Paul	32	docteur	do	[illegible]	
[illegible]SCOVICI Moïse	29	commerçant	roumaine	F/Fce	

Fort-de-France, le 5 Août 1942

Le C[illegible] de Gendarmerie, Directeur de [illegible]blique,

SERVICE DES ETRANGERS MARTINIQUE

Pierre [illegible].

Vichy French police list of Jews residing in Martinique

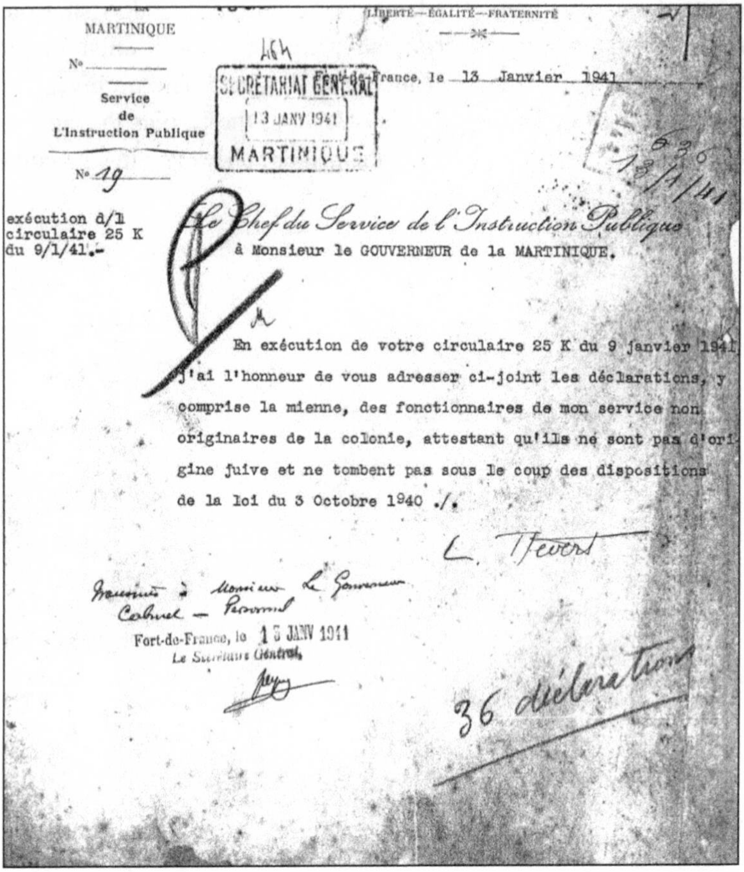

MARTINIQUE

N°

Service de L'Instruction Publique

N° 19

LIBERTÉ—ÉGALITÉ—FRATERNITÉ

464

SECRÉTARIAT GÉNÉRAL 13 JANV 1941 MARTINIQUE

Fort-de-France, le 13 Janvier 1941

636 13/1/41

exécution d/l circulaire 25 K du 9/1/41.-

Le Chef du Service de l'Instruction Publique

à Monsieur le GOUVERNEUR de la MARTINIQUE.

En exécution de votre circulaire 25 K du 9 janvier 1941 j'ai l'honneur de vous adresser ci-joint les déclarations, y comprise la mienne, des fonctionnaires de mon service non originaires de la colonie, attestant qu'ils ne sont pas d'origine juive et ne tombent pas sous le coup des dispositions de la loi du 3 Octobre 1940 ./.

Transmis à Monsieur le Gouverneur Cabinet – Personnel

Fort-de-France, le 13 JANV 1941

Le Secrétaire Général

36 déclarations

Civil servant attestation of not being Jewish

Half a century later, gendarmes still watch Jews in Martinique—not to persecute, but to protect. Concerned with anti-Semitic attacks in *la Métropole*, French authorities wish to avoid similar incidents in their island domain. And so, on the high holidays, cops in *kepi* (conical headgear made famous by French legionnaires) now stand guard outside the Schoelcher synagogue.

Yes, there is a full-blown Jewish community in Martinique, complete with kosher provisioning, Hebrew school, and *mikva* (ritual bath). Sephardim of North African birth or descent, the Jews of Martinique now number well over four hundred. Some even wear yarmulkes in Fort-de-France, where they own jewelry, luggage, and cell phone shops. They are on generally cordial terms with that other prominent diaspora group in the island's capital—the Palestinians. But the Jews are still wary, especially since several pro-independence Martinicans have embraced the Palestinian cause as their own.

"Today there are only about 400 Sephardic Zionists [here], but when there are a thousand of them, they will dominate Martinique and enslave us in our own country." These words, published in a

Entrance to Martinique synagogue

radical island magazine in the early 1980s, led to the author's condemnation in the local courts for "incitement to racial hatred." In April 2002, a pro-Palestinian demonstration in Fort-de-France included placards (one with a swastika) characterizing then Israeli prime minister Ariel Sharon as a Nazi and equating him with Adolf Hitler. The (Martinican) president of the Martinique-Palestine Solidarity declared that "the Martinican people recognize a great injustice. . . . Massacres, destruction, and genocide are going to continue against the Palestinians."

Publicly, Martinican leftists are careful to distinguish between anti-Zionism and anti-Semitism. Are they sincere? "On account of the Holocaust," I overheard a Martinican representative to the parliament in Paris say to a companion, "the Jews now feel that they can do anything." And then there is residual, old-style, pre-Vatican II, Jew-as-Christ-killer prejudice lingering beyond the coconut trees.

For sure, such sentiments are hardly representative of French West Indian feeling as a whole. Each year, there is a ceremony in Martinique's capital commemorating the rounding up of Jews in Vichy France. Afterward, French West Indian army veterans come to the synagogue for a reception. There are Black French philosemites. There is even a handful of Martinican converts to Judaism.

Vichy memorial plaque

Memorializing of the deportation of Jews in France

Army veterans (wearing medals) attending Holocaust memorial service in Martinique synagogue

Jews feel more secure in Martinique than do their brothers and sisters in France proper. Most locals are barely conscious that there are Jews on their island. Many Martinicans don't even distinguish *juif* from *syrien*—they're vaguely lumped together as off-white Middle Easterners.

Yet few Martinicans knew about Jews in the 1940s, either.

When I first went to live in the French Antilles in the early 1980s, *la question juive* was far from my mind. Anti-Semitism in the Caribbean? You might as well have said parking problems in paradise. But when you dig deep enough, you'll always find a Semitic saga. No island guarantees a vacation from the Jewish question.

Purim celebration in the French West Indies

TWENTY-THREE

French West Indies II: Aimé Césaire and My Jewish Question[1]

We arrive at exactly the same moment: he, the *éminence grise* of négritude, chauffeured by automobile; I, the wandering Jew on sabbatical, damp on my motorscooter. Rendez-vous point: the former Town Hall of Fort-de-France, capital of Martinique, French West Indies. For half a century this short, dark man served as mayor of the town to his constituents, as representative of this island to France, and as inspiration to French-speaking Blacks around the world. Eighty-eight years old and only recently retired, he was still holding matinal court in this colonial villa, long since converted into a performing arts theater.

Unobtrusively I follow behind as, hand-in-hand with his secretary, Aimé Césaire slowly mounts the curving wooden staircase to his upstairs office. Midway, he stops, apologizing to his demure and elegant assistant for his lack of stamina. She reassures him. After a minute or two he continues his laborious ascent.

He greets the staff and visitors awaiting him in the antechamber. These include a young female Japanese researcher with whom he is courtly to the point of attempting an oriental bow. On the antechamber wall are portraits of him and his island by the renowned painter Henri Charpentier. There are also gifts—*tchotchkas*—from neighboring islands.

Ushered into his spacious office, I actually see what a toll these

[1]Originally published in *Wadabagei. A Journal of the Caribbean and Its Diaspora* 6 (2003), pp. 171-182.

last fifteen years have taken. When I first interviewed him in the late 1980s, he was vigorous, sharp, and still capable of powerful monologues. Now, although he is impeccably dressed in olive green suit and matching tie, I quickly see that the great Césaire is undeniably old. Behind his trademark thick glasses with the dark frames, his eyes do not twinkle as I remember they did in the steel-and-glass Town Hall that he occupied in the 1980s. At the conclusion of our meeting, I learn why: ophthalmological surgery.

The huge wooden desk is too big for the three of us—Césaire, his assistant, and me—to comfortably converse, now that his voice fails to project as it did in his days of high oratory. His lisp—a minor defect that shocked me at first encounter, and which has always been taboo to note in writing—is now lost in the strain of articulation. I unceremoniously hunch over as much as my ice cream suit (reserved for tropical encounters) and protocol allow. Rather than answering my questions directly, Césaire responds by speaking to his assistant, ever close by his right side. Occasionally I turn to her for clarification, and the act reminds me of the ritual in speaking to African chiefs: by deference, one does not address royalty directly, and never by using the second person pronoun, but through an intermediary, and employing the third person.

I have decided in advance not to raise the subjects about which Césaire has been interviewed *ad nauseam* over the decades: négritude, assimilation, autonomy, independence. So I begin by seeking clarification about a tree.

"You spoke about it on the radio program two weeks ago," I start. Shortly, the statesman-poet will recall the names of people he knew from his Parisian lycée before the War—but for the moment he doesn't remember having been two Sundays earlier the guest of musician-comedian-radio host Maurice Alcindor. His assistant reminds him of his recent appearance on Radio Martinique. He then asks in wonder if I speak Creole, language of the humoresque radio show. "Mwen capav comprenn kreyol en ti brin," I reply. Césaire himself had been teased into speaking Creole on the show by Alcindor, prodded by the claim that many Martinicans believed that the Great Man of Martinique could not even speak the island's colloquial tongue. Césaire, renowned for his mastery of the language of Molière, took up the challenge. But in truth, he does not speak Creole well—not fluently, not as a native speaker. I wonder if, in his waning days, he regrets his malaise with Creole.

"A caller asked you about a tree," I resume the thread. "A tree called, 'ear of Negro, ear of Jew.'"

"Ear of mulatto," Aimé Césaire counters, as he had to the radio show listener.

"Why is it called that?" I ask.

Césaire takes a piece of paper—he will do this on several occasions, when an answer demands precision—and sketches the form of the tree. "The fruit of the tree, when dried, looks like a human ear," he explains. "It could be the ear of a Black, or the ear of a Jew. We could call the tree 'ear of a Human Being.' But its real name"—and here he again marks the paper with his distinctive script—"is this . . ." Whereupon the Black octogenarian hero writes out *entorolobium cyclocarpium,* the botanical name in Latin, and discourses on the etymology of the word. "Popularly, some do call it 'ear of Jew.' It depends on the prejudice of certain people."

"The reason I bring this up," I continue, "is that, having researched former French colonies over these many years, I have now come to work on my own culture and patrimony—Jewish." Both *grand homme* and *assistante* reveal involuntary looks of surprise.

"*Formidable!*" he congratulates me.

"So I have come to ask what place the Jew occupies in Martinican, in French West Indian, consciousness."

Aimé Césaire shrugs. His answer, at first, is disappointing. "This is a new thing for us," he replies. (Is it the royal "we"?) "We don't know much about it at all, *enfin.*" But then he transports us, with great enthusiasm, to his arrival at the Lycée Louis Grand, in Paris, in the 1930s.

"Up to that point, all I knew was that there were Whites and Blacks. I didn't know that there was this subdivision, Jew.

"And then my schoolmates talked about the most brilliant

professors at our great lycée. There was a great Latinist—Bloch. And a Hellenist—David." He sounds the depths of his memories for a first name—and he comes up with one. "Jacqueline. Jacqueline David. She was very pretty, by the way—very black hair, somewhat brown in complexion. She looked a bit Spanish to me, even reminded me of some of our own West Indian women. . . . If I remember correctly, she did her thesis on Thucydides, married a man of French nobility"—he then writes down her married name—"and became the first female member of the French Academy.

"As if by coincidence, our most brilliant teachers were, I then learned, 'Jewish.'" Antisemitic classmates would point them out: "'This one is a Jew; that one is a Jew.' From that I concluded that the Jews were the most intelligent ones around. . . .

"So it was in France that I first heard about Jews, *comme une espèce un peu à part* [as a group set apart somewhat]. In Martinique, nobody talked about Jews."

> the famine-man, the insult-man, the torture-man . . .
> one can at any moment seize, beat up or kill—
>   yes really kill him-
> without having to account to anybody,
> without having to excuse oneself to anyone.
> a jew-man,
> a pogrom-man
> a little tyke,
> a bum

Thus did Césaire, as far back as 1947, already integrate the image of the Jew in his path-breaking poetic declaration of francophone Black consciousness, *Cahier du Retour au Pays Natal* (*Return to My Native Land*). There are echoes of the late eighteenth/early nineteenth century Roman Catholic progressive Abbot Henri-Baptiste Grégoire, whom Césaire admired (Sepinwall 2003). Yet while the *Cahier* deplores the alienation, helplessness, and statelessness of the French West Indian, its author imagines an even more radical solution:

> To leave.
> As there are hyena-men and leopard-men,
> I would be a jew-man.

This passage was on prominent display in a touring UNESCO exhibit on Césaire that in 1998, after completing its run in Paris and Dakar, "returned" to Martinique. I listened as a guide read these lines to a group of Martinican elementary schoolchildren. The guide then went on to explain that négritude is not only about Blacks, but about the affirmation of dignity for all peoples who face discrimination. The exhibit's catalogue was more explicit:

> The Negro is also the Jew, the foreigner, the Amerindian, the illiterate, the untouchable, he who is different, the neighbor; in brief, he who, by his very existence, is threatened, excluded, marginalized, forgotten, sacrificed.

I now sound out the great Césaire about the relatively recent community of Sephardic Jews, originally from North Africa, established in Martinique these past twenty years. At first, he claims complete ignorance about it; eventually, he recalls being invited to the inauguration of the synagogue. "But we haven't heard anything about them since."

I try to tease out Césaire's views about current events, particularly regarding Bin Laden and the popular linking of the World Trade Center to events in the Middle East. "It's very complicated," he demurs. But then Césaire takes us back to his classical training, and he is again in command.

"Jesus Christ—" he starts. "He was Palestinian, wasn't he?"

"Well, he was Jewish," I offer, trying to be accurate.

"What difference is there between a Palestinian and a Jew?" Aimé Césaire asks, in search of genuine clarification.

At first, I am taken aback. But recently my wife—who is Martinican by birth, Jewish by choice—had explained this conundrum to me. For the French (including Antilleans) schooled in the

Catholic tradition, "Palestine" evokes first and foremost the New Testament name for what Jews today call Israel. Two thousand years ago, Jews *were*—in French Catholic parlance—Palestinians. In the consciousness of many old-school French, *palestinien* refers not to a contemporary kind of Arab but rather to the precursor of today's Jew.

Césaire then treats me to an erudite and detailed overview of the successive conquests in the Middle East, the Jewish diaspora, European anti-Semitism. (Ever the linguist, at one point he recites, in the original Aramaic, Jesus' last words on the cross, "Eli, Eli lama sabachtani?") "And many of the French who left their homes for the islands," Aimé Césaire avers, "were undoubtedly of Jewish origin." After his assistant evokes the name of one such family—de Paz of Sainte Pierre, the island's erstwhile capital completely destroyed by the Mount Pelée capital in 1902—Césaire claims that the spelling of another plantation near his birthplace in Basse Pointe—Eyma—also points to a Jewish ancestry.

I ask if it is true that some of the original European colonists in Martinique—ancestors of the tiny but ever potent white Martinican minority of *békés*—were Jews.

"You can check yourself," he replies, "But I have always heard that, among the many Frenchmen who left their country for the islands, many of them were certainly of Jewish origin. They fled a certain anti-Semitism of the time."

"And what happened to them," I persist.

"Why, they became French; they became like everyone else. They melted in so much that there is no longer any distinction. The religion, in any case, was not maintained."

But I want to talk about today, about how Jews and Israelis are perceived by French West Indians now.

"We hear on the radio that Israelis are racist," Aimé Césaire says, carefully choosing his words, "as if they are fighting the Arabs out of racism. This confuses the matter. They are fighting the Arabs because they have the sentiment, whether right or wrong, that the new state they have constructed—the state called 'Jewish'—is threatened in its very existence.

"It is not that I am especially for the Israelis," says the man who wrote sympathetically for the Shoah Jew, "but it's necessary to put the matter justly. What motivates them is not racism but nationalism—it's not the same thing. . . . The roots are historic, not racial. . . . The Israelis have the impression that the state that was such a challenge to build—and it is young, after all—is itself at stake. Israel's essential motivation is its will to exist. It is anguished to see its future threatened. 'To be or not to be,'" recites the classicist, in one of his only lapses into English.

And what about Durban? I ask, evoking another link between the condition of the Jew and that of the Black. What about the United Nations meeting that both rejuvenated the "Zionism as racism" charge and demanded reparations for the descendants of the slaves?

"I am against reparations," the co-founder of négritude pronounces. "What was done to us, what we were made to suffer, is irreparable. *C'est tout*. It is a historical fact. Even Arabs were slavists." What are we going to do, send a bill to the Arab world at large as well?

"Reparations would be too simple… The [African] continent certainly merits being rehabilitated, but not in the name of a circumstantial event."

Memory, on the other hand, is an imperative.

"Europeans should not forget their grave extremism, the crimes that were committed. Europe must feel responsible and aid the victim. Europe protested when Hitler arose, without realizing that Hitlerism existed before Hitler, and that the germ had already been planted: Hitler did to Europe what Europe did to Africa."

And our post-9/11 world?

"It's a strange kind of epoch we are witnessing," declares Césaire. "It is not a 'clash of civilizations,'" to invoke Huntington, "but a clash between barbarians. . . .

"The world took such a long time to put forward certain values. It would be a tremendous retreat of civilization—the end of the world—[if the situation deteriorated.] Each of us must resist fear and anguish. We must strive to cultivate hope and the will to live."

Césaire is tired; it is time to take my leave. But before walking me to the door, the afro-existentialist has an unexpected afterthought: "To understand Israel, you have to study its history. You have to read the Bible, the Old Testament."

Before departing, I compliment Césaire on his vigor. He demurs, but relativizes his age. "I recently received word that my old friend Senghor just had his ninety-fourth birthday. So I guess I'm not doing too badly."

Two months and four days later, the world would mourn the passing of Césaire's comrade-in-négritude, Léopold Senghor of Senegal.

In Martinique, talk was still abuzz about Césaire's planting a courbaril on the plantation of one of the island's prominent *békés*—a family of "Jewish origin," according to a local Sephardic historian. "No one else could better widen the roots of [the plantation]," declared the host, Hayot. "In it I see the symbol of an essential value—solidarity," pronounced the guest, Césaire.

From "ear of Jew" to West Indian locust tree, Aimé Césaire continues to plumb roots—a sensitive nerve for peoples of diaspora—on his native island of Martinique.[2]

---

[2] Césaire would die six years later, in 2008, at the age of 94.

TWENTY-FOUR

The "White House" of Judaism: Under Renovation, New Hues May Apply[1]

A Review of Edith Bruder's and Tudor Parfitt's *Studies in Black Judaism* and Tudor Parfitt's *Black Jews in Africa and the Americas*

There is an ancient ivory manor, sturdy in structure but with some weather-beaten façades. It is occupied by several branches of a venerable family who get along fitfully but co-exist nevertheless. But now new folk are clamoring at the gates for entry. They claim that the property belongs to them, too. They also say that the walls are in need of repair, and they are prepared to undertake the renovations. Some of them are clutching newly printed deeds; others say they are previous occupants, about whom the current dwellers have either forgotten or pretend to have forgotten. The befuddled gatekeepers of the house need to decide whom of these claimants —if any—to admit.

Such is the parable of the "white house" of Judaism, whose fractious residents (ranging from Ultraorthodox to Secular Humanist residents) have overwhelmingly, if unconsciously, shared one epidermal trait: whether Ashkenazi, Sephardi or Mizrachi, they are on the pallid side of the pigmentation spectrum. Increasingly, however, tenancy rights to the ancestral Jewish abode are being claimed

[1]*African Studies Quarterly* 14:1 (Fall 2013). For another comparative review that includes *Black Jews in Africa and the Americas*, see Lyons (2013).

by new Jews of color. As for the gatekeepers who by convention choose who gets into the "house of Judaism": please read on.

Each of the books here under review constitutes an essential contribution to two complementary streams of scholarship that previously have been advanced with relatively little overlap: the one on established and emerging Jewish communities in sub-Saharan Africa, the other on Black American Jews, Hebrews, Israelites. Constituted from different types of building blocks—the 2012 book an edited collection of papers, the 2013 one a compilation from a lecture series—together the two books significantly advance and reinforce the budding literature on the growing importance of Judaism among various African peoples and within a small but noteworthy segment of the African-American diaspora. This synergy is not surprising, given the collaboration of both books' authors on *African Zion*, and the integration of their previous findings in *Black Jews in Africa and the Americas*. Cumulatively, Bruder's and Parfitt's scholarship is particularly important for African studies and religious studies, both of which appear slow to acknowledge African Judaism. Case in point: a supposedly comprehensive overview on "Religion in Africa in the Past Fifty Years" at the 2012 Roundtable at the Centre of African Studies conference at the University of Edinburgh made no mention whatsoever of any Jewish phenomenon on the continent. When I tried in the Q&A to elicit some such acknowledgment or discussion, the effort was met with as much enthusiasm as a plate of pork chops served up on Yom Kippur.

The major aim of *African Zion* is two-fold: to provide an historical (two-century) overview of the evolving representation, conceptualization, and reconfiguration of Black Jews in both Africa and the United States, and to explicate how a distinct Black Jewish identity has emerged out of Africans' and Europeans' understanding of Judaism and Jewishness in the African and African diaspora contexts. To do this, editors Bruder and Parfitt provide a three-part structure for the wide-ranging essays of their book. Part I, after Tudor Parfitt's presentation of the "(de)construction" of Black Jews (evolving perceptions of African Jewish identities from the peak of the African slave trade in about 1800 to the genetic testing of the Lemba in the mid-1990s), focuses on West Africa: three chapters on the Igbos of Nigeria who have adopted Judaism or have otherwise identified with the Jewish state of Israel, and one on an even newer community of African Jews in Ghana. Part II is the most wide-ranging section of the book. Here we read of Nahum Slouschez's early twentieth-century attempts to retrospectively create a trans-African Jewish proto-empire in antiquity, and equally creative (albeit more scholarly-based) arguments for an Israelite tradition of origin for the otherwise emphatically non-Hebraic (not to mention non-Zionist) cradle of the Hausa people of northern Nigeria and Niger Republic. (Given the virulently violent nature of the Hausa-dominated Boko Haram movement, in league with Al-Qaeda and currently wreaking havoc in Nigeria, the putative Israelite Hausa myth of origin is bitterly ironic if not outright provocative.) This middle section of *African Zion* also contains chapters on Judaic scriptural, liturgical and cultural practices among the Beta Israel of Ethiopia and the Lemba of Zimbabwe and South Africa. The final section of *African Zion* presents the most challenges for actual Africanists, at least as narrowly defined. Here we shift hybridic gears to delve into the otherwise fascinating communities of Jewish-, Israelite-, and Hebrew-identifying descendants of African slaves (each with its own nuances) from New York City to Dimona in the Negev Desert (with a welcome stopover in the Caribbean, courtesy of Marla Brettschneider, for post-colonial and diaspora studies novelist Jamaica Kincaid.) The concluding chapter focuses on "black" Jews who have no genealogic connection to Africa at all: Dalits ("untouchables") in Andhra Pradesh, India.

If, by the very nature of an edited collection, the constituent parts of *African Zion* vary by tone, length, and quality, *Black Jews in Africa and the Americas* is uniformly exemplary in its evenness of form and excellence in substance. Originally conceived as a series of presentations at Harvard University (the 2011 Nathan I. Huggins Lectures), the book recapitulates Tudor Parfitt's more than two decades of investigations, from the 1984 exodus of the

"Falashas" via Sudan to genetic testing of the Lembas in the mid-1990s, into Jews in sub-Saharan Africa and the African diaspora in the U.S. and West Indies. (Parfitt is Emeritus Professor of Modern Jewish Studies at the University of London School of Oriental and African Studies [SOAS]. Edith Bruder, who under Prof. Parfitt's supervision wrote her dissertation [later published as *Black Jews of Africa*] is Research Associate at SOAS.) Parfitt's deep historical and theological knowledge affords a contextualized understanding of the sensitive topic of race in Judaism, beginning with post-Biblical interpretations (Christian as well as Jewish) of the story of Ham, the son of Noah who was (somewhat inexplicably) punished by having his descendants (later identified as African) "cursed" with black skin. By the nineteenth century, proto-anthropology had transformed this myth into the pseudo-scientific Hamitic hypothesis, according to which the more "evolved" of African tribes were of Hebrew/Israelite origin. From there, it was a short theo-historical hop to discovering Lost Tribes of Israel in the most unexpected corners of Saharan, Sahelian and Sudanic Africa. Parfitt's eminently readable exposition is as much about the internalization by (some) Africans of this belief in Jewish origins as it is about the projection of the construct by (mostly) European missionaries and early ethnologists. In the context of descendants of Black Africans in the New World, appropriation of Chosen People and Zionistic paradigms vied with Hamitic internalizations to give rise to self-identifying Black Jewish, Israelite, and Hebrew communities and synagogues in America. What remains inexplicable is why the common nineteenth-century "knowledge" (or expectation) of ancient Israelite descendants across the African continent should have been lost, subject to recovery today as a "new" and "surprising" phenomenon. Parfitt gamely moves in his book from colonial Africa to contemporary Ghana, Nigeria and Zimbabwe where (some) Sefwi, Igbo and Lemba emphatically claim Jewish ancestry. Why are these communities so energetic today? Given what Parfitt has documented about real and imagined African Israelites from time immemorial, why do students of Africa, Jewish and not, learn of them today with *de novo* surprise?

We are living in an era in which the color of Catholicism has been turning steadily darker: in Europe, for example, priests are increasingly being recruited from Africa, Asia and Latin America. Evangelical Protestantism is also expanding mightily in these regions. Is the darkening complexion of Western Christianity a precursor to the future of Judaism? The two books under review do not raise the question directly, but do provide incontrovertible elements to engage it. At the very least, the growing phenomena of Black African Jews and Jews of African descent ought to be considered through comparative religious studies lens as NRMs (New Religious Movements).

To return to the parable of the "house of Judaism": traditionally, the gatekeepers – the deciders of admission to Jewry and Judaism —have been the rabbis. Yet of all the diverse perspectives honored through publication in these otherwise inclusive treatments of Jewish identity, it is the *rabbinic* voice which is most conspicuous through its absence. It is as if the authors and editors posed the question "Is Judaism too important to leave to rabbis?" and provocatively (if not problematically) answered in the affirmative.

Not that there will ever be inter-denominational rabbinic consensus on the contentious question "Who is a Jew?" One conundrum that these books brings to mind is that it is neither necessary nor sufficient to practice Judaism in order for the Chief Rabbinate of Israel – the single most influential rabbinic authority that does exist – to consider somebody as Jewish. A vociferously anti-rabbinic overt atheist from America is still considered a Jew if her mother was Jewish; a Judaism-devout African who regularly prays, in Hebrew, in a minyan (Jewish prayer quorum) would not be considered a Jew by that same Rabbinate, absent maternal lineage or formal conversion. For sure, different rabbis of different denominations will apply different standards and come to different conclusions. Still, the unmediated voice of Judaism's longstanding "gatekeepers" is relevant, even if disagreement among them about "Black Jews" and "Black Judaism" is inevitable. May future treatments of these emerging African and African diasporic communities provide room for rabbinic voices as well.

TWENTY-FIVE

Ethiopian in the Negev: A Minor Rescue Story

You see them everywhere in Israel, in all walks of life: The aged, bearded white robed ones, tentatively meandering in sandals as if they had just been plunked down from the bush of a different century into the frenetic bus station walkway of a twenty-first-century postindustrial city. The burly, no-nonsense guy in plainclothes with walkie-talkie and sidearm at the Western Wall, scanning the crowd at the holy site for potentially dangerous infiltrators. The petite female in army uniform shlepping a rifle almost her size, chewing bubble gum and checking her text messages. Teenagers who pump gas at the station and query you in rapid fire Hebrew with words of Biblical vintage—*mezuman*, *ashrai*—that you have to deconstruct before they will fill your tank: "cash or credit?" They are all Jewish, and they all hail from Ethiopia.

In and of itself, having lived in West Africa and being Jewish provides little rapport with these ubiquitous reminders of Israel's Black African heritage. For one, most blokes from the Horn of Africa have little in common with those from the Gulf of Guinea or the Sahel or Sahara. For another, these dark-skinned Zionists are true-blue Israelis, not diaspora Jews who -whether they periodically drop in for ethno- religious love fests or never care to visit Zion—relate to the Jewish State as outsiders. And so, like many visitors to Israel, I would observe the Ethiopian Jews with a mixture of curiosity and warm-heartedness, wishing to bond with them but not having a basis to connect with any particular one of them.

Until, like an idiot, I let my wallet fall out of my pocket on a city bus leading up to the Carmel heights in Haifa.

It had already been a difficult sabbatical in the land where the Sabbatical idea first emerged, as a religious commandment. For one thing, my sabbatical coincided with the 2008-9 war with Gaza and now literally hit the university campus where I was affiliated.[1] For another, the married Israeli friends who had at first warmly urged that I take my sabbatical at that very university near their home were separating and now didn't even want to see me. Compared with such crises, international and personal, the loss of a wallet may not sound like such big a deal. But maybe on account of those other crises, losing the wallet just pushed me over the edge. They were, in any event, the reason that I had barely slept the previous night, before taking the train from the university station in the Negev desert in southern Israel to Tel Aviv and then an unplanned regional bus (because the train tracks were closed) further north to Haifa.

It wasn't just the loss of my emergency dollars and credit cards whose replacement is such a hassle, especially when one is overseas, that made me so miserable. It was the tiny but serviceable address book tucked within one of the wallet side pockets, the only comprehensive listing of numbers and addresses that I had since receiving it as a part of a wallet gift decades before. The address book was my only connection to old friends inhabiting the remaining non-Facebook crooks of the planet. It also was my only comprehensive record—in case I should ever wish to review it—of former and deceased friends.

Before leaving Haifa I, of course, made multiple inquiries with the city's bus services. I now had the phone numbers of the bus's local dispatch office and more than one for the lost and found department. I was becoming quite proficient in describing, in detail, the wallet's appearance and contents in Hebrew. But all those avenues were a dead end.

---

[1]I recount that experience in "An Unquiet Sabbatical," *The Chronicle of Higher Education* (January 23, 2009), p. B 24.

Back in Beer Sheva, the wilderness to which in Genesis Abraham banished his slave woman Hagar and their son Ishmael and later, according to the Book of Judges, constituted the southern extremity of ancient Israel ("from Dan unto Beersheva"), I now wandered aimlessly in the quiet, dusty, northeastern neighborhood of an otherwise busy city with a university named after modern Israel's first prime minister. I chanced upon the Ethiopian Cultural Center (closed, despite the posted opening hours) and wandered some more, until I came across a clutch of northeast African-looking people congregating in a makeshift plaza outside a high-rise apartment building. This, it turned out, was the Jewish Agency's Haruv Absorption Center for Ethiopian immigrants, a one-stop immigration complex including over 150 residential units. A perfect opportunity to take my mind off my lost wallet—or so I thought.

After taking in the market-like atmosphere outdoors, I wandered into the building's lobby, sat down to enjoy the boisterous atmosphere in the otherwise austere architecture, and was soon approached by a man in his mid-twenties. He wore a uniform, spoke in Israeli-inflected Hebrew (unlike what I was hearing around me), but shared the brown complexion and facial features of the building's residents. His name was Asher Aissa, and he was the security guard.

After checking into my identity and politely refusing my request to take pictures, Asher was happy to chat. He had come to Israel as a young boy, and was much more integrated into Israeli society than most of the residents and clients at the Absorption Center. We talked evenly about America and world politics, about Bill Clinton and Ethiopia, and eventually about my travels in Africa and Israel. In passing, I mentioned my recent trip to Haifa and let slip my discomfiture over the lost wallet.

For reasons I have never quite fathomed, this touched a chord in my new Israeli chum from the Horn. Asher straightened up, his face taken over with an expression of immediate concern unmatched by that of any other Israelis to whom I had explained my problem. He then sprung into action with a sense of near-frenetic urgency.

He asked for the Haifa city bus telephone numbers I had been calling (often with no reply), and proceeded to call them on his own. Asher knew the system, how it worked, and how it didn't. He figured out that there was yet another level and location within the municipal transportation's lost and found bureaucracy that no one had informed me about, and he extricated yet another telephone number. And with that, bingo, he got through to the industrial zone bus office in Haifa whose supervisor confirmed with me that, among the thousands of lost objects they were storing, my wallet was indeed among them.

What the supervisor went on to tell me confirmed what others had said: If lost on the bus, there was a good chance the wallet would be turned in, but little chance that any cash in it would remain.[2] No matter: the address book, secreted beside the tiny folded, now absent, hundred dollar bill, was still there. When I next spoke to Asher, while riding the train back down to Beersheva from Haifa, wallet and address book in hand, I only had joy and gratitude to report.

Of course, compared with the incoming rockets from Gaza and the explosion of my friends' marriage, the loss and recovery of my billfold *sans* bills was small latkes indeed. But Asher Aissa had not only rescued my wallet. My encounter with this Jewish guardian angel from Ethiopia helped rescue what had otherwise been turning into a rather unpeaceful sabbatical in the Land of Israel.

---

[2]This was a far cry from what I was told as a fifteen-year-old in Israel in 1971, when I left a wallet in an Israeli taxi: "If the taxi driver is Jewish, you'll get it back . . ."

TWENTY-SIX

Tropical Seders[1]

If there were a Guinness Book of Jewish World Records, there might be an entry for "Seders Celebrated in the Most Random Set of Countries." If so, I like to think that I'd be a prime contender.

Vanuatu is perhaps most well known in America for having hosted a slew of episodes for America's reality television show *Survivor*. But when we observed Passover there in 1991, it was one of the most obscure locations on earth. Indeed, in 1991 the then-ten-year-old-country—previously known as the New Hebrides—didn't even *have* television. Perhaps the only Jewish connection was that the musical maven duo of Oscar Hammerstein and Richard Rodgers had immortalized one of the Vanuatu islands in their Broadway hit *South Pacific*. Yet three decades later it was in Vanuatu that I too had a debut of sorts, conducting my very own Seder for the first time as a head of family—in French.

Vanuatu is an archipelago of over eighty islands, a dozen of them inhabited, strung out over five hundred miles in Melanesia. It is because most of the islanders are very dark-skinned that Western anthropologists called them Melanesian (Greek root *melas* to connote "black peoples") in the first place. For all the superficial similarities with Africans, however, the origins of the Melanesians are believed to lie in southeastern Asia, not Africa.

During the colonial era the New Hebrides was governed as an Anglo-French "condominium." For nearly one century France and Britain competed for the hearts, minds, and tongues of the is-

[1]This is an expanded version of an essay originally published in *CJ: Voices of Conservative/Masorti Judaism* (Spring 2008).

landers. After independence, the country was still riven between nominally English- and French-speaking citizens. In reality, the cleavage broke down between Protestant churchgoers and Catholic ones. Being a rare Jew made it easier to navigate Vanuatu's tricky theo-political shoals for my social science research.

France still retained a particularly strong presence in this Oceanic nation, especially in the realm of education. Indeed, the premier institution of education was the Lycée Français of Port Vila (the capital), which was staffed, managed, and funded by France's ministries of education and foreign affairs. As *mazel* (luck) would have it, the principal of the lycée at the time was a bearded, distinguished-looking Frenchman of North African descent, a Sephardic Jew named Simon Alezrah.

Simon had not participated in many Seders during his years as teacher and principal in France's far-flung overseas colonies and ex-colonies. Ours was his first, and probably only, Seder celebrated in Vanuatu. But Monsieur Alezrah also knew some fellow tribesmen (Sephardic, not Melanesian) who had relocated from the nearby French territory of New Caledonia to expand their jewelry trade. My forward-thinking wife had packed a French language Haggadah (Seder prayer and guide book) when we had taken off from Boston in January on my six-month grant with our then three-year-old daughter and one-year-old son in tow.

"And what about the matzah?" you may ask. The nearest fully-equipped Jewish community was one thousand trans-Pacific Ocean miles away, in Australia. But thanks to the ultra-Orthodox outreach of Chabad in Sydney and some additional *mazal*, for the first time my family and guests observed the mitzvah of consuming unleavened bread in the form of *shmura*, the hand-baked variety preferred by the ultra-Orthodox.

For sure, the boxes, having arrived by freighter, were beaten up. Virtually all of these round, hard, large shmura wafers had broken en route. Yet three had miraculously survived intact, sufficient to perform the *yachatz* ritual: at the Seder, I could break the middle matzah into two, designating the larger piece as *afikoman*, the driest dessert (sic) known to the human palate.

Tasty this matzah was not—but nor was it supposed to be. Matzah shmura is supposed to afflict the palate as it reminds the soul of the tough cuisine our ancestors fleeing Egypt had to endure. It is dry, crusty, jaw-challenging. It does goes well, however, with *poisson poulet*, a tender, local ocean catch with fins and scales that translates as "chicken fish." (Few of Vanuatu's other indigenous delicacies—flying fox, coconut crab, pork-stuffed lap-lap—would have passed kosher muster for the traditional Festive Meal.)

Chewing shmura on that hot and humid tropical Passover night in Vanuatu represented yet another miracle of sorts. For on account of a dock strike in Australia that held the matzah itself in bondage it wasn't until practically Erev Pesach (Passover eve) itself that the flat Brooklyn-baked, bread actually arrived in Port Vila. Moses may have had to shlep his matzah across the Red Sea, but at least he had it in tow. Ours had to be shipped clear cross the Coral Sea, with no delivery date in sight.

Mauritius is another French and English (and Creole) speaking island-nation where matzah is not found on the grocery shelves in springtime. Settled by the Dutch, colonized by the French, and then conquered by the British, this Indian Ocean republic is home to descendants of slaves from Africa and indentured servants from India. Most of the population is Hindu; Islam is the second most widely observed faith. But during World War II some of the most poignant Seders in the modern history of the "free" world were celebrated en masse here. Fifteen hundred Jews, fleeing the Pharaoh of twentieth century Europe, made it across the "Red Sea" of the Mediterranean in two rickety boats to the shores of the Holy Land—only to be arrested by British for attempted "illegal" entry into Palestine. They were deported to a detention camp on Mauritius. Thanks to the nearest Jewish community—two thousand miles across the Indian Ocean, in South Africa—they at least could rue their lack of freedom while eating the bread of affliction.

Today, one of the most popular attractions on this Rhode Island-sized island is a crocodile farm. It is owned and operated by the same man who conceived and built it—a nice Jewish *boychik* from Australia.

Owen enjoys Oceanic *yichus* (venerable family status): a not-too-distant poor immigrant ancestor had been deported from England to Britain's "down under" penal colony for some petty larceny. Within days of our arrival in 1996 to begin another grant-sponsored year abroad, Owen had somehow heard of our joining the other million people crowded on the island. He phoned us from his croc farm. By the time Passover rolled around in "winter" (remember, seasons are reversed below the equator; but temperatures in April can still rise to almost 80°), we were such friends that he asked if he could sponsor that year's Seder for all the island's Jews in our more centrally located home. (We were renting a house at the base of a volcanic crater in the quaintly-named town of Curepipe, the rainiest, most humid spot on the island.)

That Passover, we hosted about forty fellow tribesmen and friends of tribesmen. The latter included B. Suppaya Curpen, Israel's honorary consul to Mauritius, president of the Mauritian-Israeli Friendship League, and publisher of the *Mauritius Shalom Magazine*. (Mr. Curpen himself is a non-Jewish Mauritian, one of dozens of Christians and Hindus who have been to Israel on educational and training programs.) We all assembled around a single layout of adjoining tables united by white paper tablecloths.

Thanks to Owen's Australian connections, we were amply endowed with matzah and other requisite accoutrements. Owen's far-flung connections even netted us a visiting rabbi from America to lead us through the Haggadah. (He had brought along some Anglophone Seder guides; we still had the Francophone version from our Vanuatu days. As at all of our tropical Seders, celebrants shared photocopies of key passages.) But the most wondrous element of that year's Passover in the tropics were the giant frozen turkey and matzah balls that my mother cooked, froze, and flew half-way across the globe to deliver in person, even as she herself returned to New York before the Seder to spend the holiday with more homebound *mishpocha* (family). On this single point all the island's Jews were in agreement: my Mom's were the best matzah balls in all Mauritius.

In the category of "most humbling" tropical Passover experiences, my hands-down winner goes to Cochin, India. In 1987 my wife, six-month-old daughter, and I were guided clear cross the Indian subcontinent's southern plain by Abe Aboody. Abe was a Bombay Jewish book printer whom we had befriended at our year-long home in Pondicherry, on the southeast coast of India.

Abe's dark, bushy mustache contrasted with his slender, light-skinned physique and short frame. A bachelor with no family locally, he was rather lonely. Perhaps it was the distance from home, Pondicherry being a good 700 miles from Bombay. Maybe it was his sarcastic if quick and witty humor: think Woody Allen gone tandoori. In any case, Abe so needled and teased his few friends that one evening he had a blow-up with one of them, complete with yelling and shoving, in our gleaming apartment.

It happened one Erev Shabbat (Friday night). The friend was a disciple of several years standing at the Sri Aurobindo ashram, a spiritual retreat in Pondy. He was tall and lanky and always wore shorts, as befit the ascetic lifestyle of the ashram. His name was Bob Lender and he had started out as a middle-class American Jew. The four of us—Bob, Abe, my wife Loïza and I—almost certainly constituted the entire Jewish population of Pondicherry. And half of that population was fighting each other. Come Passover, there was no question of bringing Bob with us as Abe led Loïza, our then six-month-old daughter Arielle and me westward across the Subcontinent to Jew Town in Cochin.

Abe didn't actually *know* the venerable Koder family of Cochin but he was sure that they would welcome us for the Feast of Nisan. By the 1980s the three Jewish communities of Israel—Bombay, Cochini, and Bene Israel—were no longer isolated from one another, as they had been for centuries.[2] Nor was the traditional segregation between the "black" and "white" Jews in caste-conscious India still observed. For sure, residual intra-Jewish racism had not entirely disappeared. But, as I realized during a Passover service in Cochin's last functioning but still exquisite synagogue, I was one of its bearers.

The synagogue's address, appropriately enough, was Jew Town Road. Even the road sign was in a tasteful blend of blue and white stripes. Festooned with now electrified hanging chandeliers, the sixteenth century Pardeshi Synagogue was decorated with blue Chinese hand painted floor tiles. It was not large but boasted ancient copper plates, dating back at least five centuries before the synagogue's own construction, that chronicled the perquisites and powers accorded by a Malabar ruler to the person and descendants of the nascent Jewish community's leader, Joseph Rabban.

I was called up for an aliya, the honor of blessing the Torah. Unlike Abe Aboody and the Koder clan, the Torah reader was a "black Jew." "How quaint!" I at first thought to myself. As this "Funny, you don't look Jewish" character chanted directly from the Torah, I started to "assist" him, vocalizing the portion a nanosecond behind him, thanks to the Chumash I had brought up to the *bimah* (altar). (The Chumash is a book version of the Five Books of Moses that, unlike the actual scroll, has vowels for phonetic pronunciation.) With an exacerbated expression and impatient raise of the hand, the Torah reader quite appropriately shut me up. He knew Torah much better than I, and I should have known better than to distract him with my uncertain Ashkenazic tonalities. In terms of judging who is a "real Jew," he put me in my place.

Towards the end of the service, the tables were turned once

---

[2]For a scholarly perspective written by an Indian Jew, see Israel (1984). Another work published in India about the World War II experience of Jewish refugees there is Bhatti and Voigt (1999). The celebrated novel of Jewish exile in India as a result of the Holocaust is Desai (1999). For treatment of a new (1990s) Jewish community of Indian "untouchables" (like this book, within the context of Africa and African diaspora), see Egorova (2012).

again. Usually the ethnographer who records the strange and exotic, I was just as incensed as my fellow congregationalists when a group of European tourists, intrigued by us "exotic" looking prayer shawl enwrapped Jews in an Indian synagogue, started to snap pictures as we davened (prayed). I joined in the jeering of them away, even while internally confessing that I am usually at the other end of the camera.

At the Koder family Seder I was again humbled. For it was there that I met P.D. Yehudi, a thick-bearded, Orthodox man of dark Sephardic complexion and the intense eyes of the Hasid. Only he was not Sephardic; nor was Yehudi his original name. Prem Doss of Trivandrum, Kerala, was born and raised a Hindu, converting to Judaism only recently, as an adult. He brought to his Judaism

Prem Doss Yehudi and Koder patriarch at Cochin, India, Seder

an intensity, discipline, and spirituality that I humbly realized I was incapable of bringing to mine. Was it because growing up infused with Hinduism provides a head start on transcendence and the Eternal? All I know is that this Hindu *ger* (convert to Judaism) exuded a Jewish aura that greatly surpassed my Long Island-inflected Jewishness.

Martinique, April 2002. For once, there is no kosher-for-Passover supply challenge during a sabbatical year abroad. This Caribbean island has a very tight knit and well-organized Jewish community, comprised mostly of French citizens hailing from North Africa. Although eight thousand miles away, France is not only still the "mother country" but, with respect to Jewish matters, the provider of all your food needs. I can't help bursting with laughter when a visiting grandmother asks, in all seriousness and with great concern, how we Jews manage in America if we can't import matzah from Marseilles.

Rabbi Yehuda Erharar, the Jewish community's volatile spiritual leader, was born in Morocco and grew up speaking Hebrew mixed with Arabic at home and French in the street. When his family felt compelled to leave North Africa, he insisted that they move to France. When his parents then decided to make aliya to Israel, he insisted on coming to America. That's how he came to attend Yeshiva High School in New York City.

But it was in Haifa that he finished up his secondary education. After six years in Israel and army service there, he moved to Ireland for his first job, working on a butcher crew. That experience landed him the job of ritual slaughterer for the Jewish community in São Paolo, Brazil. Rav Erharar also served in Panama, as assistant to the chief rabbi there. In the meantime, he was twice ordained: once in Israel, once in Philadelphia.

So it is at this rabbi's home in the French Antilles that we attend the most multilingual of all our Seders in the tropics. (Somewhere along the line, *le rabbin* also picked up Ladino.) We eat outdoors on the veranda, the white draped table laden with colorful vegetables prepared Sephardi-style: bright orange diced carrots with raisins, spicy red onions, pickled white cauliflower, crunchy green cucumber. Rabbi Erharar insists that we take our holy day Passover lunches with him, too. Away from his family while at his Martinican pulpit, it is quite a challenge for him to prepare the Pesach dinner for dozens of guests by himself, aided only by Creole helper whom he overwhelms and mystifies with the arcana of Passover kashrut and Seder protocol.

It is at the Martinican Seder that I first learn of the medical specialty known as "victimology." Bernard Feldman, a visiting Franco-Israeli who once lived in Martinique and married a West Indian woman who herself became Jewish, specializes in the treatment of victims of terrorist-inflicted trauma.

Only at one of the Seders that I have attended overseas did I feel uncomfortable. It was the Feast of Unleavened bread of 1994. There was no dearth of matzah. Everyone had his own Haggadah. But, with hundreds of bare headed Jews at the tables surrounding me, for the first time in my life I felt out of place for wearing a yarmulke at a Seder. Such is the paradox of Jewish life on a secular kibbutz in Israel.

"Foul!" will cry would-be arbiters of my fanciful Guinness Book of Jewish World Records. "You can't count Israel among your 'random' countries for Seder attendance. Israel is the very nexus of the Jewish world!"

Point conceded. But it is only in contrast with the taken-for-granted Seder settings—in Israel as well as in America—that one truly appreciates the tropical alternatives.

References

Abitbol, Michel. 2001. "Juifs et Noirs de part et d'autre du Sahara" [Blacks and Jews from one end of the Sahara to the other]. *Les cahiers du judaïsme* 10, pp. 72-78.

Abu El-Haj, Nadia. 2011. "Jews – Lost and Found. Genetic History and the Evidentiary Terrain of Recognition." In Marianne Hirsch and Nancy K. Miller, eds., *Rites of Return. Diaspora poetics and the politics of memory*. New York: Columbia University Press.

Africa Confidential. 2009. "Israel/Africa. A business and strategic foray." 50:9, pp. 3-4.

Afsai, Shai. 2013. "Hanging Haman with the Igbo Jews of Abuja." *The Times of Israel*, April 30.

Alaezi, O. 1999. *Ibos: Hebrew Exiles from Israel. Amazing Facts and Revelations*. Aba: Onzy Publications.

Arthur, Kwame Boafo, and E. Gyimah-Boadi. 2006. "Africa's Evolving Relations with Israel." In *Israel and Africa. Assessing the Past, Envisioning the Future*. American Jewish Committee and Tel Aviv University.

Ba, Idrissa. 2006a. "La problématique de la présence juive au Sahara et au Soudan d'après Jean Léon l'Africain" [Problems relating to the Jewish presence in the Sahara and in the Sudan According to Jean Leon the African]. *Outre-Mers* 94:350-351, pp. 249-266.

______. 2006b. Présence Juive au Sahara et au Soudan au Moyen-Age: Perceptions et réalités [Jewish presence in the Sahara and in the Sudan in the Middle Ages: Perceptions and realities]. Ph.D. dissertation, Université de Paris I-Panthéon Sorbonne.

______. 2008. "Continuité ou discontinuité de la présence juive à Walâta et dans le Sahel ouest-africain du xve au xixe siècle"

[Continuity and discontinuity of the Jewish presence in Walata and in the West African Sahel from the 15th to 19th century]. *Outre-Mers* 96:358-359, pp. 147-185.

Basden, G. T. 1921. *Among the Ibos of Nigeria. An account of the Curious & Interesting Habits, Customs & Beliefs of a little known African People by one who has for many years lived amongst them on close & intimate terms*. London: Frank Cass.

______. 1938. *Niger Ibos. A Description of the Primitive Life, Customs and Animistic Beliefs, &., of the Ibo People of Nigeria By One Who, For Thirty-Five Years, Enjoyed the Privilege of Their Intimate Confidence and Friendship*. London: Frank Cass.

Beker, Avi. 2006. "*Tikkun Olam* in Africa." In *Israel and Africa. Assessing the Past, Envisioning the Future*. American Jewish Committee and Tel Aviv University.

Bhatti, Anil, and Johannes H. Voigt, eds. 1999. *Jewish Exile in India. 1933-1945*. New Delhi: Manohar.

Boas, Franz. 1923. "Are the Jews a Race?" *World Tomorrow* 6, pp. 5-6.

Bruder, Edith. 2008. *The Black Jews of Africa. History, Religion, Identity*. Oxford: Oxford University Press.

______. 2012. "The Proto-History of Igbo Jewish Identity from the Colonial Period to the Biafra War, 1890-1970." In Edith Bruder and Tudor Parfitt, eds., *African Zion: Studies in Black Judaism*. Newcastle upon Tyne: Cambridge Scholars Publishing.

______, and Tudor Parfitt, eds. 2012. *African Zion: Studies in Black Judaism*. Newcastle upon Tyne: Cambridge Scholars Publishing.

Buber, Martin. 1923/1970. *I and Thou*. Scribner: New York.

Burgogne, Michael Hamilton. 1987. *Mamluke Jerusalem. An Architectural Study*. Jerusalem: British School of Archaeology.

Césaire, Aimé. 1947/1971 (translation by Emilie Snyder 1971). *Cahier d'un Retour au Pays Natal* [Return to My Native Land]. Paris: Presence Africaine.

Chazan, Naomi. 2006. "Israel and Africa: Challenges for a New Era." In *Israel and Africa. Assessing the Past, Envisioning the*

Future. American Jewish Committee and Tel Aviv University.

Coly, Jean Michel. 2009. "Don de Moutons aux Nécessiteux. 99 moutons pour 99 pauvres" [Gift of Sheep to the Needy. Ninety-nine sheep for ninety-nine poor people]. *Walf Grand Place* [Dakar] 1193.

Decalo, Samuel. 1998. *Israel and Africa. Forty Years, 1956-1996.* Gainesville: Florida Atlantic Press.

Dent, David. 1992. "Mideast Militant. Black Palestinians." *Emerge* (March), p. 10.

Desai, Anita. 1989. *Baumgartner's Bombay*. New York: Random House.

Divon, Haim. 2006. "MASHAV in Africa: the Israeli Government's Development Cooperation Program." In *Israel and Africa. Assessing the Past, Envisioning the Future*. American Jewish Committee and Tel Aviv University.

Dorès, Maurice. 1992. *La Beauté de Cham. Mondes juifs, mondes noirs* [The Beauty of Ham. Jewish worlds, Black worlds]. Paris: Editions Balland.

______. 2003. Black-Israël (documentary film). Paris: Les Films Esdés (producer) and New York : Filmmakers Library (distributor).

______. 2008. "Identités juives et racines africaines" [Jewish identities and African roots]. In Shmuel Trigano, ed., *Juifs et Noirs. Du mythe à la réalité* [Jews and Blacks: From myth to reality]. *Pardès* 44, pp. 19-26.

Duffield, Mark. 1983. "Change among West African Settlers in Northern Sudan." *Review of African Political Economy* 26, pp. 45-59.

Egorova, Yulia. 2012. "Jewish Identity Among the Bene Ephraim of India." In Edith Bruder and Tudor Parfitt, eds., *African Zion: Studies in Black Judaism*. Newcastle upon Tyne: Cambridge Scholars Publishing.

Eilberg-Schwartz, Howard. 1990. *The Savage in Judaism. An Anthropology of Israelite Religion and Ancient Judaism*. Bloomington: Indiana University Press.

Equiano, Olaudah. 1789/1995. *The Interesting Narrative of the Life of Olaudah Equiano. Written by Himself.* Edited by Robert Allison. New York: St. Martin's Press.

Frank, Gelya. 1997. "Jews, Multiculturalism, and Boasian Anthropology." *American Anthropologist* 99, pp. 731-745.

______. 2001. "Melville J. Herskovits on the African and Jewish Diasporas: Race, Culture and Modern Anthropology." *Identities* 8, pp. 173-206.

Frank, Lawrence P. 1988. "Israel and Africa: the Era of Tachlis." *The Journal of Modern African Studies* 26, pp. 151-155.

Fried, Eli. 2006. "Soft Power and Israel's Policy of Development Cooperation." In *Israel and Africa. Assessing the Past, Envisioning the Future*. American Jewish Committee and Tel Aviv University.

Goldstein, David B. 2008. *Jacob's Legacy. A Genetic View of Jewish History*. New Haven: Yale University Press.

Greenberg, Joel. 2012. "In Israel, African Migrants Face Backlash." *The Washington Post*, June 23.

Habtu, Haile. 1984. "The Fallacy of the 'Triple Heritage' Thesis [of Ali Mazrui]: A Critique." *Issue. A Journal of Opinion* 13, pp. 26-29.

Haïdara, Ismaël Diadié. 1999. *Les Juifs à Tombouctou. Recueil des sources écrites relatives au commerce juif à Tombouctou au XIXe siècle* [The Jews of Timbuktu. A Collection of written sources relating to Jewish trade in 19th century Timbuktu]. Bamako: Editions Donniya.

Harnischfeger, Johannes. 2012. "Igbo Nationalism and Jewish Identities." In Edith Bruder and Tudor Parfitt, eds., *African Zion: Studies in Black Judaism*. Newcastle upon Tyne: Cambridge Scholars Publishing.

Herskovits, Melville J. 1916. "When Is a Jew a Jew?" *Modern Quarterly* 4, pp. 109-117.

______. 1949. "Who are the Jews?" In Louis Finklestein, ed., *The Jews. Their History, Culture, and Religion*, Volume II. New York: Harper & Brothers Publishers.

Herzl, Theodor. 1960 [1902]. *Old-New Land*. New York: Bloch Publishing Company and Herzl Press.

Hull, Richard. 2009. *Jews and Judaism in African History*. Princeton: Markus Wiener Publishers.

Hunwick, John. 2006. *Jews of a Saharan Oasis. Elimination of the Tamantit Community*. Princeton: Markus Wiener Publishers.

Israel, Benjamin J. 1984. *The Bene Israel of India. Some Studies*. Bashir Bagh, Hyderabad: Orient Longman.

Jeffreys, M.D.W. 1953. "The Jewish Origin of the Fulani?" *Bulletin de l'Institut Français d'Afrique Noire* 15, pp. 1715-1717.

Kershner, Isabel. 2012a. "Crackdown on African Immigrants Tugs at Israel's Soul." *The New York Times*, June 18.

______. 2012b. "Israeli Leader Pledges Hard Line on Migrants." *The New York Times*, June 5.

Kirsch, Stuart. 1997. "Lost Tribes: Indigenous People and the Social Imaginary." *Anthropological Quarterly* 70, pp. 58-67.

Lange, Dierk. 2012. "The Bayajidda Legend and Hausa History." In Edith Bruder and Tudor Parfitt, eds., *African Zion: Studies in Black Judaism*. Newcastle upon Tyne: Cambridge Scholars Publishing.

Lapierre, Nicole. 2011. *Causes Communes*. Paris: Editions Stock.

Lee, Richard Borshay. 1969. "Eating Christmas in the Kalahari." In Richard B. Lee, ed., *The Dobe!Kung*. New York: Holt, Rinehart and Winston.

Levi, Janice R. 2012. "The House of Israel: Judaism in Ghana." In Edith Bruder and Tudor Parfitt, eds., *African Zion: Studies in Black Judaism*. Newcastle upon Tyne: Cambridge Scholars Publishing.

Levtzion, Nehemia. 1990. *Teaching Jewish Civilization. A Global Approach to Higher Education*. New York: New York University Press.

Lis, Daniel. 2009. "'Ethiopia Shall Soon Stretch Out Her Hands': Ethiopian Jewry and Igbo Identity." *Jewish Culture and History* 11:3, pp. 21-38.

______. 2012. "Israeli Foreign Policy towards the Igbo." In Edith Bruder and Tudor Parfitt, eds., *African Zion: Studies in Black Judaism*. Newcastle upon Tyne: Cambridge Scholars Publishing.

LoBagola. 1930. *An African Savage's Own Story. A Black Jew, descended from the Lost Tribes of Israel, a Savage who came out of the African Bush into Modern Civilization and thenceforth found himself an alien among his own people and a stranger in the Twentieth Century World*. London: Alfred K. Knopf.

London, Charles. 2009. *Far from Zion. In Search of Global Jewish Community*. New York: William Morrow.

Lyons, Len. 2013. "In and Out of Africa." *Jewish Review of Books*, Summer.

Mark, Peter, and José da Silva Horta. 2011. *The Forgotten Diaspora. Jewish Communities in West Africa and the Making of the Atlantic World*. Cambridge: Cambridge University Press.

Mauny, Raymond. 1949. "Le Judaïsme, les Juifs et l'Afrique occidentale" [Judaism, Jews and West Africa]. *Bulletin de l'Institut français d'Afrique noire* B11, pp. 354-378.

Mazrui, Ali A. 1984. "The Semitic Impact on Black Africa: Arab and Jewish Cultural Influences." *Issue. A Journal of Opinion* 13, pp. 3-8.

______. 2008. *Euro-Jews and Afro-Arabs. The Great Semitic Divergence in World History*. Lanham, MD: University Press of America.

Miles, William F. S. 1997. "Negritude and Judaism." *The Western Journal of Black Studies* 27:2, pp. 99-105.

______. 2000. "Hamites and Hebrews: problems in 'Judaizing' the Rwandan Genocide." *Journal of Genocide Research* 2, pp. 107-115.

______. 2002. *Third World Views of the Holocaust. Summary of the International Symposium* Boston: Northeastern University (on-line version www.northeastern.edu/brudnickcenter/news events/past-conferences/third_world_views/)

______. 2005. "Caribbean Hybridity and the Jews of Martinique." In Kristin Ruggiero, ed., *The Jewish Diaspora in Latin America and the Caribbean. Fragments of Memory*. Brighton, U.K.: Sussex Academic Press.

______. 2007a. *Political Islam in West Africa. State-Society Relations Transformed*. Boulder: Lynne Rienner Publishers.

______. 2007b. *Zion in the Desert. American Jews in Israel's Reform Kibbutzim*. Albany: State University of New York Press.

______. 2013. *Jews of Nigeria: An Afro-Judaic Odyssey*. Princeton: Markus Wiener Publishers.

Miller, Madeleine S., and J. Lane Miller. 1952. *Harper's Bible Dictionary*. New York: Harper & Brothers.

Millgram, Abraham E. 1990. *Jerusalem Curiosities*. Philadelphia: Jewish Publication Society.

Milligan, Maren. 2008. "Nigerian Echoes of the Israeli-Palestinian Conflict." *ISIM Review* 21:36-7. Leiden: International Institute for the Study of Islam in the Modern World.

Miner, Horace. 1965 [1953]. *The Primitive City of Timbuctoo*. Garden City, N.Y.: Doubleday.

Ojo, Olusola. 1988. *Africa and Israel: Relations in Perspective*. Westview Press: Boulder and London.

Oliel, Jacob. 2007. *Les Juifs au Sahara. Une Présence Millénaire* [Jews in the Sahara. A Thousand-Year-Old Presence]. Editions Elysée Côte-St.-Luc, Québec.

______. 2008. "Juifs et Noirs en Afrique de l'Ouest, passé et présent" [Jews and Blacks in West Africa, past and present]. In Shmuel Trigano, ed., *Juifs et Noirs. Du mythe à la réalité. Pardès* 44.

______. 2010. *Mardochée Aby Serour 1826-1886. Rabbin, caravanier, guide au Sahara* [Mordechai ben Serour 1826-1886. Rabbi, caravan-leader, Sahara guide]. Editions Elysée Côte-St.-Luc, Québec.

Parfitt, Tudor. 1999/1992. *Journey to the Vanished City. The Search for a Lost Tribe of Israel*. London: Hodder and Stoughton.

______. 2013. *Black Jews in Africa and the Americas*. Cambridge: Harvard University Press.

Peters, Joel. 1992. *Israel and Africa. The Problematic Friendship*. London: British Academic Press.

Pitot, Geneviève. 1998. *The Mauritian Shekel. The Story of the Jewish Detainees in Mauritius 1940-1945*. Port Louis, Mauritius: Vizavi.

Primack, Karen, ed. 1998. *Jews in Places You Never Thought Of.* Hoboken: KTAV Publishing House in Association with KULANU.

Ross, James. 2000. *Fragile Branches. Travels through the Jewish Diaspora.* New York: Riverhead Books.

Rosten, Leo. 1968 [and 2001, as *The New Joys of Yiddish*]. *The Joys of Yiddish.* New York: McGraw-Hill.

Rubin-Dorsky, Jeffrey, and Shelley Fisher Fishkin, eds. 1996. *People of the Book. Thirty Scholars Reflect on Their Jewish Identity.* Madison: University of Wisconsin Press.

Senghor, Léopold Sédar. 1973. "Au nom des peuples souffrants" [In the name of the suffering peoples]. *Le Nouvel Observateur,* December 24, p. 7.

Sepinwall, Alyssa Goldstein. 2003. "Eliminating Race, Eliminating Difference. Blacks, Jews, and the Abbé Grégoire." In Sue Peabody and Tyler Stovall, eds., *The Color of Liberty. Histories of Race in France.* Durham and London: Duke University Press.

Serour, Mardochée Aby. 1880. *Les Daggatoun. Tribu d'Origine Juive Demeurant dans le Désert du Sahara* [The Daggatouns. Tribe of Jewish Origin Dwelling in the Saharan Desert]. Paris: Alliance Israélite Universelle (supplement to monthly bulletin).

Sissung, Maud. 1992. "Noirs, et Palestiniens" [Black and Palestinian]. *Jeune Afrique* 1637 (May 17).

Skorecki, Karl, Sara Selig, Shraga Blazer, Robert Bradman, Neil Bradman, P. J. Warburton, Monic Ismajlowicz, and Michael F. Hammer. 1997. "Y Chromosomes of Jewish Priests." *Nature* 385, pp. 32-33.

Taji-Farouki, Suha. 1998. "A Contemporary Construction of the Jews in the Qur'an: A Review of Muhammad Sayyid Tantawi's Ban Israe'il fi al-Qur'an wa al-Sunna and 'Afif 'Abd al-Fattah Tabbara's Al-yahud fi al-Qur'an." In Ronald L. Nettler and Suha Taji-Farouki, eds., *Muslim-Jewish Encounters. Intellectual Traditions and Modern Politics.* Amsterdam: Harwood Academic Publishers.

Telushkin, Joseph. 1992. *Jewish Humor. What the Best Jewish Jokes Say about the Jews.* New York: William Morrow and

Company.

Thomas, Mark G., Karl Skorecki, Haim Ben-Ami, Tudor Parfitt, Neil Bradman, and David B. Goldstein. 1998. "Origins of Old Testament Priests." *Nature* 394, pp. 138-140.

Ujah, Charles. 2006. *The Origin of Ibos. From Linguistic and Cultural Angle*. Lagos: Ezbon Communications Ltd.

Wachman, Doreen. (n.d.) "The Jews of Cameroon." On-line two-part article originating with the Jewish Telegraph Group of Newspapers—UK (www.jewishtelegraph.com).

Williams, Joseph. 1930. *Hebrewisms of West Africa. From Nile to Niger with the Jews*. London: Allen and Unwin.

Zwergbaum, Aaron. 1960. "Exile in Mauritius." *Yad Vashem Studies* 4, pp. 191-257.

About the Authors

William F. S. Miles is professor of political science at Northeastern University in Boston and former Stotsky Professor of Jewish Historical and Cultural Studies there. A five-time Fulbright scholar, Miles is the author of many Africanist works, including *Hausaland Divided*, *Elections in Nigeria*, and, as editor and major contributor, *Political Islam in West Africa*. Winner of the National Bible Contest and North American representative to the International Bible Contest, Miles is also the author of *Zion in the Desert* (an ethno-autobiography of the kibbutz movement of Reform Judaism in Israel), *My African Horse Problem* (a memoir of his and his ten-year-old son's efforts to settle an inheritance dispute in a Muslim village in the Niger-Nigeria borderlands), and *Jews of Nigeria* (the first book-length treatment of this emerging community to be published outside of Africa). Husband of Loïza and father of Arielle and Samuel Miles, William Miles lives in Seekonk, Massachusetts, near the border with Rhode Island, where he is a member of Temple Emanu-El, an egalitarian Conservative synagogue in Providence.

Ali A. Mazrui, Albert Schweitzer Professor in the Humanities and Director of the Institute of Global Cultural Studies at Binghamton University, New York, is the author or editor of over forty books in the fields of Islam and globalization, language in society, and African culture and politics. His works include *The Power of Babel* and *Euro-Jews and Afro-Arabs*. Ali Mazrui was nominated by *Foreign Policy* magazine in 2005 for a place among the top one hundred public intellectuals alive. In 2012 he was named by the Royal Islamic Strategic Studies Centre of Jordan as one of the most influential five hundred Muslims worldwide.

Arielle P. Miles, who majored in Middle East Studies and in Chemistry at McGill University and earned a Master of Arts in Teaching at Northeastern University, teaches chemistry at Newton North High School in Newton, Massachusetts.

Printed in the USA
CPSIA information can be obtained
at www.ICGtesting.com
LVHW042051230923
758652LV00002B/242

9 781558 765825